WITHDRAWN

WITHDRAWN

110 Livingston Street Revisited

110 LIVINGSTON STREET REVISITED

DECENTRALIZATION IN ACTION

David Rogers and
Norman H. Chung

New York University Press
New York & London
1983

Copyright © 1983 by New York University
All rights reserved

Library of Congress Cataloging in Publication Data
Rogers, David, 1930–
110 Livingston Street revisited.
Bibliography: p.
Includes index.
1. Politics and education—New York (N.Y.)
2. New York (N.Y.)—Schools. 3. Schools—Decentralization—New York (N.Y.) I. Chung, Norman H., 1949–   . II. Title. III. Title: One hundred ten Livingston Street revisited.
LA339.N5R6   1983   379.1'535   83-3937
ISBN 0-8147-7387-7

Manufactured in the United States of America

Clothbound editions of New York University Press books are Smyth-sewn and printed on permanent and acid-free paper.

Contents

	Acknowledgments	vii
	Preface	xi
1.	Introduction	1
2.	A Poor Hispanic District, Polarized and Only Recently Stabilized: District A	18
3.	A Showcase District, Poor and Hispanic with Early Stabilization: District B	40
4.	A Politically Fragmented, Ethnically Mixed District, Hard to Manage: District C	68
5.	A Model District with Legitimacy Now Threatened by Rapid Ethnic Succession: District D	87
6.	A Successfully Stabilized Poor Black District: District E	108
7.	A Recently Stabilized Poor Black District: District F	131
8.	A Showcase White Middle-Class District Effectively Managing Rapid Ethnic Succession: District G	150
9.	An Isolated Suburban White Middle-Class District—Doing What It Had Always Done: District H	174
10.	Different Views of Decentralization	195
11.	Epilogue	216
	Source Notes	227
	Bibliography	235
	Index	239

Acknowledgments

This book would not have been possible without the cooperation of many community superintendents, school board members, district office staff, principals, teachers, parents, civic group leaders, teachers, union officials, central board staff, and other informants associated with the New York City public school system. They gave generously of their time and insights, and we are grateful for their help. We want to thank in particular the superintendents in each of the eight districts who provided us with entrée, met with us throughout the study, and gave their reactions to early drafts. Their willingness to discuss their problems as well as successes went well beyond what we had any right to expect. We do not mention them by name in order to maintain some degree of anonymity and confidentiality, although readers close to New York City will undoubtedly recognize from the book who they might be.

Several colleagues were also helpful. Ken Lenihan provided much thoughtful advice as related to the study's conceptualization and design, to fieldwork strategy, analysis, and putting together measures of district effectiveness. He has been a source of continued support to the senior author in several studies, and his assistance on this one was no exception. Marty Rein was also enormously helpful. The emphasis given to the politics of ethnic succession is due in large part to his suggestions. David Seeley read the manuscript at different stages and provided many thoughtful criticisms that drew on his vast knowledge of public education in New York and nationally. Some of the insights in his recent book, *Education Through Partnership*, have been drawn on in the analysis to follow on how school decentralization proceeded in New York.

Several agencies provided funding for the study on which this book is based. The National Institute of Education provided a generous eighteen-month grant that enabled the senior author to devote full time during most of that period to the study and that paid for staff assistance as well. We want to thank Fritz Mulhauser, the NIE contract officer, for his very conscientious and thoughtful involvement in this project. The Exxon Education Foundation and the Ford Foundation provided grants to the senior author in the latter stages of the project to help in its completion. George Aguirre of Exxon was particularly helpful in facilitating this funding, along with Ed Meade of Ford. The senior author thanks them both for their expression of confidence in his capacity to turn the report for NIE into a book. Their joint grant, administered through the Institute of Public Administration, freed the senior author from some of his teaching obligations during the year the book was in preparation. The Institute constituted an unusually congenial setting in which to do this work. Colleagues, administrative and clerical support staff, and facilities at the Institute were very helpful. Rogers had done a previous book while in residence there, and he found his good feelings confirmed about the Institute as a stimulating, supportive place for public sector researchers. Annmarie Walsh and Howard Mantel of the Institute provided valuable colleagueship and administrative assistance. Eleanor Wentworth typed the manuscript with great facility, a winning sense of humor, and a keen editorial eye. And Xenia Duisen, the Institute's librarian, was most helpful in tracking down various sources.

The senior author would also like to thank the Educational Priorities Panel and INTERFACE for their help. They supported his work in a previous pilot study as well as in the early months of this one before the NIE funding began. Their many studies of school headquarters and their programs with community school boards and planning boards undoubtedly helped in our gaining entrée to the districts and at headquarters. The Panel and INTERFACE made a big commitment of their own resources in support of the study. Walter Armstrong, Robin Wilner, Ferne Farber, and Dina Potocky conducted field interviews, and Armstrong put together preliminary profiles on the districts. Edward Rogers did a herculean job for the final stages of the report writing, gathering archival and statistical data on the districts, abstracting from interviews and other primary source data, and writing summaries.

David Klein, close friend of the senior author, provided helpful advice and just the right touch of humor at critical stages in the project when he had lost his. Also Bill Keller read early drafts and made many perceptive criticisms.

Finally none of the conclusions of this book necessarily reflects in any way the views of the agencies supporting the study.

Preface

This book assesses what happened when the New York City school system became decentralized in 1970. As the title indicates, it is in many respects a sequel to the senior author's *110 Livingston Street*, though with one basic difference. That book constituted an analysis of the New York City public school system as viewed from *above*. It focused primarily on the workings of the public school system's central board and headquarters, as was appropriate, since the system was centralized at that time. The conclusion that book drew was that mismanagement and professional, bureaucratic politics were among the main contributing factors to the system's decline. This book, by contrast, looks at the school system from *below*, taking as its point of departure the community school districts that decentralization spawned. It examines how the districts functioned under decentralization—how they handled the ethnic succession politics that most experienced, the management styles of their superintendents, and the relationship of both to district effectiveness. As we believe the book indicates, there is no "one best way" to manage a decentralized community school district, though there are common political and administrative problems that must be resolved in some fashion if districts and their schools are to be effective.

An understanding of New York City's experiences with ethnic succession is so basic to an assessment of decentralization that it merits special early mention. New York, like other inner cities, experienced a vast influx of poor blacks and Hispanics in the 1950s, 1960s, and 1970s and a corresponding exodus of middle-class whites. By the late 1960s, leaders of the new minority populations increasingly regarded the city's public service delivery agencies, particularly the schools, as unresponsive to their needs. These leaders regarded decentralization as a strategy to rectify that situation and, in the process, to staff the schools with more minority professionals. It was felt that newly elected community school boards were likely to pursue those goals under decentralization.

Prior to the publication of this book, no systematic assessment of this important social experiment existed.* Instead, what we had were the highly partisan pronouncements of public officials and social critics, either for or against decentralization, but with little documentation. As Herbert Kaufman observed many years ago, few if any reforms in New York City government have ever been carefully evaluated, and the city's school decentralization reform is no exception in that regard.

In deciding how to go about such an evaluation of New York City's school decentralization experiment, we opted to do it primarily through intensive, in-depth field studies of community school districts. Since it was not possible to cover each one of the city's thirty-two districts in this fashion, we narrowed the study to a close look at eight districts, eight that represented a broad cross section of the city in terms of ethnic and socio-economic characteristics and geography.

We were successful in reaching such a cross section, with a couple of minor exceptions. One outer borough is not represented at all in our study; after repeated efforts, we failed to gain access to the two districts in that borough that we had originally hoped to study. One was in the throes of a big struggle with the central board and the U.S. Commission on Civil Rights, having defied both agencies in its refusal to take an ethnic census of its staff and develop new policies based on such information. The other had an able but old-line superintendent who was reluctant to have any study done that might be at all critical of the way he ran the district and related to his community school board, parents, and civic groups. As it turned out, however, that was not a major loss because we did pick up other outer-borough districts with a similar demographic composition (white middle-class homeowners, experiencing an influx of middle class and poor minorities).

---

*One partial exception is Marilyn Gittell's "School Governance," in Charles Brecher and Raymond D. Horton, eds., *Setting Municipal Priorities* (Montclair, N.J.: Allenheld Osman, 1981), pp. 181–212. See also the five article series in the *New York Times*, June 25, 26, 28, and 29, 1980, on school decentralization.

The other omission is the extreme "problem" districts that, until recently, manifested many of the pathologies that opponents of decentralization claimed would result—that is, excessive patronage and nepotism, financial irregularities, disproportionate hiring of particular ethnic and racial groups, and the undermining of professionals by community boards and local power brokers—all of which detracted from effective education there. As one might imagine, none of these districts was receptive to having an outside group take an in-depth look at how they functioned, and we were no exception.

Are these omissions significant, seriously biasing our sample and leading to an unrealistically optimistic view of decentralization's impacts? We do not believe so. Several of the districts we studied have indeed had all of the problems listed above, including one (referred to as District A) that had some of the most notorious battles in the city. Moreover, one of our districts (District D) is still in the throes of local political struggles that have undermined the efforts of its superintendents to provide educational leadership. Thus, we have looked at a broad spectrum of districts.

Our methodology was essentially that of the field-oriented sociologist and one that the senior author has employed in several studies of urban service delivery agencies, including *110 Livingston Street*. We first secured entrée into the districts through their superintendent and had preliminary meetings to construct what might appropriately be called an organizational and political map of all the main participants. We then conducted in-depth but focused interviews with these informants relating both to their particular functions and activities and to their judgments on general district issues. We averaged seventy interviews per district, including typically all nine community school board members presently serving and many from past boards; all superintendents who had served since decentralization; twelve to fifteen top district office staff; a similar number of principals; five to six teachers' union representatives in the schools (called chapter chairpersons); the district representatives for the teachers' union and principals' association; ten to fifteen parent association leaders from district schools as well as past and present heads of the districtwide body representing all parent associations; and local political and civic leaders, including elected public officials who had been involved in the district.

In addition, we interviewed roughly forty other persons who were involved in the districts, including staff from headquarters, the State Education Department, the teachers' union, the citywide United Parents' Association, the New York Urban Coalition, and academics who conducted programs in the districts. These informants provided a useful citywide and comparative perspective on the districts.

The fieldwork was done primarily during the period from September 1979 through June 1981. We had, in addition, done many interviews from two earlier pilot studies in 1978 and 1979. And, in the course of the writing, we did thirty to forty follow-up interviews, checking on the details of various district operations and on later developments. Moreover, in some instances we kept in regular periodic contact with district officials. The senior author, for example, had roughly half a dozen face-to-face interviews with superintendents in several districts.

The central question of the study related to how these districts had managed under decentralization and to whether decentralization had made any significant difference in their operations—that is, in their effectiveness. We therefore collected as much base-line data as we could on the period when decentralization began and did a historical analysis of trends in each district.* In that regard, the reader will note that the beginning sections of Chapters 2–9 highlight stages of political and administrative development in the districts as they experienced ethnic succession and the emergence of different leadership groups and coalitions.

As will be indicated, decentralization worked quite differently in the various districts, a not very surprising finding in a city as diverse as New York. Notwithstanding such differences, there were some key political issues that all districts had to handle if they were to be at all effective, and those issues constitute the core of the analysis. They relate to the politics of ethnic succession, both among various community groups and between them and the professionals. In order for decentralization to work, it was necessary that the districts and their schools gain some local legitimacy and be responsive to community interests and needs. That was, after all, one of the main rationales for decentralization as a reform strategy. And, as so many of the New York City school system's clients, critics, and staff had bemoaned in the years prior to decentralization,

---

* It was not possible to do a comparison with the predecentralization period, since the district lines were completely different then.

such legitimacy and responsiveness had been called into serious question in the 1950s and 1960s, with *110 Livingston Street* extensively documenting that condition.

The struggles of these districts, then, to provide effective education under a decentralized system were closely related to community and citywide politics over the workings of the public schools—who would run them, how, and in response to whose interests. That is one of the central themes of this book.

A particularly complex issue of this study—and of any such assessment of schools or other service delivery agencies—is how one conceptualizes and measures effectiveness. There are some relatively simple ways of doing that—for example, by looking at trends in reading and math scores, attendance, later academic achievements of students, and the like. We have provided such trend data, both for individual districts and citywide, but that is, in our view, a much too simplified approach. Other indicators are also important—such as the climate of the schools; the extent of innovation in programs; the extent to which programs are customized to the values and learning styles of students; and the extent to which closer, collaborative relations are established between the schools and local institutions, including the family. We have discussed many such indicators in this book.

Beyond that, of course, many forces other than modes of school governance and administration bear on effectiveness as we have defined it. The socioeconomic backgrounds of students are the most important of these.

One of the main features of our analysis in this regard has been to combine the use of quantitative data on the management styles of their superintendents. The qualitative data help illuminate the context in which to interpret trends in district performance.

We followed one procedure that the reader should be informed about. When the superintendents first invited us in, we made the commitment to share a draft of the section on their district with them before it went into the final version. This provided us with some of our most illuminating insights on the dynamics of these districts. All of the superintendents reacted in a responsible, cooperative fashion, despite the concerns of some that the analysis reopened issues that they would have preferred remain dead. As one might well imagine, some of these feedback meetings became quite stormy, as superintendents reacted not only to errors of "fact" in the drafts but also to what they saw as the negative political repercussions of the accurate information and interpretations that appeared. To their credit, all of them acknowledged our right to the "final word" on various issues. And we tried in every instance to maintain a balance between providing an accurate and in-depth analysis of how each district worked and eliminating any examples or personal references that did not enhance the analysis and might hurt the district. As indicated in the book, we have not identified the districts by name or number.

The reader should also keep in mind a couple of features of the New York City context in interpreting the findings and conclusions of this study. First of all, the Decentralization Act of 1969 that was passed in Albany and that established community school districts in New York was at most a compromise bill. It was worked out at the last minute following a year-long stalemate, after all parties were in a state of acute exhaustion. The powers that were transferred from headquarters to the districts were limited, ambiguous, and hemmed in by many concurrent powers that remained with the chancellor.

In addition, decentralization took place in New York under quite adverse circumstances. Not long after it was under way, the city faced an acute fiscal crisis. The cutbacks in funding, programs, and staff at the district level were, and continue to be, quite marked; and most district offices are now functioning under a vastly reduced work force and with class sizes in the schools way up from former levels.

While these are simply the realities of the urban condition, probably more acute in the case of New York City, they suggest that any positive educational developments that may have taken place in New York as related to its watered-down version of decentralization might well be magnified under a stronger plan. Likewise, some of the negative ones may well be more a reflection of this particular law and the circumstances under which it was implemented than of the concept as such.

Despite the idiosyncratic features of the New York City setting, we see this book as having relevance for school systems and other service delivery agencies throughout the nation. The conditions of bigness, overcentralized bureaucracy, and insulated professionalism that provided the political pressures for school decentralization in New York appear in varying degrees in many communities that may learn a great deal from the New

York experience. The lessons from its attempts under decentralization to develop more productive relationships between school and community thus become relevant to everyone concerned about the future of public education and public sector services at the local level. Anyone familiar with public education across the nation will have little difficulty in seeing in the history of these eight districts many of the classic problems of school systems regardless of location. The ways the problems have been worked out and the fact that different solutions may be called for in different communities provide useful lessons for educators and citizens everywhere.

110 Livingston Street Revisited

1

Introduction

New York's Community Control Controversy

The New York City public school system embarked on a critical experiment in 1970. This followed more than a decade of turbulence regarding the quality of educational services it delivered, the extent of equality in the way they were delivered to different racial and ethnic groups, and the accountability of the system to the various publics it was required to serve. Many big-city school systems experienced such turbulence. New York was not alone in that regard. As the biggest urban system, however, with by far the largest central headquarters bureaucracy, New York's came under increasing attack in the 1960s from a broad spectrum of citizen groups for its alleged failure to be responsive to the city's many sociopolitical changes. Blacks, in particular, resented the fact that the system had failed to improve the quality of education for them, either through compensatory programs or through desegregation.[1] Other groups, including but not limited to Hispanics, had also become alienated from an agency that was increasingly seen as insulated, grossly mismanaged, and dominated by professional educators who had successfully deflected and absorbed all past efforts at reform, without those efforts having had any significant impact on the schools' performance.[2]

By the mid-1960s, *community control* became the slogan and rallying cry of reform advocates. It gained wide appeal in New York City and elsewhere in conjunction with such other developments as the black power movement, various student movements, New Left attacks on bureaucratic institutions in general, federally funded community action organizations that pressed for more grass-roots power over traditional service delivery agencies, and an increasing consensus that big-city schools were indeed failing to educate large numbers of students. A series of critical events in poverty areas of New York, in combination with the activist, anti-Establishment climate of the time, gave further impetus to the movement.[3]

The movement's main targets were *professional power* and *bureaucracy*. Community control advocates increasingly saw the professional power of the educators, exercised through their strong teachers' union and supervisory associations, as working against the public interest. A prevailing point of view among these advocates was that the educators had a monopoly over definitions of professionalism (what should be taught, how, who should evaluate schools, and by what means) and had consolidated their power over the running of the New York City schools to such a point that they seemed increasingly unresponsive to legitimate demands of citizen groups for improved education. This view was particularly prevalent in poor black areas of the city.

The central bureaucracy was also seen as the enemy. Parent and civic groups throughout the city shared horror stories about their attempts to deal with headquarters staff on such matters as zoning, appointments of teachers and principals, and school construction. And other groups, including employers, universities, and community agencies, joined in with accounts of their disappointments, as they tried to develop collaborative programs with the school system or simply to secure information on the schools that should have been part of the public record.[4]

Moreover, the movement soon spread to many other big cities, although it reached its greatest intensity and had perhaps its greatest effects in New York. The movement's main goal was to decentralize the New York City school system into a series of smaller community school districts. The plan was that each district would be governed by an elected community school board that would hold the educators of their district accountable for the quality of education there and would have significant power over budget, staffing, and program decisions.[5]

Academics as well as citizen groups soon became strong advocates of this strategy, arguing that there were many potential benefits from pursuing it, including: (1) more *accountability* of the educators to their school and district constituencies; (2) more parent and community *participation* in educational decision making; (3) increasing educational *innovation*; (4)

a more *organic relation of schools to communities* in curriculum and staffing and in program *linkages* to outside agencies; (5) more *jobs* within the school system for district residents; (6) *the development of more local-level leadership*; (7) improved *legitimacy* of the schools; and, ultimately, (8) *improved student performance.*[6]

This was quite a formidable agenda, but community control advocates, at least taken collectively, clearly had all these things in mind. The fact that the movement took on all these dimensions undoubtedly contributed to the strong resistance that soon arose, particularly from educators who felt that their jobs and their autonomy as professionals were being threatened. There were clearly several sets of goals—economic, political, community development, as well as education. And the threat that the pursuit of them by community control advocates posed to groups already holding jobs and bureaucratic power soon helped to escalate the conflict over the issue that became citywide in scope and that tore the city apart.[7]

A basic goal of some community control advocates was *ethnic succession,* and it was this goal perhaps more than any other that activated strong resistance from a predominantly white educator group within the system. The New York City schools, like so many other big-city school systems and service delivery agencies, reflected waves of ethnic migration into the city in their staffing patterns.[8] As historical accounts of the system indicate, up through the early 1950s educators of Irish descent tended to predominate. After that, increasing numbers of Jewish educators moved into teaching, supervisory, and administrative positions. Then, in the late 1960s, under the banner of community control, blacks and, to a lesser extent, Hispanics were demanding that people of their ethnic background with appropriate credentials be given entry into the system.

The gatekeeper of this system was a small but powerful group called the Board of Examiners that administered all the tests for professional and administrative positions. The board became the eye of the storm during the 1960s, as minority educators and their advocates continually charged it with discrimination against minority applicants. Blacks focused in particular on the oral exam, which they claimed was biased against candidates who showed any traces of ethnic dialects, such as "southernisms," in their speech. And these were not just isolated, random complaints, since many black applicants who were turned down took their grievances to the N.Y.C. Commission on Human Rights. Moreover, many Jewish educators within the system had observed that the same discrimination had been exercised against them in the 1940s and 1950s, as their ethnic speech patterns—then referred to as "Brooklynese" and "Concourse English"—were judged inadequate.[9] The tragedy of the community control controversy was that it escalated Jewish-black tensions in New York City, largely because Jewish educators predominated within the school system at that time.

The opposition to community control was quite formidable, and it came mainly from New York City educators through their teachers' union and professional associations that argued that community control would have devastating effects on the schools. Local groups without that much of an interest in improving education would solidify their power base, they argued. Doing this would increase *segregation*, the use of *racial and ethnic criteria in staff appointments*, *parochialism* in curriculum (e.g., black culture programs), *nepotism*, and local *corruption*. In addition, they argued, breaking up the system into many small districts would be very *inefficient*, leading to much *duplication* of administrative and curriculum services, abandoning the important economies of scale that the centralized system provided. And the net result of such a politicized, racist, parochial, and inefficient system, they concluded, would be *deteriorating schools*, *heightened ethnic and racial conflict*, and *declining student performance*.

Historical Perspective

A sense of history will enhance an understanding of the community control movement and its opposition. No such attack on the fundamental assumptions on which an institution is based comes about overnight. Indeed, the crisis of legitimacy that the New York City school system experienced in the 1960s was a culmination of ongoing developments beginning at the turn of the century. And they were characteristic of all big-city school systems, not just New York's.[10]

In the nineteenth century big-city school systems, like many other service delivery agencies, were organized on a decentralized ward basis, and patronage politics determined major educational decisions. Contracts, appointments, and major budgetary decisions were often made in a highly particularistic way by functionaries of the political machine. At the same time, the schools did have some integral, organic relation to the neighborhoods, reflecting as they often did the aspirations and "old-country values" of the newly arrived immigrant groups they served.[11]

Beginning in the late nineteenth century, the municipal reform movement, led by a middle- and upper-class business and civic elite, including some academicians, swept much of that away. It helped create centralized and supposedly "professionalized' bureaucracies with strong superintendents and boards. These changes, while made under the banner of democracy, and with the claim of removing the schools from politics, in fact substituted a new brand of middle-class, bureaucratic, professional politics by eliminating arrangements for school governance at the neighborhood level. The changes replaced a particularistic "private-regarding" ethos of immigrant groups (mainly Irish, Italian, Polish, and other European Catholics and some Jews) with a more universalistic "public-regarding" one of Protestant, "native" Americans.[12]

The goal of the reformers of the time was thus not only to take over power but to do so in the name of a different (and what they regarded as "superior") set of values—those of professionalism, civil service reform, and bureaucratic rationality. They wanted to create a public education system that would effectively assimilate or acculturate new immigrant groups to an Anglo-American society. Based on the view that centralization would bring with it many benefits—especially economies of scale, area wide planning, professionalism, freedom from local patronage and parochialism, and accountability—the development in fact turned big-city school systems into isolated islands of professional power, with New York leading the way.

These developments might well have gone on unquestioned but for the fact that American cities attracted millions of new blacks and Hispanics in the 1950s and 1960s. The new groups found big-city schools unready and often unwilling to adjust to their needs. Desegregation proposals were not implemented, except on a very limited basis. And a vast array of compensatory programs failed to improve student achievement. Meanwhile, these newly arrived ethnic groups were experiencing a rise in expectations with respect to the service levels of public agencies. Thus, the climate was ripe for the community control movement described above.[13]

Many of the supposed benefits of a centralized, bureaucratic, and professionalized public education seemed not to have been realized, as previously accepted public administration and management principles from the municipal reform movement were increasingly called into question. The headquarters bureaucracies of this and other municipal agencies had become more insulated from the service delivery requirements of their diverse constituencies. Civil service, once an instrument for improved standards and performance, was now seen instead as protecting agencies from outside review and demands for accountability and as creating administrative rigidities that prevented adaptation to service demands of clientele.[14]

Moreover, public administration writers began to question centralization on broad management and economic grounds as well. They noted possible diseconomies of scale, as proliferating layers of bureaucracy in large, centralized agencies led to long delays in decision making and to waste. They formulated notions about optimum size; and they pointed up the diversity of service needs in different subcommunities in large urban areas, precluding the effective delivery of services on a centralized basis. The size and diversity of service delivery agencies in big cities, particularly in New York, thus seemed to call for a different service delivery mechanism.[15]

In brief, a centralized, bureaucratic, professionalized system of public education was seen as no longer working as its designers had hoped. Instead of producing more efficiency and economies, it brought about inefficiency and diseconomies. And instead of professionalism being promoted, nonprofessional practices were made possible by increasingly politicized educators (teachers, principals, administrators). The latter tended to externalize the blame for poor student performance; refused to police themselves; and rejected proposals for outside, lay review of the schools.

This is the context in which community control became a strategy for redesigning the New York City school system. Viewed in such a context, the movement made sense. On the other hand, there is serious question as to how clearly the movement's advocates articulated their goals and how well the goals gibed with one another.

Some Frameworks for Assessing the New York City Experience

In retrospect, the concept of community control was a complex one that included many elements, some of them potentially contradictory. As David Seeley has pointed out in his new book, *Education Through Partnership*, the concept had three different strands: (1) *minority-group power*, that is, the desire of the blacks and other minority groups to control their schools; (2) *political democracy* whereby professional educators would be accountable and responsive to their communities; and (3) *debureaucratization* that would involve much closer relationships between schools and their communities—as the schools might become less insulated and more oriented toward creating partnerships with community organizations rather than functioning as separate service delivery agencies.[16]

A big problem for the community control advocates was that the concept was ambiguous and took on all these different meanings, thus putting its supporters in a situation of making conflicting sets of demands. As Seeley has noted: "These three strands of community control obviously overlap. Each, nevertheless, has different policy and political implications, and they are so different in some respects that they represent competing causes."[17] What was particularly harmful to the movement was that as it developed much more emphasis was placed on the first two or *control* aspects relating to the transfer of political power, and less on the third or *community* one that probably had much more direct bearing on improving education. Indeed, as the educators reacted so strongly to try to discredit the movement, based on their fears that it would eliminate their jobs and professional autonomy, the community component got lost in the shuffle. Since it provided much less grist for the media mill, it got much less coverage.

And yet, this third strand, as Seeley also points out, emphasizing school-community linkages and partnerships and learning, is probably much more revolutionary than the other two, in that it would change the basic structure of urban public education rather than just shift the political controls. Moreover, although it does involve a radical shift in the educators' role and responsibilities, it might in the long run gain much more political acceptance, from both educators and other constituencies. It does not confront the educators head-on with threats to their jobs, and it provides them with more resources and supports than they might otherwise have. Moreover, in the process, the definition of who are the producers or deliverers of education is broadened considerably to include many more participants (e.g., students, their families, and community agencies). In that sense, accountability is correspondingly spread, thereby redirecting some of the demands of parents and school reformers, but it might well make more sense as a strategy for redesigning public education than any past approaches.

A Political Model: Decentralization as Facilitating Ethnic Succession

One useful perspective for assessing decentralization relates it to the political turbulence cities experience over ethnic succession. Decentralization may be viewed as a way of helping cities channel their ethnic succession politics. It does so by allowing local-level leadership to gain greater control over the management of human service agencies like public schools, thereby making their services more responsive to minority-group needs, and by providing jobs in these agencies to minorities.

All major cities, according to this view experience a turbulent ethnic succession politics, as newly arrived minoriy groups seek to attain some control over the agencies that serve them. The turbulence takes at least two forms. One is a conflict between the ins and the outs—between the predominantly white civil servants (represented through their unions and professional associations) who run the agencies and the minority populations they must serve. A second is a conflict among the different groups of outs, to determine which ones will gain such control.

In cities where decentralization does not take place, such conflicts take place anyway, but in random, "runaway" fashion, emerging in unchanneled and unstructured ways. Decentralization may be seen as helping such conflicts gain expression in more predictable ways by institutionalizing the mechanisms for handling them. That may happen, however, only if local political leaders emerge in minority communities under decentralization and establish some minimal level of consensus regarding the goals and directions of the agency—that is, regarding its programs, staffing patterns, and budget. To the extent that such leadership does develop, it both increases the agency's legitimacy and provides some social peace in connection with its functioning. It may also help orient the agency outward, to the community, resulting in closer relations to parents and civic groups and bringing about more collaborative programs with outside institutions (e.g., employers, other districts, cultural agencies, and the like). In that case, it allows for more initiatives to be taken for educational improvement efforts. Thus, the more local areas of cities (subcommunities, neighborhoods) attain some degree of social peace in connection with the functioning and legitimacy of public service delivery agencies, the more the resources of agency staff may be turned to planning and program improvement efforts, rather than to power struggles over control and turfs.

A model that may be useful in analyzing the experiences of community school districts and assessing their effectiveness thus emerges from this political perspective. It suggests that districts may be effective only if they handle the turbulence of their ethnic succession politics by having a local leadership group that is capable of coalescing the factions and developing a fair amount of consensus about how the agency works and who will run it. And it allows for the fact that some districts may reach that stage of political development while others may not. Moreover, it may further indicate the importance of analyzing the conditions under which that development in fact takes place.

A Management View: Decentralization as Facilitating the Emergence of Product Divisions

Another set of perspectives on community control comes from academic writings on managing complex organizations. Most of this literature has been developed from studies of business, but its concepts and findings apply to governmental agencies as well. Henry Mintzberg, a well-known writer in management, provides an intriguing typology of bureaucracies that synthesizes the literature and constitutes a useful framework for interpreting the dynamics of the community control controversy in New York.[18] Drawing on Mintzberg's typology, the New York City school system may be seen as having characteristics of three types of bureaucracy.

First, it is in many respects a *professional bureaucracy* in that the main production, or, in this instance, "service delivery activities" are carried out by teachers in classrooms. Given their professionalism ideology, teachers place a high value on maintaining their autonomy in the classroom and on not being subject to close bureaucratic controls by their supervisors—such as principals.

Second, the New York City school system is a *machine bureaucracy* in the classic Weberian sense. It is under strong pressure, for example, as a large government agency delivering services to a big population, to do so in a way that is uniform across the city, that shows no "favoritism" to particular groups and that is free from any taint of patronage or corruption. In this respect, it is a system containing many rules, standard operating procedures, and controls to ensure that those goals are adequately pursued. And much of the energy of the staff, particularly at headquarters, is devoted to such maintenance activity, as opposed to what might be called adaptive and developmental activity, that is, activity related to generating programs that are responsive to the unique, particularistic needs of various client groups. The pressure, then, is on maintaining the rules rather than on delivering more and better services, although there is much less of that in recent years under a reform chancellor than under one who had come up through the ranks, like his predecessor.

Third, since the New York City school system was partially decentralized in 1969, as an aftermath of the community control struggle, it has taken on many of the characteristics of a *divisionalized bureaucracy*. Just as major corporations in the business sector set up relatively autonomous product divisions, corresponding to diverse markets, so has the New York City school system, in response to the increasing political pressures of the 1960s, set up a decentralized system that is designed to be more strategically and operationally responsive than its more centralized predecessor. That is, it is designed to give the decentralized districts more flexibility and authority to customize their services to the particular needs and learning styles of their local clientele. Given the tremendous ethnic and socioeconomic diversity of New York and some of the serious questions economists have raised about diseconomies of scale in centralized urban service delivery bureaucracies—with their red tape, multiple offices and levels, and considerable fragmentation—decentralization makes sense, even independent of the political pressures that also give it some justification.

Thus, one may reasonably speak of a big-city school district responding to markets based on different clientele—for example, a Harlem or Bedford-Stuyvesant one (poor black); an East Harlem, Lower East Side, or South Bronx one (poor Hispanic); a Northeast or Northwest Bronx one (mixed, middle-class to upper-middle-class white); or a Bensonhurst, Bay Ridge, or Staten Island one (lower-middle-class white). A strong case can be made that the needs and learning styles of students in these separate areas, each generally corresponding to one or more community school districts, are in fact different.[19] Each requires a somewhat different educational program, acknowledging the fact that there are common standards that must apply to them all. More important, each has its own approach for developing the relationships of legitimacy and support that are necessary for successful schooling.

Community school districts may thus be considered as analogous to product divisions of diversified corporations, requiring the same autonomy to develop their services in adaptive and responsive ways as corporations do their products. Just as in the business sector, however, there are pressures that do not allow for as much autonomy as the divisional leaders would like.[20]

In fact, what we have in the New York City school case is three sets of conflicting pressures, corresponding to each of the bureaucratic types just described. Thus, while the districts may press hard to pull power down from central and up from the classroom, central continues to enforce rules in line with its concerns about "proper procedure." And this continues to be a constraining factor under decentralization.[21] So, too, does pressure from teachers to try to maintain their autonomy and flexibility in the classroom, sometimes in opposition to pressures from the district office, which may seek more control over their behavior.

In sum, three broad perspectives are useful in assessing how the demands for community control of the schools worked out in New York City. One conceptualizes the movement as having three different goals, often in conflict with one another. It contributes to an assessment of decentralization in terms of the extent to which these goals were realized in particular community school districts, how, and with what consequences. A second views decentralization in terms of the politics of ethnic succession. A third adopts a more managerial perspective and sees community school districts and decentralization as subject to different sets of institutional pressures. There are *centralizing ones* from headquarters that require the districts to adhere to common standards and that subject them to mandated programs and policies from central. There are *professional ones* from teachers that are in part centralizing pressures as well, such as requiring districts to comply with citywide collective bargaining agreements—but that also demand autonomy and powers (e.g., work rules, prep periods) for the classroom teacher. And there are *divisional or district ones* that seek power at that level to help customize programs to the learning styles of students in particular schools. For decentralization to work well, there must be a balancing of those powers in a way that enhances the capacity of the schools to develop programs relevant to student and community needs.

Analyzing School Decentralization in New York City

It is clear from even the most cursory look at the New York City school system that decentralization has worked out quite differently in different settings.[22] As one might expect in a city as large and diverse as New York, community school districts come in many different shapes and sizes. In student enrollment, they range in size from 36,000 to 11,000. They cover a broad range of ethnic and socioeconomic groups and are equally diverse in types of parent, community, and political organizations. In addition, they have many different kinds of boards and superintendents. Some have boards that play an effective policy role, while the boards in others have no clear sense of purpose and often hamper their superintendent and professional staff as well. In some districts there are active superintendents who provide strong leadership; in others, the superintendents exercise little initiative in running their districts.

Moreover, analyzing decentralization in terms of a standardized set of criteria is difficult to do in New York City, for fairly obvious reasons. The main one is that forces other than decentralization affect student performance. Two prominent ones in New York, as in other big cities, are its continued shift in student population and its fiscal crisis and consequent cutbacks. White and minority middle-class students have left the public schools in large numbers, while poor minority ones have increased correspondingly as a proportion of total enrollment. Several districts examined in this study have undergone shifts in population of this particular sort since decentralization began in 1970. If decentralization were in fact having a positive effect on student performance, the best it might do in such districts would be to minimize the extent of decline.

The districts have been hampered in that effort, however, by the city's fiscal cutbacks.[23] Declining resources for the New York City schools have hit the districts very hard since the mid-1970s. The numbers of staff available to the districts have shrunk considerably in recent years, contributing to increased class size and to more disorganization in schools at the start of each school year, as the nature and timing of the cuts are not always predictable sufficiently in advance. In addition centralized personnel policies greatly restricted the districts' flexibility in dealing with cutbacks.

These are some of the reasons for interpreting the data with caution. Also, any analysis of decentralization will benefit from using *process* as well as *bottom-line indicators* of effectiveness. Indeed, one may learn much more about long-term trends and prospects for organizations by just looking at process indicators than by using only bottom-line ones.[24] We have thus gathered data relative to them as well, including the following: (1) the extent of fit or *congruence* between the schools and the community—for example, in curriculum, staff orientations and skills, and collaborative program linkages of schools with outside agencies; (2) the extent of success in *bringing in state and federal funds* for new programs; (3) the extent to which *neighborhood stabilization* is enhanced through district-initiated desegregation programs, school improvement efforts, and the development of alternative schools; (4) the extent to which *job opportunities* exist for parents and other community residents as paraprofessionals and neighborhood workers and to professionally licensed staff (teachers, supervisors, district office administrators) of previously unrepresented ethnic groups; and (5) the extent to which *schools* have emerged under decentralization more *as community institutions*.

Our central focus is on the management style adopted by various districts, the conditions for its adoption, and the effects it had on the district's performance. We defined management style for purposes of this study in two ways. First was in terms of how the superintendent behaved in relation to a series of *critical tasks and relationships,* including: (1) *curriculum and instruction;* (2) *district office-school relations;* (3) *district office–professional staff relations;* (4) *district office-community relations;* (5) *district office-headquarters relations;* and (6) *the internal structure and workings of the district office itself.* There are obviously many other ways of describing the management tasks of a superintendent, but we found these to be particularly germane for our study.

Second, we looked at the *orientations* of the superintendent, with management style being defined as the broad approaches the superintendent used in dealing with critical tasks and relationships, superseding what was done on any particular one. In this regard, we are concerned with whether the superintendent was *more participative or authoritarian, more entrepreneurial or efficiency-oriented, more politically accommodating or adversarial, oriented more toward running the district in a formal bureaucratic manner or as a more informal, organic system,* with these orientations transcending any particular management task and usually being transferred from one to the other.[25]

Obviously, the management style in a district does not exist in a vacuum, and it is shaped in important ways by what we have called the *context*. We mean by that a district's *demographic characteristics* (e.g., who lives and goes to school there); its *political characteristics* (e.g., who are the main interest groups and coalitions); and its consequent *educational leadership group* (e.g., what constituencies and organizations are represented on the community school board, what kind of superintendent they select, and how they define their role and his in running the district).

Thus, while we acknowledge that management style is partly a function of the orientations and skills the manager brings to the situation, it may be a function of the situation as well.[26] What kind of superintendent is appointed to a community school district is directly related to the politics and values of the district, as channeled through its board; and, if the board does not reflect those considerations in its decision, having selected a different kind of superintendent whose orientations and skills do not fit the situation, he may change to adapt to that situation or he may leave, voluntarily or otherwise. In addition, he may well have taken the job in the first place because he saw the district as a place in which his style would be particularly appropriate. These are, at least, some assumptions on which the study is based.

Lay versus Professional Authority

A particularly important issue under decentralization relates to *professional versus lay authority*.[27] The matter of appropriate powers of school boards and professionals, with the former assumed to be the *policymakers* and the latter the *implementers* of that policy, has always been fraught with ambiguity; and in the case of community school boards and their superintendents in the New York City system, it takes on added significance. Some boards have taken on administrative as well as policy functions, often leading to much conflict with the professional staff. Other boards assume almost no role of any kind, in either policy or administration, with the superintendent and his staff making policy and running the district. The problem of reaching a balance appropriate for each district has been particularly acute under decentralization. There have been many instances in the New York City system of what the professionals refer to as "meddling" boards and others of "rubber-stamp" ones; problems have resulted in both cases, as the case studies that follow will indicate.

This issue takes on particular significance in the New York City community school district system, since decentralization was mandated to bring about more *accountability* and *responsiveness* of educators to their clientele. Advocates of community control clearly wanted more lay authority, but they also wanted better education; and the problem of working out an appropriate balance between such lay and professional authority so that better education does in fact result is still an issue, after more than ten years' experience with decentralization. The case studies that follow shed some light on this, and the concluding chapters suggest solutions.

A final comment is in order regarding measures of *student performance* and what they mean as reflections of how decentralization went. One problem with using reading and math tests, the traditional way of assessing student performance, is that the tests keep changing in New York, as they do in many other cities. Also, the administration of the tests has been a subject of much controversy. In some schools there may be much more prepping and "teaching to the test" than in others. In some, there have been cases where only higher-achieving students would be given the tests.

One must thus interpret these data in context, and as long as one is aware of such conditions, the data may be useful in indicating some of the possible impacts of decentralization. They are useful, however, only in conjunction with other effectiveness indicators. For example, some districts have not improved their reading scores in line with citywide trends but have nevertheless initiated many productive programs under decentralization that were less prevalent under the old, centralized system. Those districts may still be cited as examples of how decentralization helped to improve effectiveness. Furthermore, when one takes into account the fact that some of these districts have lost many high-achieving middle-class students, with major demographic shifts, such interpretations make sense.

The Order of the Chapters

The substance of this book consists mainly of analytic case studies of eight decentralized districts. We use the term "analytic" because we did much more than simply describe what happened. We also provided interpretations as to why the same district was more effective at different times, and why districts differ in that regard.

We generated a number of hypotheses and have tried to pull them together in as systematic a way as we could. That is done in Chapter 10, in which we develop a preliminary model of the prerequisites for district effectiveness, acknowledging that effectiveness itself has many dimensions.

We end the book in Chapter 11 with a statement of some of the unresolved problems under decentralization and with recommendations for change. Some of these recommendations simply urge public policymakers to take a much closer look at particular issues—for example, on whether functions that have remained centralized might better be decentralized to the district level—while others are much more specific in their focus.

No single study, regardless of how well conceived and extensive, will answer all the important questions on an issue as complex as public school decentralization. But this one should at least, we hope, help clarify many of the issues and indicate which further ones require more study.

2

A Poor Hispanic District, Polarized and Only Recently Stabilized: District A

Our first district reflects in quite dramatic fashion the ethnic succession politics that gave rise to decentralization as a reform strategy. Located in a small, rapidly changing area of the city that had experienced an exodus of white middle-class residents and a big influx of Hispanics, its public school population is now 74% Hispanic, including, in addition, 14% blacks and 7% Asians, most of them from low-income, working-class families.[1] There remain many white residents in the area, however, who, along with white educators, have been active in school politics, usually in opposition to community control. Indeed, this district was one of the most politically polarized in the city until the late 1970s, reflecting a power struggle between whites and Hispanics over jobs in the school system, over who would run the district, and over what kinds of programs it would have.

Most of the themes indicated in our model relating school decentralization to ethnic succession are highlighted in this district's experiences. Several years before decentralization there had been much political protest over the schools in the district and turmoil within the schools, as minority parents were organized through antipoverty agencies to deal with the limited educational services being provided for their children.[2] Decentralization simply provided more established channels for the expression of that protest politics.[3] Community school board elections and meetings, particularly when the latter dealt with critical decisions on budget, staffing, and programs, were examples of such channels. And, as this chapter will indicate, it took almost a decade of decentralization before the district reached a degree of social peace concerning the workings of the public schools. It was only at that point, in the late 1970s, that a more collaborative relationship developed between minority parents and educators, replacing the intense political conflict that had existed before. This change facilitated, in turn, the emergence of an effective superintendent who has the strong support of local power groups—the community school board (CSB), the district's educators, and parent and community organizations. And he and his board are now pursuing an educational improvement strategy that may well upgrade quite substantially the quality of public schools in the district.

The case thus illustrates one type of political development scenario under decentralization, namely the emergence of strong local leadership following a prolonged period of conflict and turbulence within the community and between the community and professional groups. This chapter describes the conditions that gave rise to this delayed political development, and it indicates how the district's politics affected its management at different stages.

Demography, Neighborhoods, District Characteristics

This district's political problems resulted in part from the fact that it was treated in gerrymandered fashion, as a small segregated district. A top staffperson recalled: "The district lines were drawn in a way that built a wall and stigma with *us* as the people that *they* in the neighboring district didn't want. We felt like lepers."

The district has had the smallest student enrollment of any in the city, both at the start of decentralization and more recently. Thus, it had 18,411 students in 1970 and only 11,386 in 1980, with at least some of that decline attributable to its political instability, as parents increasingly enrolled their children in parochial and private schools.[4] The geographic area covered by the district is also very small, constituting a limited portion of its borough. Its ethnic politics, however, has been at least as turbulent as that of larger, more ethnically diverse districts.

Three separate sets of neigborhoods exist. One is mostly white middle class; many of its residents are young, single people who have moved in recently, including a fair number of artists and writers. For the most part, they have not been involved in school politics. A second is Orthodox Jewish, mainly elderly residents, who have lived there for several generations. A third is a new Hispanic area, including many families with children attending public schools. The last two are both low and lower middle income areas. "The Orthodox Jewish and Hispanic neighborhoods each feels a sense of desperation," reports a journalist who writes about the district and lives there. "Each feels the other will soon become dominant, and this creates a sense of great fear, while the middle-class area has much less of this desperation." The Jewish population's concerns are compounded by the increasing voter registration among Puerto Ricans in recent years.

The district's educational politics reflects these differences. "It is basically a fight between Puerto Rican leaders and the Jews," explains a local resident. "The former want to have a say in local government, while the latter say, 'You are not really qualified.' And both see the CSB as a vehicle for patronage and jobs."

Meanwhile, both poor neighborhoods have been threatened by a gentrification trend in which poor residents are being forced out, as young middle-class people move in and restore deteriorating housing. Indeed, housing in these neighborhoods has deteriorated so much that it has become a target of considerable arson, further displacing the poor.

There were two coalitions, then, that had been vying for power under decentralization. One was an anti–community control group, representing white educators and Jewish community organizations. It has dominated the CSB until the most recent 1980 election. The other coalition represented Hispanics and includes antipoverty agencies; parents, tenant groups, and community control activists; and various other organizations, such as unions with a large minority membership and social service agencies.

The most militant community-control-oriented groups, however, have been largely displaced in recent years by a parent-community coalition that has played down divisive ethnic issues and tried to appeal to groups whose main interest is in improving education rather than hiring more minority educators. These moderate groups had been repelled in the past by the tactics of the militants. They have a much more pragmatic orientation than the militants had.

CSBs and Superintendents: A History of Turbulence

The political turbulence that continued in this district during the first years of decentralization is perhaps best reflected in the actions of its various CSBs and superintendents. The district has gone through three distinct periods: (1) one in which Hispanics and community control advocates gained control of the CSB and appointed a superintendent who espoused that cause; (2) a period representing a reassertion of white educator control such as existed before decentralization; and (3) a recent period of political stability, with the CSB and superintendent both expressing a moderate problem-solving approach in running the district.

The first CSB of 1970 had six whites and only three minority members, but two of the whites soon resigned and were replaced by minority people, changing the entire balance of power. When community control advocates gained a 5 to 4 majority in 1971, they selected as superintendent a Hispanic male with prior experience in the Ocean Hill-Brownsville struggle. This is a very good case with which to begin an assessment of decentralization. In this instance the district took advantage of its increased powers to select a strong superintendent who would, in turn, exercise his powers to the hilt. Districts could not do this before decentralization, and this was to be a test case of what would happen when they tried. Indeed, this energetic and aggressive superintendent, a strong community control advocate himself, made extensive staff and program changes during the four years in which he served. He appointed many Hispanic principals, assistant principals (APs), and teachers; built up a large bilingual program; and increased minority parent participation in school and district affairs. In addition, he made this district the first in the city to have its own locally controlled lunch program.

His forceful style in pursuing these strategies in a previously white-controlled district reactivated considerable concern among the educators and their organizations—the United Federation of Teachers (UFT) and the principals' association. As mentioned above, the district had a history of confrontations between poor Hispanic parents and white educators, dating back to political organizing of parents by antipoverty agency staff in the 1960s; and the superintendent's strategies rekindled that conflict. The white educators were particularly concerned about protecting their jobs, which they believed were threatened under new bilingual programs.

CSB meetings were marked by physical confrontation and violence, as militant pro- and anticommunity control groups squared off against one another. "It was a war zone," reported one union official. "Teachers had to be escorted into the schools, in some instances by armed guards. The parent associations were taken over by the superintendent's cronies. One principal was literally broken by the PAs." A Hispanic activist recalled: "There was terrorism on both sides. And, in all the fighting and bickering, education got lost. There was no room for education anywhere." This district thus became quite polarized, as the superintendent appointed more minority educators and moved to alter the district's "power structure."

The extent of polarization becomes quite clear as one compares the two sides' markedly different accounts of those years. From the white educators' perspective, this Hispanic superintendent's strategy was one of "illegal appointments" of "unqualified" Hispanic educators, involving blatant racism and anti-Semitism, and leading to an erosion of "professionalism." Community control advocates, on their side, saw the strategy as one of opening up opportunities for qualified minority educators; introducing increasingly "relevant" programs to meet the unique needs of Hispanic students, thereby significantly improving education; and establishing a more open, community-based school system.

One can see from these views how divided the district was. It had split into two organized camps whose political struggle consumed their energies. And the superintendent contributed to the conflict by adopting an adversarial posture vis-à-vis white educator groups. As one Hispanic activist observed: "He refused to make any compromises and did not take a broad perspective. He focused only on one constituency, and he was not the type of person that could halt the feuds. In all the fighting, education got lost. That is why I felt that he was not the right man for the job. He was too much into polarizing the groups so that nothing was accomplished and much of what he wanted that was right got lost."

It did not take long before the teachers and principals sought to regain control over the CSB so that they might remove this superintendent. They were successful on both counts. Thus, through intensive political organizing among the white voters in the district, they prevailed in the 1973 CSB election, changing the balance of power back to one of white, proeducator domination. The new board then charged the superintendent in a court suit with discrimination against whites in staffing decisions. Although he was vindicated of these charges, the CSB was able to dismiss him as superintendent. He left at the end of 1974, but the CSB, instead of replacing him with somebody who might deescalate the conflicts, appointed an anti–community control educator with a style that was also polarizing. This superintendent was an outspoken defender of white educator interests and dismantled all the bilingual programs, repeatedly turning away funding for new ones as well. In addition, he dismissed most of the Hispanic and black educators his predecessor had appointed.

Moreover, the new superintendent kept the district polarized by treating minority parents and educators with little consideration. "He was very sarcastic, very insensitive to parents," reported a Hispanic CSB member. "He ran the district with the CSB in secret, and we never had the whole story on anything. He was 100 percent behind destroying the bilingual program, referring to it as an Hispanic organizing service." "He and the majority on the CSB sent back $280,000 of bilingual education money," reported a moderate white CSB member. "When I asked him why, he said there is nothing to worry about, because all it means are jobs for Puerto Ricans."

From 1973 through 1977, this CSB and superintendent supported white educator interests and opposed those of community control activists. The general policy was one of reestablishing "professionalism," which for the board and superintendent meant appointing mainly monolingual white teachers and supervisors from civil service lists.

In brief, this district had two activist superintendents in its first seven years under decentralization, representing extreme positions, and their polarization styles kept it in continual turmoil. Neither had any skill or interest in stabilizing the politics, and their adversarial postures made it difficult to secure the kind of educator-community collaboration and staff continuity necessary to sustain a coherent improvement strategy. The Hispanic superintendent did initiate many new programs that met educational needs of students and that probably contributed to their improved performance, but he negated the programs with his confrontational style. His successor had no coherent strategy other than to dismantle new programs and defend the interests of white educators.

The stalemated politics that resulted might have continued, except for the fact that the second superintendent got into trouble with his CSB over his loose style of administration. More specifically, the 1977 CSB found serious financial irregularities with the district's food programs; and although the board agreed with its superintendent's pro-teacher orientation, it forced him to resign. As one CSB member explained: "He left rather than being indicted. There was an awful lot of money missing and unaccounted for." This superintendent's style was also a factor in his resignation, as the CSB increasingly realized that it needed another superintendent who might run the district in a less adversarial manner.

The superintendent the board then selected, a white principal from within the district, had a completely different style from that of his two immediate predecessors. Although not an advocate of community control, having honored the UFT strike of 1968 over that issue, he did not support the tactics of the white educators either. Rather, he wanted to cool off the district's politics. In fact, he had turned down the superintendency several years before, on grounds that the district was too polarized to be managed effectively. His style is a *balancing* and *stabilizing* one vis-à-vis district constituencies. And he had always played that kind of mediating role. At the time of the 1968 teachers' strike over community control, for example, he worked with all sides to try to reopen the schools with a minimum of disruptive conflict. Later, under decentralization, he had often shuttled back and forth between the Hispanic superintendent and white educators, at the superintendent's request, to help attain better communications.

Since this superintendent was appointed in 1977, the district has turned away from "no-win" political battles between teachers and community control advocates and focused much more on education. The CSB has also been an important factor in this development. The most recent CSB, for example, elected in 1980, represents for the first time a more balanced group, with a majority interested in educational program improvements; in parent participation; and in the employment of professionally credentialed, minority educators. Even though there is only one Hispanic on this board, several of its white members are committed to the above-mentioned goals. The board is, in that sense, moving in a more moderate direction than its predecessors were, responding both to Hispanic and to white educator constituencies.

This combination of a more moderate board and a superintendent with a similar set of commitments and style are hallmarks of the district's most recent period of more social peace concerning public education. There has thus been a gradual increase in the power of moderates on the CSB, after each of the polarized union and community factions became burned out through years of struggle while also losing local constituency support. The precipitating critical incident was the second superintendent's poor management, but it seems likely that some other reason for forcing his resignation might well have been conjured up had this one not been available.

Since assuming office, the superintendent has become a major force in the district's improvement efforts. While he is not single-handedly responsible for the many changes that have taken place in recent years, his style has certainly contributed to bringing about these changes, and it is to a consideration of that style that we now turn.

Managing a Divisionalized Bureaucracy

One purpose of decentralization was to provide enough administrative authority to community superintendents for them to be able to develop programs that were responsive to student needs. Superintendents could do that only under conditions of political stability. Otherwise, their energies would be so taken up in dealing with community conflicts and in trying to broaden their own political base that they would have little energy left for exercising much educational leadership. But even if they were fortunate enough to manage in a politically stable district, they had to have the administrative skills and educational expertise to take advantage of that. The most recent superintendent in District A has both—a stable district and needed leadership skills. And it may well be that his skills have further stabilized the district's politics.

This superintendent's style is much more collaborative than adversarial. It has helped bring participants together rather than fragment them. As a professional educator, he has effectively refocused the district's attention from the divisive conflicts of the past to educational planning and improvement activity.

The change in political climate is particularly noticeable in the district's shifting power structure. The two power groups described above—

a white educator coalition bent on maintaining their power and a community control group wanting radical change—have all but disappeared, having been replaced by newly organized parent associations and new educators not caught up in past conflicts. Seventeen of the district's eighteen principals, for example, have been appointed since the mid-1970s.

A further reflection of the changes relates to bilingual education, formerly one of the district's most divisive issues. Rather than take a strong ideological stand for or against bilingual programs, the superintendent has worked to improve them. Soon after taking office, he appointed a Hispanic as bilingual director, who is highly trained in that field and is a staunch advocate of bilingual education. Since then, the superintendent has made other Hispanic appointments—as district office staff, teachers, paraprofessionals, and school aides. And he and his director have substantially increased the number of proposals put in for bilingual programs, roughly doubling the size of their bilingual staff and tripling the numbers of students served by the programs. While he has not appointed nearly as many minority educators as some community leaders want, the district has reestablished an affirmative action policy in staffing decisions.

Most important, this superintendent has pursued a low-key but task-oriented approach to issues that has improved both the political climate and the educational programs. Indeed, over the past couple of years, he has kept the district on a more even keel than it ever was before.

CURRICULUM STRATEGY

A big problem in many inner-city minority districts, particularly those with much political conflict, is that of developing a coherent, standardized curriculum so that all students have at least some common educational experience. This superintendent has done that. He has moved to *consolidate* the district's many reimbursable and city-funded programs into a single package, and to set *minimal standards*. He has done so through a new district advisory council composed of parents, teachers, principals, CSB members, and district office staff that he set up in 1980. And they have been developing a standardized curriculum for the entire district in reading, writing, and math that went into effect in September 1981. He and his council are using the central board's curriculum guides for this purpose, and they have also visited several other districts to learn from their experience with curriculum planning. At the same time, this superintendent, like many others, leaves the way they reach those standards up to individual principals—for example, whether they emphasize traditional or more informal, open classroom approaches.

Particular attention has been paid to reading, to prekindergarten programs and the early grades, to getting more outside (federal and state) program money, and to consolidating the management of funded programs. The district now has new, large pre-K and day-care center programs, and it has expanded bilingual education considerably, after several years of inactivity. Indeed, for the first time in several years, it is much more in compliance with court orders to have such bilingual programs for its non-English-speaking students than before. As in other districts, perhaps the biggest emphasis has been placed on improving reading, and much teacher training has accompanied this effort.

Other curriculum changes are also taking place. Title I and Pupils with Special Educational Needs (PSEN) programs, for example, which constitute the bulk of outside funding, no longer involve pulling students out of regular classrooms for separate instruction somewhere else in a school building. The superintendent has ordered that practice discontinued, as he saw the stigma it involved for participating students who were at least implicitly defined as failures by such a procedure.

In addition, the superintendent is now establishing an information system indicating that supplies, textbooks, and other curriculum materials are available in each school and in the district office. This system will help in allocating them more efficiently in the future.

All these developments indicate an orientation to educational improvement that was not present in this district before decentralization and was not possible during the first years of decentralization; given the political climate. In brief, politics constrained leadership in the past, and until that politics was worked out to achieve some legitimacy for the schools, and some consensus within the district about policies, it was not possible to address critical education problems in any sustained way.

At the same time, working out the politics is a necessary but not sufficient condition for educational effectiveness. The professionals must then provide some coherent direction and develop good programs. That is now taking place in District A. Such curriculum initiatives were always possible under the old centralized system though there was little incentive to push such reforms through the bureaucracy. Under decentralization there is more pressure from the community to make changes that will improve education and they may be undertaken in the districts with more knowledge of local conditions and more community and educator participation, providing the political climate permits that. It now does so in this district, and the superintendent and his staff are taking advantage of that fact.

DISTRICT OFFICE AND SCHOOLS

One of the assumed benefits of decentralization was that local districts would provide the schools with needed technical assistance and monitoring so that they would not have to depend on a distant central bureaucracy that was often slow to respond. That kind of supportive relationship now exists between the district office and schools. The superintendent has a keen understanding of school problems, having served as an educator in the district for many years, and he relates well to his many educator colleagues there. As a result, the principals see him as supporting their efforts. "He has taken an enormous interest in the schools," reported one principal, "and he visits them often. He really knows what is going on in each school in this district."

Although advocates of decentralization hoped that district offices would play such a supportive role, its opponents argued that they might simply become mini-bureaucracies in their own right and impose programs in as equally a top-down and rigid way as headquarters had under centralization. In fact, principals in some districts still have that perception of their district office. This district no longer has that problem, however, as the superintendent has pursued a collegial rather than a bureaucratic style in relation to his schools. "Principals make the educational decisions for their schools," a union official reported. "The superintendent has introduced districtwide guidelines, but the schools have a lot of room to develop their own programs." The superintendent explained his strategy: "I am now working on standardizing the curriculum, with scope and sequence objectives. But I do not want the district to be Big Brother."

A different perception prevails on these issues among some remaining Hispanic leaders who retain the community control viewpoint of earlier years. From their point of view, there is no big push from the superintendent and his staff for minimal standards, for enrichment programs, or for monitoring the schools. As one such leader noted: "The turmoil has stopped, but the question is, what has replaced it? Has the superintendent done anything to make education better? I don't think that there has been any real movement toward change."

This perception obviously has a reality for the people who hold it, but it must be interpreted in the political context previously noted. The people who espouse it are no longer a significant force within the district. "We no longer hear from these Hispanic leaders you mention," reported the superintendent. "They don't have any constituency or voice now. The power structure in this district is the parents, not the political clubs, the old educator coalition, or this Hispanic group."

DISTRICT OFFICE AND COMMUNITY

Decentralization was meant to open up the schools to more parent and community involvement, making them more responsive than before to local concerns. It did not work out that way when the district was in political ferment. Under the Hispanic superintendent in the early years of decentralization, the political conflicts that his new programs generated—and particularly the fears of white educators that there would be a takeover by community-control-oriented militants—activated the educators and prevented parents from organizing. And the next "pro-professional" superintendent actively excluded parents from having a voice. The result was that no parent association network of any significance existed in this district until the late 1970s.

The situation has changed in recent years, however, as the present superintendent has established more collaborative relations between minority parents and the district. Shortly after he took office, he formed a president's council of PA heads from each school and got them to meet on a regular basis. "We never had much parent participation before," he said. "There was no president's council. It had never been encouraged. The Hispanic superintendent only wanted one group of parents to participate. There are now pro- and anti–community control people on that council, sitting at the same table. They are no longer into a battle. And the principals and PAs work together well."

Indeed, as indicated above, one of the main power groups in the district now is parents. They have become organized during the last few years, and their voice is heard more frequently. It is a voice that expresses a pragmatic concern about improving schools rather than about issues of power, control, and jobs, as was the case before. "There is a real community out there," explained a top district office staffperson, "composed of parents. They are smart, and we have to earn their respect. We meet regularly with every PA head, and their concerns are nitty-gritty ones. They want more security in the schools, and they want better education. We have PA presidents here who put in a lot of time. There are even some who bring kids back into the schools from the parks where they play hookey."

The superintendent, in turn, regards parents as his primary constituency. "I don't own these parents," he said. "I have to keep earning my credibility with them by what I do." The extent to which he has been doing that is evidenced by the fact that parents campaigned hard for him in the spring of 1980 when his contract came up for renewal. He had not initiated or even encouraged their campaign for fear it might stir up past conflicts. The resulting CSB vote was 9 to 0 to give him a three-year contract, and the parents' efforts had obviously helped.

One critical incident illustrates these points. A few years ago, the parents in one of the schools were furious about a headquarters announcement that it would be closed as an economy move. Those parents began organizing to stage a public protest, and when the superintendent heard about it, he asked them to hold off until he explored the matter with the chancellor. He then informed the chancellor that the closing of the school would open many old wounds. It was in a Hispanic area whose residents would see white-area schools as the favored ones, since none of the latter was scheduled for closing. The chancellor understood the point and promised not to close the school, provided there was no demonstration. If there was, he argued, it would appear that he had caved in to political pressure, thereby inviting much more public protest from other districts. The superintendent then went back to the Hispanic parents, told them the school would not be closed, and urged them to call off their demonstration. "They were skeptical," he reported, "but I told them I was putting my position on the line, and they agreed. They and I knew that it was my job if the chancellor closed the school. He didn't, and I won their respect as a result." There were other, similar incidents; and over time, they built up his credibility even more.

DISTRICT OFFICE AND PROFESSIONAL STAFF

Managing a divisionalized bureaucracy in a public sector agency such as this is different from doing so in business, in that this is also a professional bureaucracy. The main service delivery activity is carried out by teachers and principals who regard themselves as professionals, with a code of ethics and body of knowledge similar to physicians and lawyers. Given their professional self-image, educators desire considerable autonomy and prefer to be managed in a collegial rather than bureaucratic fashion. They are therefore likely to resist formal rules and controls that limit their discretion in the classroom.[5]

The problem of a superintendent managing a community school district is compounded by the fact that the interests of educators and those of community groups often come into conflict. The superintendent is consequently caught in a cross-pressure situation between professionals who want autonomy and job security and parents and community activists who want better schools. The latter tend to blame the teachers and principals for what they regard as school deficiencies. Maintaining a balance between lay and professional pressures, then, is a critical managerial problem for community superintendents.

It is particularly critical in poor minority districts where cultural and class differences exist between the educators and the parents. One of the main goals of decentralization was to help bridge the gap, to make the schools a more integral part of the community, rather than an alien, "colonial" agency. The title of the Ford Foundation Bundy Report, *Reconnection for Learning*, which Mayor John V. Lindsay commissioned in 1966 to propose a newly decentralized school system, reflects this concern.

District A is a classic example of a poor minority area where this educator-community conflict was played out in acute form, thereby limiting the prospects that decentralization might result in improved education. And the first two superintendents' orientation toward the professionals only made things worse, as already described.

That situation has changed quite radically, however, since the present superintendent arrived in 1978. He has maintained close relations with the educators without alienating parent and community groups. He brought in many of the district office staff, and the principals are colleagues he has worked with for many years. Not only does he support their schools, but he also sometimes calls on them informally to help him deal with districtwide issues. One such issue was a budget deficit he inherited that he had to negotiate about with headquarters. Being new to the position, and not having a district office staff he had worked with before or that had budgetary and accounting skills, he called on several principal colleagues he felt did have such expertise, as well as knowing a great deal about district programs. And they worked effectively with him in resolving some of the budgetary problems.

His relations with the UFT have also been cordial. The UFT reps are aware of his refusal to cross their picket lines in the 1968 strike over community control, and the behavior of people during that strike has much symbolic significance for the union throughout the city. In addition, the UFT has not had any conflicts with the superintendent over working conditions and assignments. "With this superintendent," explained the union rep, "the UFT contract is respected. So we can turn our energy to other matters." Another noted: "He is doing a good job. The district is quieter. It is possible to teach again. He is a good educator who is not here to foment a revolution. The educational process is back in this district."

Given the conflicts that existed before his appointment, this superintendent has thus handled the district's constituencies with much skill. Even his predecessor, a strong UFT supporter, was seen by that constituency as acting against the educators' interests because of his style. "He polarized the district and caused a lot of hatred," explained a union official. "He was a man of strong convictions who believed in stating them very forcefully," he continued, "and that didn't heal the wounds."

In brief, it is possible in a poor minority district, with a favorable political climate where moderates are in control, for a superintendent to make peace both with the professionals and with lay constituencies. Indeed, that is one of the keys to making decentralization work, and when it takes place, many more sustained improvement efforts on a districtwide basis seem possible than under the old centralized system.

DISTRICT OFFICE AND HEADQUARTERS

One of the big managerial uncertainties in running a divisionalized bureaucracy such as the decentralized community school district system in New York City stems from relations between the divisions and headquarters, which are often quite problematic. The divisions want more autonomy to tailor services to their unique markets, while headquarters wants more control to ensure that the divisions' performance follows its policies. That conflict has existed citywide since decentralization began. It was much more prevalent in the early stages, however, as the boards sorted out their respective powers, and there has been much more collaboration in recent years. Since it has settled down politically, relations with headquarters have improved considerably. Headquarters staff, for example, have helped to train district personnel in proposal writing for bilingual and reading programs that have resulted in outside funding, even though such programs might compete with citywide ones that headquarters had developed. And we already cited the case where the chancellor rescinded an order that one of the district's schools be closed.

The district, in turn, has helped headquarters. In addition to its improved performance, it has made available some of its underutilized buildings for headquarters use. As a result, what had traditionally been an adversary relationship is no longer that, and there seem to be prospects for much collaboration for many districts.

DISTRICT OFFICE BUREAUCRACY

Opponents of decentralization argued that it would simply establish 32 separate district bureaucracies that would function in the same obstructive way in relation to their schools that headquarters had in relation to the districts. We have already indicated the supportive role that this district office has begun to play.

In addition, it has been streamlined considerably, owing in large part to the city's fiscal crisis and its cutbacks in staff. Through the early years of decentralization, the district office had a very large staff, particularly in funded programs, and that created problems. White educators felt that those jobs were used as patronage for minorities, whereas community control advocates regarded them as opportunities for engaging in more affirmative action in district appointments.

This superintendent has totally reorganized the office, reducing the number of staff in a period of fiscal cutbacks and consolidating many positions and departments as his colleagues in other districts have done. As one district staffperson reported: "We reduced the staff in my unit from nine to four. We consolidated the management of our two biggest outside-funded programs into one position. There were too many chiefs and not enough was being done before." The superintendent explained: "The district office used to be very fragmented. I am consolidating it now. The disorganization of the office was simply a symptom of broader chaos in the district. I am getting the office back on an even keel where we can have some efficiency."

While this is not to make a virtue out of declining resources, posing as they do a further uncertainty and a basis for community agitation and less services, they do force a decentralized community school district to reassess its management. Before, when state and federal funding were more plentiful, minority areas like this one added many district office and school staff. That had many obvious benefits, including more potential services to students and more jobs. On the other hand, the programs became unwieldy and fragmented; they established special program turfs; and they thereby deflected the energies of some staff and local residents away from education and into empire building. These developments, in turn, resulted in considerable waste and shattered expectations, as the programs did not always lead to the kinds of results in terms of improved student performance that they were meant to have.

Under decentralization this district has gone a long way in developing both a management structure and procedures that make it likely for future funding increases to have more payoffs than was the case in the past. The fact that decentralization has led to the appointment of superintendents who are more oriented toward their district and its schools than their predecessors were, largely because of their being held accountable by their elected CSBs and local constituencies, has made them more attentive to improving district management than seemed to be the case under the old centralized system.

Recent Developments

Since the fall of 1981, this district has moved ahead in its pursuit of a rational planning strategy. It involves the participation of the CSB, the superintendent and his district office staff, principals, teachers, and parent and community leaders in setting goals and developing programs. The planning is being done with the assistance of academic consultants from Teachers College of Columbia University who are experienced in such efforts. At this writing, not all of the above-mentioned participants are as actively involved as the district would like, and it is hopeful of having them all included by the end of the school year. "We intend to go out into the community with posters in the spring, to get more parents and community groups involved in this planning," reported a CSB member who is particularly active in the strategy. "We still just have a small number of parents. But we are going to get more of them out in the coming months. We no longer have any problems with the teachers. The principals are a harder nut to crack. But we do have 60 to 70 percent of them with us now and hope to get the rest. I am an optimist and think that we can get this going and become a model for other districts."

One other remaining issue that this board member and others are still concerned about is staffing. Although community conflict over the appointment of minority educators has abated, and although more minority educators have been appointed, there remain some fundamental differences on this matter within the CSB. "There has been a big political shift in a positive way," reported a CSB member, "but we still have staffing problems. Our biggest weakness now is staff appointments of insiders who are payback appointments. The old coalition of white educators and the local Democratic club is still very powerful here, and the superintendent has to take them into account. As a result, staff appointments have been less than desirable, and no outsiders have been brought in. A recent appointment was deadlocked in a 4 to 4 vote, and then the principals used strong-arm tactics. Our candidate was an outside person, while the superintendent proposed an insider, the wife of a principal in the district, whom we felt was a very weak candidate. The outside person we proposed lost out."

In brief, this district has still not worked out its ethnic succession politics in a way that is satisfactory to some of its CSB members. In view of how polarized it had been throughout most of decentralization, that is not surprising. Yet, it has moved ahead, despite some remaining problems; and the conflicts that continue are at least being handled in a contained fashion that makes them minimally disruptive of the many positive improvement efforts that have been under way since 1978. That in itself is a feat of some significance, even though the district has yet to reach the kind of consensus on staffing that might be ideal.

Indicators of Student and District Performance

Despite all the political instability in the early years of decentralization, this district improved in its reading scores at every grade from 1971 to 1979.[6] Like the other districts, the largest gains were made in the higher grades, which had been furthest behind in 1971. The improvement for each grade level is shown in Table 2.1. When we compare the improvement in District A with that shown citywide, we find that it outperformed the city schools as a whole in terms of the size of the gains. The comparisons are shown in Table 2.2.

Thus, despite all the political struggles, educational improvements were taking place. The community-control-oriented Hispanic superintendent, despite his polarizing style, had introduced new programs that may have been responsible for many of the gains. In fact, most of the gains took place in the period from 1971 to 1975, when he was in office. For every grade, the gains were much greater during that period than since then.

TABLE 2.1

Reading Scores for 1971 and 1979

Grade	1971	1979	Change (+/−)
Two	2.3	2.5	0.2
Three	2.6	3.3	0.7
Four	3.2	4.4	1.2
Five	3.6	5.2	1.6
Six	4.9	6.1	1.2
Seven	5.0	6.4	1.4
Eight	5.8	7.7	1.9
Nine	6.9	8.2	1.3

TABLE 2.2

Changes in Reading Scores (1971–79)

Grade	District A	Citywide	Differences Between District A & All Schools (+/−)
Two	0.2	-0-	0.2
Three	0.7	0.1	0.6
Four	1.2	0.6	0.6
Five	1.6	0.7	0.9
Six	1.2	0.6	0.6
Seven	1.4	1.0	0.4
Eight	1.9	1.1	0.8
Nine	1.3	1.1	0.2

In 6 out of 8 grades, those gains were more than double those that took place in the more recent period. We would expect that an increasingly upward trend may soon be in evidence in the next few years, as the politics has become stabilized enough for the present superintendent and board to have an impact.

One must not, however, discount the fact of this district's demographic stability. Like all minority districts, it has a high rate of pupil mobility, but it is stable in terms of the types of backgrounds of its students.[7] There are not that many more poor minority students there now than there were before, when decentralization started, and that is probably an important factor in facilitating the improvements in reading scores.

The same general improvement took place in the district's math scores, both in comparison with what they were in 1971, and in relation to the citywide trend. They went up from 4.4 in 1971 to 5.3 in 1975.[8]

It has taken place, however, with a minimum of initiative on the district's part until very recently in the area of securing outside funding. Indeed, during the period from 1974 to 1977 this district was notorious for turning back bilingual monies to which it was entitled, for reasons we have already discussed. Those bilingual programs had become so much the center of the district's political conflicts between the UFT and Hispanics that the union-oriented superintendent and his CSB refused to accept such monies, rather than hire increasing numbers of bilingual educators as the programs required. And, in comparison with all other districts of its type—that is, those with a predominantly poor Hispanic population—it has generally been the lowest in terms of the amounts of reimbursable funds it received. In fact, many Hispanic educators from this district have sought positions in others over the past several years, where more bilingual programs were in operation.

As for average daily student attendance, it went down considerably, from 85.2% in 1971 to 83.5% in 1975, but it then went up to 84.8% in 1979.[9] The district was well above the citywide average of 83.6% in 1971. It went below the citywide figure in 1974 and 1975, and it has been slightly above the figure since then. Much of the ethnic confrontation took place during the earlier period, when parents sometimes kept their children home rather than have them face the upset and occasional violence that existed then. Again, as the district has stabilized politically, we would expect attendance to continue to improve somewhat.

Data for this district are available only for the last three years on its record in placing its graduates in specialized high schools, and they present a mixed picture.[10] In the aggregate, the performance in 1980 is about the same as in 1978, though there are counterbalancing changes for the different high schools. Thus, the number placed in Stuyvesant High School shows a steady downward trend from 20 in 1978 to 3 in 1980, as it does for the High School of Music and Art (from 14 to 2) and for the High School of Performing Arts (from 3 to 1). Those admitted to Brooklyn Technical, on the other hand, increased from 35 to 71. Brooklyn Tech has thus emerged for this district, as for many others, as the elite high school that has admitted sharply increasing numbers of minority students.

One of the most contested issues in the district, as we have described, has been the employment of minority educators, and it experienced much larger short-term changes than any other district in the city.[11] During the period from 1971 to 1975 there was a dramatic increase in the proportion of Hispanic and black educators, followed by almost equally as marked a decrease over the next couple of years. The overall trend, however, has been one of increasing numbers of minority educators. Thus, in 1971 the district had 4.2% blacks and 4.8% Hispanics in all professional positions; and by 1978, that number had increased to 11.6% for blacks and 14.5% for Hispanics.[12] That trend is also likely to continue, as the district increases its bilingual programs and as power on the CSB gradually shifts to community-oriented members.

One would expect on this basis that vandalism rates would begin to reflect such changes in the backgrounds of district educators, particularly given the fact that this was the issue that raised the most furor. The general picture thus far has been one of slight improvement.[13] The number of broken glass panes has gone down from 5,300 in 1971 to about 3,000 in 1978. Unlawful entries are up slightly, from 66 in 1971 to 69 in 1978; and there were 2 reported fires in each year, with the number fairly constant in the years in between.

Our general forecast or expectation for this district is that it may well improve on many student and school performance indicators in the future. It is unlikely to change demographically, and it has the political stability to handle its ethnic succession problems without many disruptions. It is surprising that the district did as well as it did through its many struggles, and it is likely to do better now that those struggles have abated.

3

A Showcase District, Poor and Hispanic with Early Stabilization: District B

Our next case is one of the most exemplary, "showcase" districts in the New York City school system, indicating the potential of decentralization to facilitate significant educational improvements, provided that many political conditions are present. Although this district has a somewhat similar student enrollment to that of District A, it settled down politically much earlier. And it went on to become one of the most effective districts in the city, often cited publicly as such by the chancellor and other headquarters officials. Indeed, in reading scores it has improved its ranking from 32d of the 32 community school districts to 18th since 1973.[1]

Unlike District A, this district had lost almost all its white population by the early years of decentralization, its local residents being roughly two-thirds Hispanic and one-third black, with the public schools reflecting that ratio.[2] Partly as a result of this factor, there was no big community power struggle between white educators and their local constituencies on one side and minority residents and educators on the other. While the district did replace several white principals with Hispanics and blacks, leading to some bad feeling within the local principals' association, it also appointed whites to supervisory and administrative positions, and it has many white educators at all levels. In fact, it has one of the most ethnically integrated staffs of any district in the city. The political disruption over its hiring more minority educators was thus minimal.

The main ethnic succession politics that took place here in the 1960s and early 1970s was of a broader, communitywide nature, as power within the local Democratic party machine passed from white to Hispanic leadership. The only ethnic conflicts centering on the schools were between Hispanics and blacks and between different factions of Hispanics. But even these were quite insignificant after the first few years of decentralization with respect to potentially disruptive effects on the schools.

Indeed, the hallmark of this district's experience was its early social peace in connection with public education issues, which was due largely to the success of one of its first CSB presidents in coalescing the political factions. He generated much consensus on district policies and helped to recruit and later supported an able superintendent who has provided strong professional leadership. The many innovative programs and effective staff that this superintendent has put in place have, in turn, contributed to an extraordinary performance for this district under decentralization.

The political scenario here, then, is one of early stability, allowing for strong professional leadership; many educational improvement efforts over a long period of time; and an impressive record in terms of student achievement and other such indicators of effectiveness. This chapter describes how and why this district moved so quickly through what we regard as necessary stages of political development for a community school district to become effective, and it indicates what productive initiatives were undertaken once the district's political problems were brought under control.

Demography, Neighborhoods, District Characteristics

This district is in the residential and cultural center of New York City's Puerto Rican population. Historically, however, several ethnic groups have dominated the area, including residents of German, Irish, Jewish, and Italian backgrounds. By the late 1960s, it had become a largely Hispanic area (60%), with a significant black population (35%), and some remaining Italian residents. The latter are an aging population, and the children of the few remaining younger families attend parochial schools.

Since decentralization began, many Puerto Rican residents have moved out—some very poor and the others an upwardly mobile, working class. They have moved to the city's outer boroughs and to the suburbs. They are being replaced, meanwhile, by middle-income blacks in new cooperative housing and high-rise apartment complexes. Hispanics remain the majority, however, and still hold the balance of power.

The public school enrollment essentially reflects the district's general population, and there has been little ethnic change since decentralization. Total enrollment, however, has declined steadily, as it has in many other districts, from more than 21,000 in 1970 to roughly 13,500 in 1980, making it one of the smaller districts in the city.[3] This decline has resulted from the big out-migration of Hispanics and from an influx of middle-class blacks who have few school-age children.

School utilization rates, in turn, reflect these enrollment changes, having declined from 87% in 1970 to 60% in 1979.[4] That has contributed to central board pressure to close some of the district's most underutilized schools. The district has responded, in turn, as many others have, by locating new alternative and bilingual schools in existing facilities and by attempting to attract outsiders from other districts to these schools.

Politics, CSBs, and Superintendents

Unlike many middle-class districts, there was strong support for decentralization in this one in the late 1960s. Some of the citywide community control leadership came from there and waged protests against the central bureaucracy in its schools. Like many inner-city poverty areas, those served by District B experienced considerable turmoil during the late 1960s in their antipoverty agency politics. Federal antipoverty programs had activated community organizing among previously unorganized groups; and the early stages of that process were marked by many leadership struggles that carried over into school politics and that involved severe conflicts between blacks and Hispanics over who would control the programs and benefit most from their services.

Over time, two developments stabilized this district. One was an informal agreement between Hispanic and black leaders to divide up the turf, thus permitting a sharing of new federal funds. This was done by having school district lines drawn under decentralization so that one district was in an area having a predominantly black student population and the other in a Hispanic one. And the agreement was that each would have a superintendent reflecting the district population.

Nevertheless, black-Hispanic conflicts continued until 1973, when an able, young Hispanic leader was elected to the new CSB and soon became its president, a second important development. Almost singlehandedly, he coalesced the politics, largely through his positions on the boards of key antipoverty agencies. Since some members of the CSB owed their jobs in these agencies to him, he had some leverage over their votes. Also, he rarely pressed ahead on a policy decision until he had a broad-based consensus to do so.

In addition, he helped increase the district's resources by having it declared a bilingual one, by virtue of its large Hispanic enrollment. This accomplishment qualified it for increased outside funding and thus opened up many classroom, supervisory, and administrative positions to Hispanics. At the same time, white and black educators were also appointed. The political stability that resulted from these initiatives was to help a good deal in establishing a setting within which educational improvements could take place.

Perhaps the most important decision of this CSB president and his colleagues was their selection in 1973 of a young, dynamic superintendent who was an outstanding educator and who soon made many educational innovations in the district. As one of the few Hispanic superintendents under decentralization, he reflected the values of this community, having grown up and taught there, and having recently run summer programs there.

The CSB president soon established a consensus on his board that they would function only as a policymaking body and would let the superintendent actually run the district. There was an understanding that the superintendent would be held accountable for the educational performance of the students, but only on a year-to-year basis, with little CSB interference during the year. The district thus set up a buffer between the superintendent and his CSB, thereby permitting him to move ahead on educational improvements without having to be overly concerned about district politics. As the CSB president reported: "I set up a wall between the CSB and the administration so that the educators would do their job and I mine. I effectively established a shield to prevent tampering by the board. If we have no expertise in education, we should simply select a good administrator and hold him accountable."

From 1973 on, then, the district moved to a new stage of political development, from the extreme factionalism and instability of the early years under decentralization to much more stability. Several conditions associated with school effectiveness accompanied this change, including: (1) *a CSB consensus that its role was to set policy and not be involved in administration;* (2) *much delegation of administrative authority to the superintendent and professional staff;* (3) *a consensus as well between the CSB and the superintendent on such role definitions;* and (4) *a resultant freeing up of the superintendent' resources for educational improvement activities, rather than for jurisdictional struggles with his board or constituency building in the community to establish his legitimacy.*

The political equilibrium that this district developed so early under decentralization has been maintained. The superintendent is now completing his eighth year in that position and has maintained an able staff who have helped him upgrade the district's programs and administration. The one exception to this pattern that seemed significant at the time and now lessens in importance was a brief revolt beginning in 1977 against the CSB president and, by indirection, against the superintendent as well. It began when the CSB president declined to run in the 1977 elections, moving on instead to the City Council, though it had been building up before then.

The main issue that brought together a temporary coalition opposing the former CSB president and his policies was his political style. His opponents disliked what they regarded as the unilateral way in which he ran the board, referring to him as a "power broker" and "dictator." Furthermore, they argued that he had used his position to strengthen his power base and that his actions as CSB president were a calculated means of helping him to achieve higher office. Running as a "good government," "antiboss" group, to "get politics out of education" and promote more "parent and community participation," this coalition included all those participants who felt left out of power before—some black and Hispanic parents, dissident Hispanic leaders, and newly disfranchised white ethnic politcal leaders. They elected a majority to the 1977 CSB and gave the superintendent a difficult time for the next year or so, before factionalism within their own group and their inability to function as a policymaking body limited their power.

After the former CSB president left, the new board made the superintendent's management style the big issue. It regarded him as the former CSB president's man and as functioning in the same unilateral fashion.

It continually criticized his style of not consulting with his CSB on administrative matters and finally established a policy in late 1978 that all budget decisions, staff appointments, new programs, grant proposals, and even routine purchasing decisions had to be cleared through the board.

Although for a time it looked as if the stable political climate that had developed so early under decentralization was about to become unhinged, with the board no longer serving as the superintendent's buffer, and with his authority seriously undermined, the net result was quite different. By the end of the academic year (June 1979) in which the board's actions to limit the superintendent's authority reached their peak, its own internal factions and ineptitude got the better of it; and when one of its members used what some of his colleagues regarded as "sneaky" and "underhanded" tactics to try to unseat the incumbent president and get hmself elected to that position, several board members, including its president who had previously challenged the superintendent, made peace with him. Since 1979 the CSB has once more delegated much administrative authority to the superintendent and has continued to renew his contract for long terms (three years) by New York City standards, thus allowing him to continue his many programs to improve education in the district.

The superintendent's strong support from the district's main constituencies—parents, teachers, principals, and distict office staff—has also helped maintain his position. That support is a result, in turn, of his impressive performance in improving education and student achievement, as well as of his political skills.

Indeed, this superintendent is by far the most important factor in District B's extraordinary success under decentralization. It has become a showcase district largely because of his leadership, which has become so widely recognized that in late 1981 he won a highly publicized award from a New York City foundation as one of the outstanding administrators in all city government. No other community superintendent had ever won such an award; and it is to a consideration of this superintendent's management style, which was the basis for the award, that we now turn.

Managing Effectively in a Decentralized District

District B's superintendent may be characterized as an *outsider*, "new-style" superintendent, in contrast to the *insider*, "career civil service" types that headquarters had commonly selected in the past. But he was an outsider only in the context of traditional staffing policies of the New York City Board of Education, not of the community. He had actually lived and taught in the district and had close ties with many community organizations and leaders. Moreover, he was young, energetic, and entrepreneurial; had many program ideas; and was ready to search out programs and staff from anywhere to improve the schools. He had an irreverence toward the system's bureaucratic procedures and was thereby willing to use the flexibility and powers of a community superintendent under decentralization to the hilt. His style was thus one of removing constraints for those educators pursuing new programs. He followed it with skill and enthusiasm. And he was an articulate, upwardly mobile Hispanic male who symbolized the aspirations of his community.

Creative entrepreneurship was thus the hallmark of the superintendent's style. This took place in several ways: (1) establishing a network of what are now *19 alternative schools,* mostly at the junior high level; (2) setting up a further network of *bilingual schools,* from kindergarten though junior high; (3) developing a *districtwide reading program,* which the chancellor has selected as one of four exemplary such programs for other districts to follow; (4) *securing unprecedented amounts of federal and state funds for new programs;* (5) engaging in *creative noncompliance* with Board of Education procedures, *through aggressive budgeting and staffing strategies* to initiate all these innovations; (6) making continued efforts at *removing bureaucratic constraints* to further support the programs; and (7) making systematic efforts over the past couple of years to *upgrade regular schools* that are not part of any of the new networks.

In brief, this district illustrates how it is possible under decentralization to make significant curriculum improvements. The style has been one of exercising as much initiative as the system will allow. As one district staffperson noted: "I don't consider any day a success unless I maneuver around five or more headquarters procedures. This indicates to me that I am really accomplishing something. The system as it presently works prevents good things from happening, and the only way to run a good operation is to break these rules. From our point of view, it's a question of what is more important—the rules or the kids. We have chosen the kids."

Studies of innovation in organizations indicate that different styles and structures are needed at different stages. In the early initiation stage, it is important to have a flexible style such as this superintendent had, bringing in diverse experts who may contribute new program ideas.[5] At a later implementation stage, however, one must use a more bureaucratic approach. This involves paying more attention to structure and to administrative details of program management, particularly to monitoring and evaluation, with subsequent program and staff improvement made as the results so indicate.

Many managers have skills in one or the other area; few are strong in both. In his first several years in the district, the superintendent was stronger in *innovation* than in *careful administration*. He excelled in establishing a climate for new programs, in attracting new staff and resources, and in finding ways around bureaucratic rules to get the programs in operation. Although he had an equal concern with program results, his commitments and skills at implementation were not as strong as at getting programs started.

The superintendent was aware of this imbalance and in late 1978 hired a management consultant to help him improve. The consultant presented him with the following diagnosis: (1) The superintendent had *too broad a span of control* and had become *overloaded* with requests from many people. He therefore needed to delegate more. (2) He was too *nondirective* in handling staff; and *roles in the district office needed to be defined more sharply*. People didn't know who should report to whom. And all ended up converging on him. (3) He was very *creative at innovating and stimulating others* to be, but he was *less attentive to planning, to administrative detail, to monitoring and follow-up, and to providing district office support to schools*.

The consultant's prescriptions followed directly from this diagnosis. He recommended that the superintendent *delegate more*; that he *establish a top management planning group* that would eventually include principals; that he *streamline the district office* by clarifying roles and reporting relations, encouraging more cooperation ("lateral relations") among staff, and consolidating positions for greater efficiency; that he *train his staff to follow the same management improvement strategy* he was following; and that he *have the district office provide more monitoring, technical assistance, and follow-up support to principals*.

During the past few years, the superintendent has made changes in line with the suggestions. For obvious reasons, not all the recommendations took hold. First, it is difficult for people to change their style in more than incremental ways. And it may be more worthwhile for managers to build on their strengths than to move in radical new directions. There was also the problem of the managerial skills of his top district office staff. While dedicated to serving him as best they could, they would have needed much administrative training to fill the new roles prescribed for them by the consultant. The district did not have the resources for that. Second, the consultant left a few months after making the recommendations, and there was the usual lack of institutionalization that often results when consultants leave at an early stage of their work. Finally, the uncertainties of a big-city school district like this—for example, in levels of funding, staffing, and student enrollment—notwithstanding its political stability, called into question some of the recommendations. For example, management researchers indicate that organizations in such uncertain environments may do best by adopting just the kind of *nonbureaucratic form* that this superintendent did. In fact, the organization of the future is often portrayed as an *adhocracy*, with *loosely structured roles* and a *flexibility of organization* such as existed here.[6]

CURRICULUM STRATEGY

Some districts have taken more advantage of their flexibility under decentralization than others, depending on whether they have worked out their politics and on whether they have a superintendent who provides innovative leadership. This district ranks high on both counts and has engaged in much curriculum innovation as a result.

Contrary to many poverty-area districts where parents demand traditional, "back-to-basics" approaches, however vague and ambiguous that slogan may be, this district has been unusually experimental. Thus, the two biggest programs are its 19 alternative schools, accounting for roughly 20% of its total enrollment and its network of bilingual schools, accounting for another 20%. Moreover, there are other alternative programs as well, made possible through the district's vast federal and state funding.

The net result of this experimental approach has been to create a situation of competition among three types of schools—alternative, bilingual, and regular. Although not originally planned this way, the development of these alternatives has established the equivalent of an intradistrict voucher system where schools compete for students and where parents have considerably more options than is usually the case. Principals in regular schools feel threatened by these alternatives, since they may lead to declining enrollments and to consequent staff and budget cuts. "Principals feel the alternative schools are taking their kids away, and they are jealous," reported a district staffperson. "Ultimately, the game is one of numbers and power. They want as many students as possible."

Responding to such competition, several regular school principals have made their programs more attractive. Some have started mini-schools, while others have developed new enrichment programs. They have written brochures and have actively advertised their new programs to attract students. The superintendent is in this sense *orchestrating a diversity of programs* in a way that all may be enriched. At least, this has been one of the alternative education strategy's unanticipated consequences.

Another result of these alternative schools is that they are attracting increasing numbers of white middle-class students from outside the district. The schools have received much publicity through the press—such as the *New York Times,* the *Post, New York Magazine,* and education journals—as well as through informal word of mouth throughout the city. And since white middle-class parents in New York City have always been reluctant to send their children to large junior highs, those being problem schools throughout the city, more of these parents are now actually clamoring for admission to District B's alternative schools. At present, they account only for roughly 400 of the 2,000 students enrolled in those schools, but even that number is large for such a poverty-area, minority district, and it has been increasing.

These alternative schools have thus become, in essence, unzoned *magnet schools,* providing a 1980s version of *reverse open enrollment* that has inceased *ethnic integration.* That is taking place in an area of New York City where it would never have been predicted, desegregation having been written off as a lost cause there and in other big cities, and certainly never to be expected in the form of whites voluntarily traveling into poor minority areas. Most important, these schools are a direct result of decentralization. They would never have been started but for initiatives taken by the superintendent and his able associates.

Given the fact that District B's alternative schools have become perhaps New York City's most dramatic showcases of effective educational innovation under decentralization, they merit a brief treatment. An analysis of how they work may provide a model for other decentralized districts and may help suggest how innovation can succeed in such an inner city school setting.

A Success Spawned by Decentralization. The alternative schools constitute smaller schools housed within existing ones. Each has from 50 to 200 students, its own organization, staff, parent council, and a separate reporting relationship with a district office administrator rather than with the principal. They are in that sense autonomous schools within schools, emphasizing individualized learning, a humanistic relation of school staff to students, intensive remediation for underachieving students, out-of-classroom as well as traditional learning experience, and concentration on a particular curriculum and/or career. Their staff emphasize teaching basic skills by focusing the curriculum on a particular subject or skill in which students already have some expertise and self-confidence, including the performing arts, science, mathematics, language arts, and sports.

Each of these alternative schools was started by a teacher, who either sought out the superintendent and the alternative schools administrator and presented the idea or was instead sought out by one of them. Regardless of which way it went, these schools began in a distinctly *bottom-up fashion*. A teacher had a conception of how to run a good school, was usually already putting it into practice in a particular classroom, and wanted to develop and implement it further.

While conclusive evaluations do not exist, the district did contract with a research organization to assess how the alternative schools have done. The data suggest significant improvements in student performance.[7] Thus, a report by Community Arts Resources, Inc., of September 1979, on 6 of the alternative schools concludes that 5 of them now have students performing at or about national norms in reading. As the authors of that study state: "What is of particular note is that these centers are generating this performance in a school district that in reading achievement traditionally has ranked at or near the bottom in a city that, taken as a whole, ranks well below the national norm in standardized testing."[8]

They further report an increase of 56% of the graduates of these schools being admitted to specialized science high schools (Bronx High School of Science, Stuyvesant, and Brooklyn Technical) from 1977 to 1979, 1977 being the first year a systematic effort was made to increase the number of graduates accepted to such schools. As the authors report: "The A.E.C. [alternative schools] students comprise 26% of the District's seventh through ninth graders. However, in 1979, that 26% produced 45% of the District's acceptance from the Science High Schools, 65% of the Private School acceptances, and 74% of the Music & Art and Performing Arts High Schools' acceptances. These percentages clearly reflect a level of success that is high relative to the District taken as a whole."[9]

One simple explanation for these findings is that the better students in the district opted to attend one of these alternative junior highs rather than a traditional one. This would then be a self-selected population in alternative schools that had "creamed" the better students, much as receiving schools under various open enrollment plans had historically creamed the higher-achieving minority students who opted for them.

Other data on changes in scores on standardized reading and math achievement tests in 1975 and again in 1978 indicate substantial improvements among students in the three alternative junior high schools that had been in existence that long.[10] Thus, the mean reading score went up 3.3 grade levels in one alternative school and 2.7 in the other two, compared with 2.2. for the entire district and 2.1 for the city at large. And mean math scores went up 2.0, 2.1, and 2.5 for these three schools during that period. While problems of interpreting these data are enormously complex, given changes in the tests and their many reliability and validity problems, the findings gibe with qualitative data on these schools. Those data indicate that the schools have helped many East Harlem youths become high achievers in high school and college. Many of these students return to the district, reporting on their later successes and expressing much satisfaction with the education they received there.

As one of the alternative school administrators reported: "By and large our kids do very well after they leave. Many go to specialized high schools and private schools. They would never have done this well had they gone to a regular junior high. The ability of our teachers to pick up on these kids is not possible in the regular junior highs. It is hard to quantify that, but that is our experience."

These schools have been successful for a number of reasons, including:

(1) the superintendent, (2) the district office administrator and support staff, (3) the director and staff in each school, and (4) parents and students.

The superintendent has been the key to the entire operation. He actively recruited several of the teachers who started these schools, and he then provided a receptive administrative climate within which the teacher could further develop and implement the idea, ensuring that bureaucratic and resource constraints were overcome. "None of this would have happened except for the superintendent," explained the district administrator for the alternative schools. "And he more likely would not have been here under a centralized system."

One of the most supportive things the superintendent did was to appoint a supervisor from the district to a new district office position as administrator of the program, and to provide him with an able associate as well. The support they have provided has been extensive, including meetings with teachers to help in the early formulation of their design for the school; follow-up sessions with the superintendent; organizing parents at each school and through a districtwide network; providing teacher training and curriculum materials; providing continued assistance to the schools in securing needed supplies, staff, and additional students; mediating, where necessary, between the school and the principals in the building where it is housed; lobbying for higher salaries for school directors and for independent status for the entire network of alternative schools; publicizing their successes; and constantly mobilizing support from district and citywide groups.

The program depends heavily on the teachers, and their dedication is most impressive. Many stay late. They often visit students' homes. They sometimes hold staff meetings on weekends, and they do much work during the summer in preparation for the next year. The teachers are there by choice, so one should not be surprised by these actions. Nevertheless, they are deeply committed to these schools and their students.

A critical factor in the success of these schools and in the commitment of teachers to their success is the fact that teachers have such a strong voice in the development of their programs. These schools are in many respects *teacher-* as well *student-* centered, and that fact contributes to teachers' sense of ownership about school programs.

What is further striking about the relation of teachers to these schools is the strong support the union provides, even though teachers work incredibly long hours, way beyond what is specified in the union contract. "The union rep for the district comes to our school regularly," reported one alternative schools director, "and she thinks the things going on here are some of the most exciting in the city. I take it that the union does not feel the contract is being violated, since the teachers who are here are doing things because they want to." Another school director explained: "My staff works as though they never heard of the UFT contract. People want to teach here, and they don't think in terms of a nine to three day. They don't complain, because they feel productive and happy. We don't even follow UFT staff procedures."

As for the curriculum in these schools, there is a strong emphasis on the basic skills, through approaches that build on students' strengths and areas of self-confidence. The schools that specialize in the performing arts, for example, have developed close relationships with dance and theater groups in the city and have professionals in these fields working in the classrooms. One of these schools takes several week-long tours every year—to the Midwest and the South—during which its students perform publicly. These schools combine both professional training (e.g., in music and acting) and an academic program in basic subjects. One other school, whose curriculum focus is writing skills, has its students write and stage their own play. Still another, concentrating in science and marine biology, has developed close relations with the Bronx High School of Science, using its lab on a weekly basis, as well as with the Bronx Botanical Gardens and other such institutions.

Many of these programs are not that new, but their richness—combined with a dedicated teaching staff and an individualized, humanistic approach to students in a small school setting, with much back-up administrative support—produces effective schools. Parents are also deeply involved in these schools, and one of their contributions has been help with fundraising so that many of these enrichment activities might be continued.

Bilingual schools are another important alternative program, accounting for up to 20% of the district's enrollment. And there is now an extensive network of bilingual centers throughout the district, including 8 in elementary schools and 2 bilingual junior highs. The program has considerable federal funding and has, in addition, much teacher training, some of it in collaboration with Hunter College, that has a bilingual staff development program. Since District B is such a center of Puerto Rican culture and has a large enrollment of Puerto Rican students, the bilingual program there takes on particular significance.

Political controversy about bilingual education is widespread in New York and elsewhere, both on the merits of different approaches and as to whether there should, indeed, be any such program at all. Two approaches around which controversy has raged are (1) *maintenance* ones that emphasize instruction in the students' native language and include a lot of material on their cultural heritage and (2) *mainstreaming* that emphasizes English as the primary language (e.g., English as a Second Language programs). The conflict is more than just a philosophical one, since it involves jobs as well. As we saw in District A, white educators and their union often vehemently oppose bilingual programs that require teachers to have a mastery of Spanish, fearing that they will be replaced by Hispanics. Moreover, bilingual programs are vulnerable in other respects, since they usually serve the lowest-achieving students whose reading scores are likely to reflect that. Bilingual educators are therefore often in the position of having to defend their programs, fearful that they may be abolished. One such defensive posture is to develop a rigid philosophical justification for the particular approach they follow. And, in many districts, bilingual programs have been on shaky political ground.

District B has been fortunate in this regard. Its bilingual programs have strong local support from the superintendent and the board. While the philosophy is a maintenance one, the district also teaches English quite intensively, starting with the early grades, and it is doing more of that. After many years of modest results, the programs have begun to have a significant impact on student achievement. As the superintendent reported in 1981: "In addition to one bilingual junior high where the reading scores are extremely high, we have three bilingual centers where they are way up, where 35% to 45% of students are reading at grade level. In total, two of our eight centers are way up, and three others have shown improvement as well. In those where we see promising gains, not only is the English performance way up, but the Spanish is also."

A big factor in the success of the district's bilingual programs is the political support it has given them. The strong CSB president of the early years of decentralization had the district designated a bilingual one. He and his CSB selected a superintendent who has placed a high priority on improving bilingual education, secured much state and federal funding, and provided a lot of district office support—for example, in curriculum development and teacher training. One of the most productive things the district does is to maintain cooperation among the various bilingual centers so that they may learn from each other. "We have a coordinated effort through our network," explained a bilingual staff person in the district office, "so that we try to avoid service duplication and have a lot of information sharing. We try to spread the expertise of one school throughout the district."

Parents are also important to the programs' support. The district office has maintained active parent councils in the various centers who meet monthly with the staff. And parents are encouraged to talk with teachers about how their children are doing.

The majority of students in the district, however, are enrolled in regular schools rather than in these enriched alternatives. As one might expect, many staff in the regular schools have felt neglected by the district office and have been particularly sensitive to the positive media coverage the alternative schools have received. Staff in the regular schools have felt threatened by the presence of these other schools that compete with them for students. Both the alternative and bilingual schools have been active in attracting students, and their numbers have begun to show it.

This competition, while functional—for example, it provides more options for students and teachers and encourages the regular schools to improve—has contributed to conflict as well. The alternative and bilingual schools are housed in regular schools, and arguments over space, over staff, and over the sheer presence of their students have been common. "The principal feels it is his building," reported an alternative schools director. "He can bother you on petty things, like sharing of secretaries, scheduling of the lunchroom and gym, where to put misbehaving kids, and sharing the auditorium for performances." A district office staff person explained: "Having to share the same house is a problem. What does a principal of a regular school get out of it? He gives up control, and the school may take away some of his students." Regular school principals thus feel much resentment and jealousy.

Managing effectively in a district with so many options, and with the competition and conflict that goes with that, requires a delicate balancing strategy. On the one hand, the superintendent has wanted to give strong support to these alternatives, since that has been one of the most expeditious ways of bringing in good programs and significantly improving student performance. And yet, he has also had to deal more directly with this strategic constituency that still constitutes 60% of the district's students.

After giving considerable attention to the alternative and bilingual schools in the early period of their start-up, the superintendent and his staff have provided much support in recent years to the regular schools. This has coincided with his increased emphasis on having the district office play a much more active, administering role in the district, in contrast to his more entrepreneurial style of the past. The latter is still strong, but he has complemented it by doing much more monitoring and provided more district office assistance to the regular schools, particularly those with the lowest reading scores. "I have been much more active in watching those schools with reading scores in the lower ranks," explained the superintendent. "We work with the principal and make available a structured program in reading to help raise those scores. While I continue to delegate to the schools, there is much more accountability, and if the bottom half schools with the lowest scores don't improve, after we provide help, we take more drastic corrective action." This action has involved providing even more curriculum assistance and, in some extreme cases where that doesn't work, replacing the principal.

The fact that the district has improved its rank from 32nd to 18th among the 32 districts in reading, much of that coming in the past few years, suggests that the regular schools are getting much more attention. Indeed, one of the main reasons for the improvement relates to the district's *comprehensive reading program.*

The superintendent hired a new reading coordinator shortly after he arrived in 1973, and she has been there ever since. She and her staff service the regular and bilingual schools. And some of the district's success in recent years is due to their efforts. She has consolidated most of the reading programs, and in that sense, there has been a fair amount of *comprehensive planning* in this area. It has generally been done in a centralized way, with the superintendent and coordinator urging the schools to follow whatever approach to reading the district office favored at any given time.

The district's most recent reading program, which has attracted citywide attention, is called STAR (structured teaching in the area of reading). It got under way in 1978 and has been successful enough to be selected for widespread use throughout the city. The focus is on teaching *reading strategies* by directing the student toward a larger context. For example, if the selection read is fiction, students are alerted to think holistically about such elements as the plot, the main characters, and the author's thesis. If it is nonfiction, students are directed to the central themes, the author's biases, and the purposes of the work. "These are broad thinking and reading strategies that efficient readers follow intuitively all the time," explained the reading coordinator. "And our model is the efficient reader who does these things anyway."

Since the program has been in effect, reading scores in the district have continued to improve. It seems unlikely that this recent improvement is due just to other, extraneous factors (e.g., changes in the citywide reading tests, new policies of the chancellor).

Managing Professionals in an Innovative, Divisionalized Bureaucracy

Advocates of decentralization hoped that the added flexibility it provided to districts and their schools would result in more sustained curriculum innovations than the old centralized system provided. And some districts like this one clearly took advantage of that flexibility, for reasons already indicated: they handled their ethnic succession politics, achieved relative social peace, hired able superintendents and other staff, and effectively insulated them from outside interference—though still holding them accountable for their performance.

Even those conditions would not have been enough, however, if the district had not gained the cooperation of the professional staff. Effective management of the professionals, then, is a critical task in running a successful district under decentralization.

Perhaps the most striking aspect of District B's experience has been its collaborative relations with the teachers' union and principals' association, despite its having engaged in many departures from traditional staffing procedures. New Hispanic and black principals were appointed in more than half of the district's schools; many staff were brought in "off the lists," on certificates of competence and per diem and consulting lines. Yet, neither the teachers' union nor the principals' association staged any significant protests.

Board policies and the superintendent's style have much to do with this effective managing of the professionals. The CSB and the superintendent are committed to establishing an ethnically balanced staff, unlike their counterparts in some minority and white districts, and the professionals are aware of that. Thus, the total staff (teachers, principals and APs, and district office personnel) changed from 81.4% white, 5.1% Hispanic, and 13.4% black in 1970 to 45.5% white 27.1% Hispanic, and 28.4% black in 1979.[11] While some white educators felt threatened by the changes, it was clear that "merit" as well as "ethnic representation" were foremost in staffing changes. Indeed, many white educators were appointed during this period, and some minority educators who did not work out were transferred or removed from their positions. As the superintendent explained: "Before, we had an almost all-white group. A lot of the white principals who left were very near retirement. We now have an integrated staff, and our appointments have been made with ethnic balance in mind. But we do not take unqualified minority educators. Sure, we make mistakes just like anybody else, but we go about rectifying them."

In addition, all the things the superintendent did to improve the district made it a better place for the educators, thereby increasing their cooperation. He and his staff brought in substantial amounts of outside money for new programs; he constantly encouraged teachers to come to him with ideas they wanted to put into practice; he was very effective at removing bureaucratic constraints so that they could in fact implement ideas that he and his staff felt had merit; and his whole approach was to give teachers more and more of a *voice* in developing school programs. His nonconfrontational style contributed to cooperation as well. He never publicly criticized the educators if they disagreed with his policies.

The one limited exception to this pattern of collaboration was the district's relations with the principals' association in the early years of decentralization. Several white principals were encouraged to take early retirement or were transferred out of their schools, usually being replaced by minority successors. One such principal whom the CSB and superintendent felt was no longer able to run his school effectively was allowed to collect his salary while simply sitting in the district office for a few years, to qualify for his pension. He and the principals' association tried to make a cause célèbre out of his case by representing it through the media as a reflection of unwarranted ethnic politics in the selection and firing of staff. They also charged that it reflected a general policy. In actual fact, he had been a competent "traditional" principal who was unable to function well under decentralization.

That was a short-lived protest, however, and the district's relations with the professionals remain collaborative ones. The district has demonstrated that it is indeed possible for a minority area to pursue a policy of ethnic succession in staffing under a decentralized system without any major political disturbance. It was hard for the professionals to challenge a district that hired educators from all the main ethnic groups; that hired credentialed minority staff; and that acknowledged "mistakes" when they occurred in appointments of the latter, just as it did in staffing decisions on whites. All these policies established a climate of collaboration and trust that has contributed to the district's successes.

DISTRICT OFFICE AND HEADQUARTERS

While managing local politics and the professional staff are clearly essential in developing an effective community school district, it helps to have headquarters support as well. District B was masterful in that regard, pursuing a strategy of what might be called "playing the system." It involved taking initiatives in budget and staffing practices that some, perhaps many districts were hesitant to follow. On the budget, for example, the district's business manager maintained a flexibility in funding allocations to various programs so that the district could shift funds around according to need, without having to clear the details with headquarters and risk long delays. And on staffing, it successfully negotiated an agreement with headquarters whereby it could recruit all educators from off the civil service lists, to ensure that promising new programs would be well run.

The superintendent's style of *removing bureaucratic constraints* was reflected in these practices, and it was one of the hallmarks of his effectiveness. While some of his counterparts in other districts adopted a lower-risk strategy in this regard, he and his staff took advantage of the *loose coupling* of headquarters-district relations to stretch their powers to considerable limits.[12] That required the informal support of headquarters administrators, some of whom had enough confidence in the district and enough commitment to decentralization to provide it. And, when the district demonstrated its capability by improving student performance as much as it did, this reinforced that support.

Many districts complain that their options remain quite limited under decentralization, since so many decisions on staffing (e.g., collective bargaining agreements, personnel policies) and budget are made centrally. While these complaints are valid, there is flexibility in the system for those willing to bend the rules. And District B illustrates what can be done to take advantage of that.

DISTRICT OFFICE AND COMMUNITY

Advocates of decentralization had hoped that it would help make the schools a more organic part of their surrounding communities, and we found considerable evidence for that in District B as well as in other districts we studied. The argument was that by having the flexibility both to recruit staff sensitive to the culture and learning styles of students and to develop more collaborative programs with other local agencies without having to keep clearing them through headquarters, community school districts would more likely customize or tailor their services to meet local needs. That has happened in quite dramatic fashion in District B, as it has in varying degrees in the others we studied.

The superintendent and some of his professional staff, for example, have deep roots in this community and are strongly committed to its economic and political development. This has been reflected in their involvement in community agencies and even in the district's electoral politics.

On a more educational note, the programs reflect both much more collaboration with outside agencies (local and citywide) and a customizing to fit local needs. To illustrate: the district has developed an alternative school in environmental studies as a joint venture with an adjacent white middle-class district, in one of the latter's facilities. Extensive further programs exist in collaboration with hospitals, museums, theater groups, and academic high schools outside the district.

A typical example of this community-oriented outreach approach is the superintendent's unique new project to convert an existing high school in the district that had a long record of failure under central control to a community school whose curriculum will be upgraded significantly and closely integrated into that of the district's elementary and junior high schools. A new magnet junior high specializing in math and science will be housed with the high school, and the latter will build on that. And there is to be a two-year community college program there as well. This project has thus begun the revitalization of a failing school that was a blight on the area and indicates the promise of decentralization for community development under strong local leadership.

By contrast, parent involvement has been less extensive than decentralization advocates had hoped it would be. In this minority district, as in so many others of its kind, there has been limited parent participation in the school. There has been no active district wide parents council as there is in many middle-class districts; and the key educational decisions have been those of the superintendent and his professional staff. Yet, they clearly express the "general will" of the community, as evidenced by the many effective new programs and staff, the considerable outside funding they have secured, and the improved performance of students.

Poor minority parents, particularly Hispanic ones, seldom get involved in public school affairs in significant numbers. They did to a much greater extent in the 1960s, when federal funds were available for that purpose—for example, for parent training and organizing through antipoverty agencies. When the money dried up, however, parent participation also declined markedly.

While the reasons for such limited parent participation may vary from one district to another, there are common ones as well. In a declining economy, these parents have all they can do just to survive. Many have more than one job, and they have little energy left for involvement in public school affairs. In addition, for many Hispanic parents, their culture encourages a deference to authority figures like teachers and principals. These parents would be ill at ease as activists.

Yet, as schools in districts like this one become a part of their communities under decentralization, and as some parents become more middle class in outlook and style, there may be more parent participation in the future. A parent support structure has in fact begun to develop in this and other minority districts over the past couple of years, in part to protect programs in a period of continuing fiscal cutbacks.

District B's superintendent, for example, formed a parents council in 1980, and parents are now on districtwide CSB committees. In addition, he maintains informal relations with parent leaders, to compensate in part for the absence of established parent organizations in the past. "We never use the power of our professionalism," he explained, "to keep parents out."

One lesson from this and other minority districts, however, is that parents do not necessarily have to participate actively in school decision making for decentralization to work. "It may be a copout for the professionals to say that there must be massive parent participation to have an effective district," explained a district staffperson. "That may be too much of a burden on minority parents." Indeed, this district has been effective without a lot of parent involvement, as the superintendent has developed programs almost exclusively through his professional staff. While that does not fit the goals of community control advocates, it has worked well in this district, as it has in several others.

What may be needed for the future are new roles for minority parents under decentralization. One traditional role they have played in this district, where they have otherwise been quite inactive, has been to exercise their *voice* on important staffing decisions. The renewal of the superintendent's contract and tenure decisions for principals are examples, and on several occasions that parent voice has made a difference. As for other roles, the reader is referred to our analysis of two poor black districts, E and F, for some intriguing recent developments.

Conclusions

The question arises in analyzing a "success case" like this one as to its replicability. Are there any lessons from its experiences that may apply elsewhere, at least to other inner-city districts with similar student populations? Several factors, in retrospect, contributed to this district's successes.

As this chapter has indicated, the superintendent has served in the district since 1973, as have many top administrative staff. That has facilitated a more systematic and coherent approach to curriculum than might have been the case had there been a high rate of turnover. Staff continuity per se obviously does not guarantee innovation and better planning, as the experience of the New York schools before decentralization indicates. It helps a great deal, however, if other conditions are also present.

One condition is administrative leadership. The main theme of this chapter has been to indicate how critical the superintendent's leadership has been to the district's success. He attracted some of the most professional proposal writers and educators in the city, and we found no other minority district that brought in more outside funds or developed more effective new programs and schools. Most important was *the supportive climate* he established for teachers and district office staff. He consistently played the role of facilitator for their schools and programs—cutting through red tape and helping them secure needed resources.

A final condition for this district's success has been its *declining enrollment*. That has provided the space needed for the development of alternative and bilingual schools. In a period of fiscal crisis, when districts were being pressed from headquarters to close underutilized schools, there was no way they were going to be permitted to acquire new facilities for experimental programs. This district, however, like several others, was able to turn its declining enrollment into an advantage, by using underutilized space for new programs.

Declining enrollments also provided an additional incentive for the district to search for more outside funding, since city funding was decreasing commensurate with that demographic trend. The superintendent would have sought outside funds anyway, given his style, but his efforts got added impetus by this development.

In sum, staff continuity, leadership, and declining resources were among the key factors in this district's success, along with the political factors mentioned earlier. And the first two factors are, in many respects, manipulable variables, amenable to public policy interventions. There is no reason to assume, for example, that as skilled and unique as this superintendent is, there aren't others available who might be recruited and/or trained to be as effective in at least some other districts as he has been here.

Indicators of Student and District Performance

Given the many positive developments in this district under decentralization, have they made any difference in how well students perform? Have the district's many successes in securing outside funding led to better results in the classroom? We have already reported on the reading score improvements in the alternative schools, but how about the district as a whole? What has happened there?

TABLE 3.1

District B
Reading Scores for 1971 and 1979

Grade	1971	1979	Change (+/−)
Two	2.3	2.6	0.3
Three	2.7	3.2	0.5
Four	3.2	4.2	1.0
Five	3.7	5.0	1.3
Six	5.0	5.8	0.8
Seven	4.8	6.3	1.5
Eight	5.5	7.4	1.9
Nine	6.2	7.7	1.5

It appears that the district's educational programs described in this chapter have had a big effect. In all 9 grades, pupils improved their reading scores between 1971 and 1979, with the greatest gains occurring in the higher grades, possibly because they were furthest behind in 1971, but possibly also because that is where the alternative schools have concentrated the most. The reading scores and the net change for this district are shown in Table 3.1.[13] Most important, the district's gains were greater than those made citywide. Table 3.2 compares the two, indicating that this district outperformed the city as a whole at every grade level.

What other explanations, besides the special form of decentralization that took place in District B, could account for the fact that it did better than the city as a whole? One possible explanation might be selective migration patterns, but this district has been subjected to the same migration trends as the rest of the city, with upwardly mobile families leaving the district or sending their children to private and parochial schools. A second explanation relates to an artifact in such time series data known as the regression effect. That is, extreme scores (above or below the mean) tend to regress toward the mean, just as a matter of chance. This alternative explanation might be plausible if our conclusion were based only

TABLE 3.2

Changes in Reading Scores (1971–79)

Grade	District B	Citywide	Difference Between District B & All Schools (+/−)
Two	0.3	0.3	0.3
Three	0.5	0.1	0.4
Four	1.0	0.6	0.4
Five	1.3	0.7	0.6
Six	0.8	0.6	0.2
Seven	1.5	1.0	0.5
Eight	1.9	1.1	0.8
Nine	1.5	1.1	0.4

on a change or a difference from one year to the next. But our conclusion that District B outperformed the city as a whole is based on observing a slow growth over an eight-year period. It is not based on one year's change.

How, then, does one account for the better performance in District B compared with the city as a whole? We would suggest that the many initiatives pursued by this district's superintendent, reflecting his management style, may well have contributed. The district has had an extraordinary record, for example, in securing outside funding, and that was a result of the superintendent's leadership, which we described earlier. He hired some able proposal writers, and they were successful in getting their programs funded. Thus, the district brought in more than $10 million in outside funds in 1978, ranking it as the 4th highest in the city.[14] While some of this was in noncompetitive grants, owing to the district's having a large proportion of low-achieving, minority students, including many Hispanic ones, the district has secured substantial funding through the competitive Emergency School Aid Act (ESAA) and other programs as well. These successes seem to have paid off in student performance. Indeed, in the 1977–78 year, more than 40% of its total budget came from reimbursable funds, far surpassing 30 of the 31 other districts. What is particularly striking is that this is one of the smallest districts in the city in total enrollment, having decreased from 21,379 in 1970 to around 13,000 in 1979.

By contrast to the district's reading scores, there has been only a very small narrowing of the gap in its math scores relative to citywide trends. Math test data are available only for fifth graders, the other grades not being tested, and in this district the average score has moved up from a little above fourth grade level to fifth grade level during the period from 1971 to 1979. Meanwhile, the citywide trend has been from 5.4 to 5.9. There has been greater improvement than for the city as a whole, but it has not been as dramatic as in reading.[15]

Attendance data do show a significant upward trend, however. In 1973, when the present superintendent took over, the district's average daily attendance was 83.3%, below the citywide figure of 85.6%. By 1979 the district had gone up to almost 87.0%, while the citywide rate was around 85.09.[16] Again, some of this improvement may well have been the result of the new programs the superintendent and his staff initiated.

Another indicator of student performance relates to the rate of placement of its graduates into the city's elite, specialized high schools. New York City has 5 such high schools to which students are admitted only after passing an entrance examination. After much controversy in the 1960s, in which minority-group leaders charged that these schools were too elitist and should be closed down, admissions requirements were modified to let in more minority students, but the standards have not changed much since then. And some minority districts apparently do much better than others in placing their students in these schools. A district's location affects such placement rates, but its programs may also play an important role.

District B has a particularly impressive record in this regard. Thus, it placed 59 students in these schools in 1975–76, the first year in which data were collected, while that number increased to 180 in 1980.[17] It placed 16 students in the High School of Music and Art in 1975 and 41 in 1980, while the number gaining admission to the High School of Performing Arts increased from 5 to 12 during that period. Both increases were probably reflecting the district's vastly enriched programs in those areas. Its tutorial programs with the Bronx High School of Science in which its students visited that school on a regular basis were particularly important in those admissions. If one adds to this the many students from this district who have gone on to academic private schools, the figures are even more impressive.

District B is thus a prototype of a district that did well under decentralization. Its politics stabilized relatively early; its CSB selected a "new-style," community-oriented superintendent who brought in many new staff, much outside money, and many new programs. All those positive developments have been reflected in student performance.

If this district had become more of a community-oriented one, as we also pointed out in this chapter, that should have been reflected in its vandalism rates as well.[18] In fact, they point strongly in that direction. Thus, during the period from 1971 to 1978, broken glass panes were down from 5,150 to 2,600, unlawful entries from 160 to 95, and fires from 14 to 3. This confirms what many observers of urban schools have known for a long time—that those minority-area schools regarded locally as community institutions, rather than as "colonial" outposts manned by outsiders and not oriented toward community needs, are likely to be treated with more pride and respect. They thus have more legitimacy. District B is an example of this, having moved a long way toward making its schools legitimate social institutions. Notwithstanding some continuing problems, decentralization is clearly working in this district.

Moreover, all this is taking place with increasing staff integration as well. As indicated earlier, under decentralization this district has thus become one of the most integrated ones in its staff of any in the city.

4

A Politically Fragmented, Ethnically Mixed District, Hard to Manage: District C

Our next district is one of the most ethnically and economically diverse ones in the city. Encompassing a large section of an outer borough, it has been very difficult to manage, raising serious questions as to whether any district of that size and diversity could ever be run effectively, regardless of the skills of its CSB and superintendent. It has a student population of roughly 15½% white, 51½% Hispanic, and 34½% black, and that has remained relatively stable since decentralization began.[1]

Unlike either District A or B, this one never settled down politically, and it remains sharply divided to this day. Its community boards have been very factionalized, reflecting interest-group divisions in the wider district. Moreover, these boards have been deeply involved in patronage politics and administration and have increasingly limited the authority of their superintendents, three of whom have served since decentralization began. The first two, both of them regarded as among the ablest in the system, took early retirement rather than keep dealing with the district's turbulent politics. The most recent one, who has served since 1976, has been given only a series of one-year contracts, and he has yet to establish himself politically.

Thus, none of the conditions for district effectiveness that we found in District B and are now beginning to affect District A exist here. There remain too many ethnic groups that have not worked out a consensus on how the district will be run and staffed. The energies of both the CSB and the superintendent are focused much more on power struggles and constituency building than on educational planning.

Nevertheless, despite the politics the district has several able principals and some good schools. The schools run themselves, and much of this reflects the district's commitment to local option. This made sense, given the diversity of populations served. It also helped insulate the schools from the negative effects of district politics. Had that politics developed in the direction of more consensus, however, the schools would have been much better served.

Demography, Neighborhoods, District Characteristics

There are five distinct areas within the district: two devastated poverty areas in the South Bronx, one Hispanic and the other black; a transitional area in the center undergoing rapid ethnic succession; and two fairly stable white areas in the north that also contain some low-income housing projects. The poverty areas have experienced much housing decay and arson since decentralization began, with many of their former residents moving up to the center of the district, reflecting a general south to north migration. There are no more viable neighborhoods in some southern areas, while those in the center and even the north are trying desperately to maintain what they have, as low-income, minority populations move in.

As one might expect, there is much animosity between the populations of the south and the north. Middle-class northern areas have repeatedly told the district office that they are the "forgotten group" who also have rights that must be respected. Meanwhile, those in poverty areas have kept demanding more services and saying that the northern-area communities, whom they referred to as the "country clubbers," were really the favored ones. And center-area residents claimed that they were the abandoned group, noting they were the only ones who had made integration work.

These differences have made the district very difficult to manage. One former superintendent recalled: "When I went to the middle-class areas, they would give me a hard time, and then when I went to the south, they would, too." Another explained: "This was really five districts in one. It was quite a job, balancing off all these groups."

While all these areas have community organizations actively involved in school district affairs, those in the north are particularly well organized. The most powerful, often superseding parents on matters like electing CSB members, are political clubs, the Catholic church, and property owner associations. The political clubs have been consistently influential, and a majority faction on the 1977 board was commonly referred to in the district as "the Chippewa Five" in explicit recognition of that club's role in electing these people.

Other interested groups have also been active, including unions, parents, and community action agencies. The teachers were effective, for example, in electing CSB members on some of the early boards to oppose policies of the then superintendent, whom they regarded as being antiunion. Parent associations, on their side, have influenced some district staffing decisions—hiring principals and bringing up "incompetent" teachers on charges.

Traditional parent associations, however, have been inactive in the district's poverty areas, which have been represented instead by a militant community action group. It has been a major force under decentralization, getting several minority principals selected and securing funding for and then running bilingual, after-school, and breakfast programs. It packed the halls at CSB meetings in the early 1970s, before other groups had become so mobilized, and it worked effectively to secure the necessary CSB votes on actions it wanted taken.

The district thus has a variety of interest-group conflicts, which is not surprising, given its diversity. These include the north versus the south, the white middle class versus poor minorities, Hispanic versus black in the south, and Catholic versus Jewish. The latter conflict is much less visible than the others, existing around high-level staff appointments, including the superintendency. One CSB faction, for example, did not support the appointment or the continued tenure of the present superintendent who is Jewish, endorsing instead a Catholic who had been a college administrator from outside the city. The church and political clubs were reported to have pressed for that appointment.

Notwithstanding this diversity of interest groups, two main coalitions have emerged in recent years, one supporting the superintendent and the other opposing him. The loosely joined coalition that supports him includes parents, teachers, principals, district office staff, and some CSB members. The latter are usually parents or are education-oriented, rather than being affiliated with a political club.

The groups opposing the superintendent include political clubs, churches, and some minority leaders and CSB members. One interest these participants have in common is their opposition to the superintendent's staffing policies. He is a strong advocate of using civil service lists for selecting staff, and he places a high priority on retaining classroom teachers and, if necessary, limiting the number of paraprofessionals and teacher aide jobs in the face of budget cuts. By contrast, the CSB member most opposed to the superintendent has worked tirelessly to make sure that these jobs for community residents will be retained in a period of fiscal retrenchment.

CSBs and Superintendents: Emasculating Professionals

This district's experiences under decentralization may best be analyzed in terms of the separate period of service of each of its three superintendents. The trend has been one of increasing subversion of the superintendent's professional authority, with the present board allowing the superintendent almost no opportunity to exercise leadership.

The first superintendent was the predecentralization incumbent. One of the ablest educators and administrators in the system, and a liberal on race and class issues, he was also a person of candor and high integrity. Thus, when the board president first offered him the position, the superintendent hesitated. The board members were almost all from the north, he told them, while the main district problems he wanted to address were in the poor minority areas in the south. He finally did decide to accept, however, after gaining assurances that those problems would be addressed.

By and large, his relation with the CSB was a good one. As he explained: "They kept to policy matters and let me run the district." Yet, this board, like many others in the early years of decentralization, was extremely active. Several of its members had a missionary sense about their role, in ways that limited the superintendent's authority. "It was common," reported a district staffperson, "for an evening meeting with the superintendent to drag on until after midnight before the board finished discussing the items its members put on the agenda. Then they would call on the superintendent to indicate the matters he wanted to discuss. That became wearing for him over time."

Much more important was the militancy of minority parents. They put tremendous pressure on the superintendent to respond immediately to their demands for relief from overcrowded schools, for more minority staff, and for more programs. In one instance, he indicated to parent leaders and to the chancellor (who he demanded come to the district) that he would picket in public alongside the parents until a commitment was made to build a new school. Although his highest priority was improving education in poor minority-area schools, he still became a target of protest, simply as the community superintendent. And when action from the central board was slow in response to minority parent demands for relief from overcrowding, he and a central board staffperson were locked in a school. The angry parents who did that threatened not to let them out until a bulldozer appeared across the street, breaking ground for the construction of a new school. At that point, he decided to retire.

Ironically, this able, progressive superintendent, long known within the system for his support of minority-group interests, and a strong advocate of decentralization, became its victim. Parents had turned their rage against him, assuming that he had the power to respond quickly to their demands. He didn't, and they had the wrong target in terms of the political realities of the situation.

The next superintendent was a man who had been his predecessor's deputy. Before taking that position when decentralization began, he had done an exceptional job as teacher and principal within the district. He then did the same as deputy and soon gained the enthusiastic endorsement of the CSB. A tireless worker, he was also a masterful politician and was effective in dealing with even the most militant community groups. As a top district staffperson recalled: "He was a thick-skinned guy, a handsome guy, and a consummate politician besides. He could sell heat on the equator." And yet, even this superintendent who seemingly had the political skills necessary to manage in such a turbulent district, was to experience a burnout after a few years and was also to retire prematurely.

Before leaving, however, he did many impressive things. Having learned from his predecessor's experience, he constantly reached out to minority leaders. As one such leader explained: "He had so much rapport with the community, and that was why he was such a good superintendent. Would you believe it that he often came down here and taught in our classes in the late afternoon, after he was done in the district office? And he gave us a breakfast program until we got our own funded. He would even call me at night, before an issue was to be discussed with his board, to find out how we felt about it."

This superintendent provided educational leadership in other areas as well. He developed many reading programs, math labs, and bilingual programs. He and his staff wrote one of the first bilingual proposals in the city. He set up three alternative schools for students about to be suspended from regular schools. And he started some imaginative programs with unexpended funds. One year he used such funds to send 150 students to London for a week. Another year, he sent 120 students to Washington. In still another, the district rented a boat, and students went out for a day of fishing. All these trips were used as educational experiences—in social studies, science, and the like. As one district office staffperson explained: "These experiences will undoubtedly stay with the kids for the rest of their lives. The ideas were the superintendent's, and the CSB told him to go to it. Otherwise, this money had to be returned to the city."

As the city's fiscal crisis deepened in 1975, this superintendent found it increasingly difficult to sustain many programs. He recalled with disappointment: "My biggest problem was the cutback in 1975. Many of my exciting projects had to be terminated. We had an art center and music programs at Carnegie Hall and Lincoln Center. A lot of that stuff went by the wayside in the face of the cuts.

The superintendent's frustrations went well beyond the cutbacks, however, as he faced increasing constituency problems. Although he did well with various parent constituencies, he had much less success with the unions, particularly those representing the teachers and custodians. He had pressed to eliminate the right of custodians to work at schools of their choice. And he accelerated the district's efforts to transfer out or reassign those teachers who were unable to function well in the classroom. The union leadership resented these demands on their rank and file, as they saw how responsive he was to parent concerns.

Meanwhile, he began having problems with two CSB members who regarded his enrichment programs as superfluous in a period of fiscal cutbacks. Both were quite conservative, had disagreed with his approaches all along, and finally found justification (with the cutbacks) to be even more critical than before. "These two people gave him the most trouble," reported a CSB member who supported him strongly. "Both actually drove him out of the district through their harassment. They felt he ought not continue art, music, and culture as part of the regular school program. They wanted the funds for those programs spent on basic education."

Over time, then, the job had fewer satisfactions for him, and in 1976, he suddenly resigned, much to the surprise of people in the district, and much to the dismay of many. A district staffperson summarized well the superintendent's disenchantment with the job: "The fun went out of it for him. For a long time he got a lot of enjoyment in the job. There were all those great programs—London, the boat trips, and he was good at getting groups together. He kept this place from being another Ocean Hill-Brownsville. But by early 1976, with the budget cuts, the fun programs had gone. He was taking more criticism from the unions. And some of those conservative parents who didn't like his programs got to him. Since the economics were all in favor of his leaving [reference made to his pension], it made a lot of sense for him to get out."

After the second superintendent's resignation, his deputy, in turn, was appointed, and the CSB made certain not to provide him with a long-term contract. It has given him instead a series of one-year contracts, providing him with none of the job security required to exercise effective leadership. And for the first few years, it designated him only as "acting" superintendent, further limiting his authority.

In brief, District C illustrates the conditions under which professional leadership is not possible. This is a district whose first two superintendents were victimized by its turbulent politics, even though both had such outstanding skills and were so strongly committed to decentralization and to improving the schools. It was for this reason, in part, that we noted earlier that this district seemed almost unmanageable, given its size and the diversity of its interest groups. It has never settled down politically, and we suspect that no superintendent, regardless of leadership abilities, would function effectively in this setting. Too many groups were vying for power, and demographic change was taking place too fast and in too broad an area to permit the local consensus building required for that to take place.

CSBs have, in turn, reflected this turbulence. They have become increasingly factionalized, have been deeply involved in ethnic patronage and administration, and have abdicated their policy role. This is a district almost without a functioning board, and with few coherent policies. Parents and educators have become quite dispirited as a result, as they have watched the board flounder around without ever taking on any clear direction and without allowing its superintendents to exercise leadership either. As one principal observed: "To be a superintendent in this district is putting yourself on a stake. They will roast you here. It's castration. True professionals get ripped to shreds." A parent leader noted: "Nobody is happy with this board. They have not done a thing. They are always fighting among themselves. They never do their homework. It is a total waste of time."

The deterioration in the district's political climate seems to have reached a new low in recent years, under the present superintendent. He and his staff estimate that up to two thirds of his time is spent in struggles with a faction on his board over who has what authority. As the board refuses and/or is unable to set policy on critical matters like budget, staffing, curriculum priorities, and building use, the superintendent sometimes does so on his own, informing the board after making his decisions. The board then accuses him of usurping its authority, questions the efficacy of his decisions, and then fails to generate enough consensus among its members to formulate positions itself. When the superintendent tries to minimize conflict by waiting for the board to provide him with guidance on critical issues, board members then accuse him of failing to exercise effective leadership.

The superintendent's own version of the situation aptly summarizes the leadership vacuum that district politics had produced. "My problem here," he explained, "is that I appeared tentative at times, but that was a result of my political situation with this inactive board. If I take any initiative, I am damned for trying to make policy. But if I don't, I am damned for not exercising leadership. So I lose either way. Where I see it as necessary, where an issue is important enough, I do take action, and then let the CSB react. But I have to be tentative at best on important issues, because of the nature of this CSB."

We have found that districts tend to be effective when the CSB delegates much administrative authority to the superintendent and plays mainly a policy role, when there is agreement between it and the superintendent on role definitions as related to policy and administration, and when the board itself reaches a consensus on these matters. The failure of boards to generate such a consensus often contributes to problems on the first two issues, and this district illustrates these problems to an extreme degree. Because of the differences we found between this superintendent and his board, no educational or policy leadership is possible.

Managing Under Extreme Turbulence

In most districts, one can describe and analyze the superintendent's management style in some detail, as it relates to educational improvement efforts. The politics surrounding the superintendent's conflicts with his CSB in this district is so all-pervasive and consumes so much of his time, however, that we will have less to say about his management style than about those in the other districts studied. He hasn't had the political base or time to really develop one.

CURRICULUM STRATEGY

There is no coherent or unified curriculum style emanating from the district office. The superintendent has been too involved in a politics of personal survival to have developed one. Instead, each principal is left to run the school as that principal's philosophy and local need dictate, which has resulted in a wide diversity of curriculum emphases. At one extreme is a highly publicized, open education school in the arts, reflecting the philosophy of its creative principal and of the parent group who had a strong voice in selecting him. It draws students from all over the district. At the other extreme are some traditional schools in conservative areas.

Since this district has a number of able principals, several appointed by the first two superintendents, this strategy of letting them determine curriculum priorities in cooperation with parents has resulted in many good programs. One of the perhaps unanticipated consequences, then, of the leadership struggles between the superintendent and the CSB is that the schools have been left to run themselves.

Even if the superintendent had more authority, he would probably have followed this strategy anyway. Although the district has had three different superintendents, there has been much continuity in the approach of giving the schools autonomy. As the present superintendent explained: "I basically support the philosophy of my predecessor that principals should set the educational philosophy for their school in consonance with local parent need. When I was a teacher, I resented people coming in and telling me what to do. I believe principals have to have certain prerogatives as educators and managers. We allow them to run their schools subject to our review. Only if they make decisions that may violate district policy, as related, for example, to the union contract or bilingual programs, will I come down on them."

The superintendent and his staff have pushed hard to have minimum standards for all schools and have emphasized reading, writing, and oral communications skills. There is now a districtwide testing program in reading, which the superintendent initiated. He also works closely with the principals to help each school set up its own reading and communications skills programs, and there is a districtwide committee composed of the superintendent, district office staff, and principals that is working on this. As one principal explained: "Our superintendent is extremely involved in forming reading standards for the district as a whole and works closely with principals. The aim is to get each principal to set up a reading program that is appropriate for their own particular school. He set up a committee on which my colleagues and I participate." Several other principals concurred in this judgment.

Given the conflicts between the superintendent and his board, however, there is an understandable difference of opinion on how much educational leadership he is in fact providing. One board member, for example, even invited in a reporter from the *Daily News* a couple of years ago to document what he regarded as scandalously low reading scores in the district. As a principal reported: "That board member is out to get the superintendent. He and a state senator from the district were the ones who sent the *Daily News* into the district office to interview the superintendent and write the article. That reporter arrived there in the limousine of the senator. It was a vicious article whose aim was to slander the superintendent."

The result of the article and the controversy it sparked was that parents from all over the district wrote angry letters to the *Daily News*, protesting what they regarded as an effort mainly to slander the superintendent rather than to shed light on problems. Another result was an intensification of the superintendent's original program to improve reading. The incident further indicates how district politics has permeated its operations.

Two curriculum areas the superintendent has stressed in addition to reading are math and science. He has initiated a marine biology program and several math instruction training programs for teachers from the district office. He has also supported programs in the arts. And he meets monthly with his principals and makes many unannounced visits to the schools.

There have been fewer district office initiatives, however, than under the second superintendent, partly because of continued budget cuts. In addition, the present superintendent has purposely cut back on programs he felt were spread too thin to have much effect. He has thus pursued a strategy of administrative and program consolidation that matches the fiscal situation. "My predecessor's strong suit was in curriculum," he explained. "He started many programs. When I took over, I found there were so many programs that the district schools couldn't follow through. To correct this, I cut back on a number of these programs. He ran an open office, and as a result, we had a lot of things, good and bad, going on. My own preference is to be more analytical and skeptical. I want people who have ideas to sell me on a concept. If the idea is sound, I'll go for it."

In brief, the district has no single educational philosophy but rather has many approaches to programs that reflect, in turn, the diversity of principal styles and community interests that exist there. Beyond that, enrichment programs have, of necessity, been cut back, and there is a strong emphasis on basic skills training. There is much less curriculum innovation now than under the previous superintendent. But that reflects fiscal cutbacks as well as the superintendent's preferences for programs that proved effective in the past. A major point is that the politics of CBS-superintendent relations casts as much of a veil on this issue as it does on most others.

DISTRICT OFFICE AND SCHOOLS

Given this district's diversity, the schools have been left to run themselves to a large degree, and decentralization to the school level has been quite pronounced. Despite the politics that has prevented the superintendent from exercising much educational leadership, the district still has many good programs, resulting in large part from the initiatives of several of its able principals.

The district office does, of course, play some role in the schools. Because of the strong push to improve reading, math, and other basic skills, there has been planning, monitoring, and technical assistance relative to programs in those areas. In addition to a districtwide committee of principals that meets monthly with the superintendent to discuss district policy on curriculum, particularly reading, the superintendent visits schools regularly. "I like to visit schools unannounced at every opportunity I have," he explained. "That way I get to see actual school and teacher performance. In monitoring the school, I don't want to supplant the principal. I believe strongly in allowing for local option. I want my principals to run their schools, and the less a principal needs to involve me, the better it is for all concerned."

The principals support this approach and respect the superintendent's efforts to provide some educational leadership in a politically volatile situation. One respected principal explained: "People like the superintendent because if he says something that's it. He tells the truth and does not try to placate people. He is very forthright. He meets with parents and asks principals for their opinions." Another observed: "He is a competent, highly principled person. He is being upset by the CSB. But he is extremely involved in forming reading standards for the district and works closely with principals."

DISTRICT OFFICE AND PROFESSIONALS

The professional staff, then, including principals, teachers, and district office personnel, are very much a part of the superintendent's coalition. A former teacher and supervisor in the district, he maintains close collegial relations with them. He helps principals develop programs. His districtwide policy committee of elementary school principals meets monthly to discuss curriculum issues, and he provides training for principals trying to transfer out ineffective teachers who fail to respond to efforts at helping them upgrade their skills.

Moreover, the teachers' union leaders see him as fair and supportive, despite his "tough-guy" role under the previous superintendent in relation to bringing up unsatisfactory teachers on charges. As a top union official reported: "He runs the district on an up-and-up basis. Once a month for two hours, the UFT members are invited in, and they can speak openly on issues that concern them. People with new ideas are encouraged to develop them, and he will scrounge up money for them. He works for teachers and not in opposition to them. He is extremely responsive to grievances. At times he has made decisions against the UFT, but I still respect his judgment because it is what he believes to be right and not based on political considerations."

One of the main reasons for the union's support is the superintendent's traditional staffing policies. He strongly opposed a minority board member's attempts to retain more paraprofessionals and teacher aides, at the cost of having fewer teachers, in the face of budget cuts. And he is a big proponent of using civil service lists for staff appointments. "I used to get calls all the time from politicians recommending people for jobs," he explained. "Since I feel jobs should be assigned on merit, I would tell whoever called that what they were asking was out of bounds. After the political clubs and politicians heard this a couple of times, they stopped calling me."

The superintendent was thus able to gain the strong support of his professionals through a combination of curriculum, monitoring, and staffing practices. Although these practices alienated some community constituencies—for example, a white ethnic group in the north associated with political clubs and the Catholic church, and minority leaders in the south—he has persisted. He sees them as pushing for patronage, while they regard his approach as simply another form of it, in this case for "insider professionals."

DISTRICT OFFICE AND COMMUNITY

The superintendent's way of handling this constituency problem has been to reach out increasingly to parents who are not part of those community groups. He has become more responsive to parent grievances and in recent years has pressed to give parents a voice in school decisions. As one of the most influential parent leaders explained: "He is open to parents. They have been given the right to voice opinions and have a say in evaluating teachers' performances. This has helped bridge the gap between the professionals and parents, so that the professional is not just up there and the parents ignorant down below. There are many committees that parents participate in. Every parent group in every school has a parent room. Very often there are parents at the district office. There is a lot of involvement."

One of the superintendent's most critical decisions in this regard was his appointment in 1979 of an influential parent leader to a newly established district office position, in charge of recruiting parents for service on parent advisory councils in schools. This move helped a great deal in solidifying parent support for his administration, particularly since the woman he appointed had opposed many of his policies and those of his predecessors in the past—as a former CSB member and districtwide parent leader. As might be expected, CSB members who wanted him out and opposed his staffing policies regarded the appointment as a blatant example of patronage and cooptation. One board member cynically observed: "He put her on the payroll to get her support and that of parents in his effort to renew his contract."

Notwithstanding that view, this appointment has given parents more of a voice and increased their participation. "Since she came on here," the superintendent reported, "there has been a 50 percent increase in attendance at parent council meetings. She had led workshops of parents in training them on questions they should ask their principal. Sure, many principals were uptight when I appointed her, but she has done a great job. And decentralization requires parent input."

The CSB, by contrast, has not treated parents with the same responsiveness or concern, even though some board members are parents themselves. As one parent leader bemoaned: "Nobody is happy with this board. They have not done a thing." A district staffperson summarized the frustration parents had experienced trying to deal with the board: "Parents have become very vocal and educated in this district. But they have been totally frustrated by the CSB. It ignores them totally. Parents know a lot and are tired of the CSB ignoring them. We had a parent group who visited a district on Long Island where they use a computer to do teaching. The parents were extremely impressed in discovering a new method of teaching which seems to be yielding positive results. They came back eager to try it out and proposed that money be allocated for that purpose. Our parent advisory council had put in the work to find out what they wanted and they recommended it, but it was totally ignored. The parents had gone to that district at the suggestion of staff in the district office."

The political conflict in this district between the superintendent and his board has thus resulted in parents being used in that struggle. The superintendent sees parents as a way of enlarging his political base, as well as a means of improving programs and district responsiveness. The board, meanwhile, refuses to acknowledge the legitimacy of many parent groups where it sees them as tools in the superintendent's fight for survival. In that respect, the parents are caught in the middle of a power struggle that most of them were not responsible for, and they experience needless frustrations in trying to deal with the CSB as a result.

DISTRICT OFFICE BUREAUCRACY

The same conflicts between the superintendent and the CSB that exist on matters of staffing and parent interests also exist in relation to district office staff. The latter are a mixed group in terms of backgrounds and loyalties. Some are holdovers from the past, having gained their appointments under previous boards and reflecting particular ethnic constituencies; several are new people that the superintendent has appointed to buttress his power. From the vantage point of board members who oppose him, new administrative assistants he has appointed are simply part of his patronage network. As one board member complained: "We can't even allow a deputy superintendent's position to be created to help him run the district, because he feels the board will try to groom that person for his job. So he operates instead through a series of assistants, and, as a consequence, the office is run in a very haphazard manner." From the superintendent's perspective, however, he is trying to develop a competent staff that will be loyal to him.

As in other districts where the CSB has been in conflict with its superintendent, board members in this one have at times contacted district staff directly on some issues, without informing the superintendent. This practice became so blatant a few years ago that the superintendent wrote a letter to all district office staff directing them not to talk with board members without first discussing the matter with him. He has thus been trying to develop a staff that would be responsible to him first and would work collaboratively with him. Since he inherited staff hired by previous boards and who had a political base themselves, it was not easy to form his own group.

The problem is illustrated most dramatically in connection with one key staffperson. As a parent leader and former CSB member recalled: "We had a Title I director here who was terrible, a patronage appointment from the original CSB. It took us a long time to get her out. We asked for a staff investigation of Title I here and the man from Albany who had to deal with her over the years did it. He found much noncompliance on her part with Title I guidelines, and we eventually had to pay back $45,000, after it became apparent that money was disappearing and had been misspent or taken."

In brief, the quality of district office staff in this highly politicized district has been affected by that politics, and it has not been easy for the superintendent to pull together a group who would work collaboratively with him. He has made some inroads in that regard, but his future and that of his successors probably depend in large part on securing a stronger mandate from the board than he has had in the past. It is unclear whether or not that will be forthcoming.

Conclusions

Decentralization has not had the positive impacts on this district that it has had on the others we have discussed. CSBs have progressively deteriorated, as power has gravitated away from parents and civic-minded people to those supported by political clubs, the Catholic church, and other groups. We have attributed the problems not so much to personalities, though they obviously play some role, as to the situation. The district may well be too diverse to be manageable as a single entity. It clearly does not have the *social peace* that decentralization advocates argued would result from that reform, having become more rather than less turbulent under decentralization.

Nevertheless, even in this district there are some very good schools, most of them in the central and northern areas. The district office has been taking some productive initiatives in providing support for basic skills and other programs. It is difficult to say whether the district's performance would be better, and to what degree, were the board a more effective one that hired a superintendent it had confidence in and delegated to him or her the amount of authority needed to lead the district. That clearly has not happened here, and the extent of parent and staff demoralization may well have hurt the district in ways that will show up in the future, in student performance. What we have in this case is the absence of the prerequisites for district success that exist in the districts previously described.

Indicators of Student and District Performance

We have characterized this district as one that has experienced much political turbulence and instability under decentralization, particularly since 1976, under its present superintendent. We have attributed this turbulence in part to the tremendous size and diversity of the district, rather than to any demographic changes. While there have been some such changes, they are minimal compared with most other districts in its category that have both white and minority students. Blacks increased from 31.6% to 36.9% and Hispanics from 45.4% to 50.0% during the period from 1970 to 1978, while whites declined from 22.6% to 15.2%, but again, those are not significant changes.[2]

Trends in reading scores seem to have reflected those in the district's politics. From 1970 to 1975 the district did better than the citywide trend, closing the gap at every grade level. While its scores never caught up to those citywide, they were quite close by 1975. Since then, by contrast, the district has lost ground relative to the city as a whole.[3] Thus, from 1975 to 1979, the gap has increased for 6 of the 8 grades on which data are available. This suggests that it may well have lost what momentum it had in those early years. While the fiscal crisis of 1975 may be seen as having contributed to the district's problems, this district was not harder hit than any of the others, so some other factors may be operating. We would suggest that the district's volatile politics and the increasingly tenuous position of the superintendent have made themselves felt.

Table 4.1 compares the trend in District C's reading scores with that citywide. As indicated the district has done only a little better than the city as a whole. The district's turbulent politics of the past several years may account in part for this limited improvement.

Data on attendance show that trend as well. Average daily attendance was 85.3% in 1971 and dropped to 84.8% in 1977, compared with a

TABLE 4.1

Changes in Reading Scores (1971–79)

Grade	District C	Citywide	Difference Between District C & All Schools (+/−)
Two	0.1	-0-	0.1
Three	0.6	0.1	0.5
Four	1.1	0.6	0.5
Five	1.0	0.7	0.3
Six	0.6	0.6	-0-
Seven	1.4	1.0	0.4
Eight	1.7	1.1	0.6
Nine	0.9	1.1	(−0.2)

slight increase citywide.[4] And again, the gap widened since 1975, when the district was just about the same as the city.

And yet, vandalism indicators do show a decline. In fact, on every indicator, the district is doing better.[5] Broken glass panes have thus declined from just under 10,000 in 1971 to 5,750 in 1978. Unlawful entries have declined from 153 to 110 during that period. And fires decreased from 6 to 3. Thus, the district has improved in some respects, though there is the falling off in student achievement.

Indeed, as we have discussed in this chapter, there has been much public controversy about low reading scores in the district. One CSB member complained to the press about this condition a couple of years ago, and it still seems to be a contested issue.

As for trends in district staffing practices, there has been an increase in the proportion of minority educators. Considering all categories of professionals, blacks are up from 8.0% to 21.0% and Hispanics from 2.9% to 15.0%, both fairly significant increases.[6] And they are distributed evenly across the various levels. Thus, black principals are up from 12.0% to 24.0% of the district total in that category, while Hispanic principals are up from none in 1971 to 10.3% in 1978. A similar pattern exists for teachers, with the proportion of blacks up from 7.7% to 13.2% and of Hispanics from 2.7% to 7.8%. Perhaps these changes toward greater minority representation may have something to do with the decreasing incidence of vandalism in the schools. People in the communities may perceive schools with increasing numbers of minority educators as more "legitimate" than they were before. And as we already discussed, activist parent groups and antipoverty agencies representing minority interests have been successful in this district in their efforts to have more minority educators appointed.

5

A Model District with Legitimacy Now Threatened by Rapid Ethnic Succession: District D

While most districts in New York City have settled down politically, having experienced their political turbulence in the early stages of decentralization, District D has had the opposite experience. Located in a formerly white middle-class area in an outer borough that had been fairly stable demographically and thereby insulated from changes going on elsewhere in the city, it lost many of its former residents in the 1960s and 1970s and experienced a large influx of poor Hispanics. When decentralization began, this district's close-knit coalition of district office staff, teachers, parent and civic groups, and CSB members adapted well to the change. They had collaborated before decentralization and simply deepened their close relationships when it got under way. Like many other white middle-class districts, they already had an infrastructure of parent and community groups involved in the schools, and they grafted decentralization onto that structure. In brief, social peace and good school-community relations were not things that this district had to develop. They were already there, and the district was widely regarded among New York City educators as one of the very good places in which to serve, with its many high-achieving students and its network of supportive community and parent groups.

The professional staff, in both the district office and the schools, reflected the district's demography. Many New York City teachers, principals, and district office staff lived and served there, as was the case in other white middle-class (outer-borough) districts, and appointments to supervisory and administrative positions were often made from among people who had worked in the district a long time.

They were by no means a complacent, status-quo-oriented group, however. When decentralization came along, they took advantage of the greater flexibilities it provided, like their counterparts in some other districts, to build an enriched and innovative educational program. And the curriculum materials they produced soon became widely recognized as among the best in the city. Throughout most of the 1970s, this was known among city and state educational administrators as one of the model New York City districts. Moreover, it was working in an increasingly difficult demographic and political setting. Throughout the 1970s, the district changed radically in population and public school enrollment from having a large white middle-class student population and a stable black one with many of them middle class or working poor, to becoming a predominantly Hispanic district.

As this change took place, the district came under increasing criticism from Hispanic educators and political leaders, many of whom lived outside the district, for what they regarded as its failure to be responsive to their group's interests. These leaders demanded more appointments of Hispanic educators and more bilingual programs. During one period, in the 1979–80 school year, they staged several public protests at CSB meetings over the failure of the district to appoint a Hispanic principal in a school located in a Hispanic area. And they succeeded in electing several people to the CSB in 1980 who were supportive of these demands, including a militant Puerto Rican Nationalist who had led the community organizing efforts of this group in the late 1970s.

We have, then, a different political scenario in District D from the others discussed thus far. It had early social peace and then temporarily postponed its ethnic succession politics through a process of professional insulation. The superintendent and the CSB ran the district without paying much attention to the politics of ethnic succession and are now in the throes of having to deal with it.

Demography, Neighborhoods, District Characteristics

District D has a population of more than 300,000 residents.[1] Prior to the demographic changes indicated above, it included a series of white working-class and lower-middle-class communities to the south and east (mostly Irish and Italian), living in old two- and three-family dwellings and row houses and some in tenements and apartments. To the north and west, a more middle- and upper-middle-class population resided in cooperative apartments, in middle-income and luxury buildings, and some in large homes. The district's Jewish population was concentrated in these communities, with many Catholics living nearby, usually in more modest circumstances.

The biggest ethnic changes have taken place in the south and east, with whites moving out of these areas and poor Hispanics moving in. Meanwhile, neighboring communities in the north have remained fairly stable, although they too have experienced an influx of poor minority residents on their south and east fringes.

The public school population has reflected these demographic changes. Since decentralization began in 1970, whites have declined from 48% to 22% of total enrollment, and Hispanics have increased from 27% to over 50%.[2] Moreover, these new Hispanic students are from overwhelmingly low-income families, compared with the middle-class whites who have left.

In addition, enrollment has increased from 27,000 at the start of decentralization to roughly 30,000 now, imposing a severe overcrowding condition in the southern-area schools where rates of utilization are often 110% or more.[3] In fact, the district has one of the highest utilization rates in the city and has had the biggest enrollment increase since 1970 of any district. Many overcrowded schools in the south have new annexes to absorb the overflow, and some students have been bused up to underutilized, northern-area schools, but the overcrowding still exists.

Blacks are the one stable student population. They constituted 22% of the district's enrollment in 1970 and now constitute about 25%. Many live in the northern areas and have not faced the problems that Hispanics have. There is a substantial black working and middle class in these areas that has been absorbed into the district, and racial conflict is minimal. Moreover, the district does have four black principals and some blacks in district office staff positions, providing some indication to blacks of its commitments to hire competent minorities. By contrast, there is only one Hispanic principal, and while there are some Hispanics in the district office, there have not been enough appointed either there or in the schools to satisfy the demands of some Hispanic leaders.

Political History

When community control became an issue in the 1960s, parents and educators in this district were quite apprehensive. UFT officials report that roughly 5,000 teachers lived in the district at that time, and they did not want decentralization. Furthermore, they were joined in this view by parent groups who did not have the resentment about the public schools that parent and community groups had in minority areas.

Long before decentralization, the district's superintendent and UFT rep had developed a well-organized network of parents and civic organizations to support the schools. A districtwide educational forum of parents and principals had been established in 1950 to discuss educational policy issues, and there also existed a council of parent association presidents.

These groups, along with the district's educators, changed their minds about decentralization, once it was a reality, and the educators initiated many new programs under decentralization that gave it the reputation as a model district, referred to above.

The CSBs, in turn, have until recently supported the professionals, owing largely to the fact of the board members' backgrounds. District D, like many others, has had an unrepresentative board. Up to seven or eight of its nine members have generally been from the most affluent areas in the northern end of the district. This group of white, professional, middle- and upper-middle class board members has played a "buffer" role, deferring to the superintendent's "professional" judgments. The majority on the board had a more "public" than "private"-regarding ethos and were more interested in supporting broad educational improvements than in responding to demands from minority groups for more representation in staff appointments. Moreover, with one exception, all the CSB presidents since 1970, took the position that their superintendent was the education leader of the district and that they should support him strongly. The fact that the district's more affluent population voted in greater numbers in CSB elections than did low-income minority groups made it possible for the board to keep perpetuating itself and its point of view. The result was a district with a strong superintendent whose board deferred to him on both policy and administrative matters.

As for the district's interest groups, there have been two main coalitions since decentralization began, with a third likely to emerge in the near future. Each coalition ran its own slate in CSB elections. By far the most powerful is a parent-educator group that includes the teachers' union, the principals' association, and parent organizations, a remarkably inclusive collection of interests. It has long been dominated by people from the northern end of the district, many having been in public school affairs since before decentralization.

The less powerful coalition is a parochial school one, sponsored through the district's many parishes. Since the district is roughly 58% Catholic, this coalition has understandably wanted to have its interests represented in district decisions. In addition to pressing for the parochial schools to get their share of Title I funds, the group has pursued many other issues on which its parishes have strong positions. They include having more discipline in the schools, making prayer part of the day's activities, eliminating sex education, opposing many desegregation programs, and having homosexual teachers removed. There is actually little conflict between the two coalitions, however, since the district has always provided funds to the parochial schools' satisfaction, as prescribed by law, while the conservative church positions on the other issues have not been that much of a focus for debate. "There is a good relationship between the district and the parishes," explained a CSB member. "The superintendent made every effort to keep them on his side."

The politics of the district, at least until late 1980, may thus be characterized as a stable one, with a large, well-organized majority in control and a less powerful group trying to shape district decisions and having enough success to minimize their inclination to stage any public protests. Meanwhile, there is an emerging third coalition representing Hispanic interests, which are increasingly reflected in the most recent CSB that was elected in 1980. It remains to be seen what role they may play in the future, and much depends on what the superintendent does.

Managing Under Increasing Ethnic Succession and Turbulence

From 1972 through 1981, District D had an active, energetic superintendent who "took charge" and pretty much ran the district with board and community support. He had extraordinary leadership skills and was able to set policies and develop programs as he and his staff saw fit. This worked out well for most of his years in office, but conflict has been building since the late 1970s, as the district has become more Hispanic and as people claiming to represent that constituency have increasingly questioned district policies and programs.

This superintendent articulated his educational philosophy for the district, developed a highly professional staff, initiated and effectively implemented many new programs in collaboration with them, built an informal but strong administrative support structure for the programs, maintained close relations with the educators, and reinforced support for the programs through an extensive network of parent and community organizations. As a result of this leadership, the district developed into one of the most productive in the city, putting together programs, curriculum materials, and staff development efforts that often went far beyond anything headquarters had done. It was an impressive effort, indicating the many educational improvement possibilities that decentralization can facilitate, when local conditions are right, and when given the needed political support citywide.

CURRICULUM STYLE

This superintendent's philosophy is what he and his staff refer to as humanistic, open education. It places much emphasis on individualized approaches to instruction, on experience-based learning, on nontraditional classrooms and learning contexts, and on the affective as well as the cognitive-intellectual development of the child. It has been shaped by the superintendent's enthusiasm for John Dewey's concepts, for open education, and for alternative schools. It stresses informality and flexibility in curriculum and the importance of participation by teachers, students, and parents as well as principals in developing school programs. Such approaches clearly fit the values of some of the district's more affluent and middle-class areas, but they were also used in poverty areas.

One contributing factor to the district's widespread use of this approach was the superintendent's staffing strategy. He gathered around him administrative and curriculum staff in the district office and supervisors in the schools who agreed with his educational philosophy and helped him apply it. During his administration, eighteen principalships became vacant, and in most cases he filled them with former assistant principals from within the district. The same was true of his district office staff. To illustrate, the six top district office professionals, including the superintendent, had been in that position an average of almost twelve years and in the district itself an average of fifteen years. No other district we studied came close to that in the extent of continuity.

The main curriculum and program initiatives the superintendent and his staff have developed include experimental junior high schools; extensive open education programs; learning centers and resource rooms; considerable integration between reimbursable and tax-levy programs; district-office-initiated programs in reading, math, science, the arts, early childhood, health education, drug prevention, career education, and bilingual education; principals' conferences in various district schools; school-based and districtwide parent-teacher curriculum committees; and the development of numerous curriculum bulletins on such diverse topics as energy, the space program, the criminal justice system, and reading. This is, in brief, an extensive array of educational improvement efforts that decentralization has helped facilitate. "Many of these things didn't happen before decentralization," reported a district office administrator who originally opposed that change. "Our regular staff meetings dealt mainly with the superintendent going over administrative matters, telling principals about various headquarters rules and policies, and checking to see if they were being followed. They were boring and tedious meetings, and they didn't cover matters of curriculum and programs. Under decentralization we can make our own curriculum policies, and we now deal with issues of substance."

Some of the junior high school programs are among the most dramatic. One of these programs, which became a prototype for others within the district, has been at a predominantly black and Hispanic school. Located in a devastated poverty area, this school was plagued with low reading and math scores, high truancy rates, severe discipline problems, low teacher morale, and much student and community hostility toward the school and its principal.

The superintendent first visited the school in 1972, got a sense of what the teachers' complaints were, and set in motion several changes that not only reversed its decline but also established a model program that later was transferred to other JHSs in the district. Acknowledging the community's desire to have a minority principal, he first appointed one of the APs, a white Orthodox Jew, as interim, acting principal until he could find a minority one. That principal, working closely with several creative teachers, soon put together a nondepartmentalized, student-centered, individualized program that developed in the students a much more positive attitude toward the school. He and his teachers created a "family-type" atmosphere in the classroom by personalizing teacher-student relations; and teachers developed close contacts with the students' homes. After six months, the students and their parents voted unanimously to retain the principal rather than have the superintendent continue the search for a minority one.

Treating these students in a caring and humane fashion and in a nontraditional classroom setting was a key to the programs' success. The school eliminated specialized subject-area departments and provided more of a community climate for students by keeping them in the same classroom setting, with the same teachers for all subjects. There were also many out-of-classroom learning experiences, involving frequent trips to plays, movies, and museums. One of the highlights of the year in this regard is a two-week trip to a YMCA camp in the Catskill Mountain area northwest of the city. Teachers accompany the students there without extra pay and conduct programs in science, environmental education, and sensitivity training.

In 1976, three years after this program was in operation, the school developed a second one along similar lines, also begun at the initiative of some of its creative teachers. It is another alternative, mini-school program that focuses the curriculum on student interests, emphasizing reading and math skills through an individualized approach. The same "community" and "family" climate of the original program exists in this one.

The results from these programs are quite positive.[4] Thus, students participating in the first one had averaged a gain of 2.0 years in reading scores by the end of the school year. Meanwhile, students in the second gained 2.2 years in their reading scores, and those in both have a consistent record of better than 90% daily attendance. Although there are only a couple of hundred students in both programs, reading scores of the entire school have improved steadily since 1973. Those of ninth graders, for example, went up from 6.6 in 1973 to 8.0 in 1978. Those of eighth graders went from 5.9 to 7.4 during that period, and of the seventh graders from 5.2 to 6.6.

The program has now been extended to several other junior highs in the district and to some elementary schools as well. These developments are a direct result of initiatives taken by the superintendent and his staff, as they saw how successfully the program worked out in the first school, as well as in response to requests from other principals as they, too, saw the results.

Open education programs have been similarly extensive. The superintendent and his staff initiated a wall-less, open education junior high in one poverty area with similarly positive results, and many elementary schools have adopted open education approaches to learning as well. "We have 4,000 kids in open education," the superintendent reported in 1978, "and we trained all the teachers."

Unfortunately for the district, central board staffing directives, forced on the system without its having any control over the situation, decimated its open education program. Budget deficits have forced districts to eliminate many teaching positions, and teachers have had to be "excessed" out on the basis of seniority. Open education teachers have generally had the least seniority and are therefore the first to be let go. In addition, the U.S. Office of Civil Rights (OCR) has required that New York City desegregate its teaching staff, causing even more turnover among open education teachers. To work effectively, then, decentralization, requires much more local flexibility in staffing than was provided in this case.

The district has undertaken other program initiatives as well. It has learning centers and resource rooms within many schools, for example, for its early childhood programs and for various subjects like math and science. It has an audiovisual resource center within the district offices as well as one with extensive material for programs geared toward gifted and talented students, including bilingual students.

Still another significant program strategy has been the district's integration of state and federally funded programs with city-funded ones. Many districts have not coordinated these programs, but this one has done so in a productive way for many years. It uses state and federal funds to develop new programs that fill in gaps from locally funded ones; and it then institutionalizes those outside-funded programs that work well by making them a regular part of city-funded efforts. While this is how such outside funding is meant to be used, it often does not happen that way elsewhere.

One of the strengths of the district's programs has been its highly professional staff of curriculum directors, whom the superintendent recruited and who work well together. These people all share the superintendent's educational philosophy, and they are active in initiating new programs for schools, providing technical assistance and support, and informing principals of developments in their fields that might be incorporated within schools.

Several aspects of the superintendent's management style are evident in the way these curriculum directors function. They are given much autonomy and flexibility. They work very closely with one another, building on each other's materials. They function as service providers to the schools and provide much technical assistance to principals and teachers. And they work within the district's open education philosophy. The superintendent delegated to them as much as he did because he had recruited them with full knowledge of their commitment to his philosophy. While he keeps in close touch with what they are doing, he knows that they are developing programs in consonance with policies he has set for the district.

Still other initiatives the superintendent has undertaken relate to the professional development of principals and teachers. He meets monthly with the principals, for example, and holds most of those meetings in particular schools where model programs exist. He also pursues a strategy of peer support, with principals helping one another, as each takes turns hosting a session at his or her school. "We have principals' conferences at schools, in small groups," explained the superintendent, "so it gets to be more of a living thing and not just discussions around a table. That is being done now at the assistant principal level as well."

There is a strong emphasis in the district on releasing the creativity of staff as well as students, and that priority of the superintendent relates directly to his professional development programs with principals. Rather than imposing particular programs on them or visiting their schools unannounced and in an explicitly controlling posture, the superintendent makes clear to them his interest in helping them with school problems, as they see them. And he tries to encourage the principals to follow the same participative management style that he does. "I have told principals that they have to release teacher creativity as I do with them," he explained. "That means that they should sit down with different groups of teachers, ask them their problems, and work with them on those problems. I trained our principals to do that."

The superintendent also provides incentive grants to further encourage the principals to develop innovative programs. To qualify for such funds, principals must indicate explicitly their school development plans and how the program whose financial support they are applying for fits with those plans. Under such an arrangement, it soon becomes apparent both to the superintendent and to the principals which ones are doing effective planning and which are not; and for the latter, the visibility of their limited efforts becomes in itself an incentive to improve.

Teacher in-service training is equally extensive. The curriculum coordinators do much of that, and the district office serves as a valued resource for teachers who come there after school and on vacations to review curriculum materials, meet in small groups, and write proposals. "We have teachers in and out of here all summer writing mini-grants," a top district office staffperson reported. "We encourage them, as do their principals, to develop programs."

The superintendent has extended this participative style to parents and students as well. There are both school-based and district-wide parent committees that work on developing curriculum bulletins. In addition to getting some parent input, these committees are an important vehicle for the principal to explain school programs to parents, to secure their support.

Students are also given a role in the district. Reflecting the superintendent's philosophy, he and his staff have actively encouraged schools to set up student organizations in every grade. In several cases, student input has made a difference. As the superintendent notes: "I have met with students since 1972, and they have had a big impact on the district. Teachers sat in on many of these meetings, because some were afraid that students would delve into personalities and be critical of them. Students have been instrumental, for example, in changing the social studies curriculum. They said that social studies was dull, old stuff that was not relevant, and I had them suggest what they wanted. I have even asked kids in a kindergarten class what was wrong with their school. In one school we had a complaint that the security guards were very mean, and we made some changes. In others we had doors put on toilets and required vendors to come in with garbage cans so the yard wouldn't be littered. The students feel they have some say in how the school is run."

In sum, this is a district that has developed a highly professional staff under the superintendent's leadership, and they have demonstrated the many possibilities of decentralization. Their curriculum materials, staff training, and integrated approach to educational improvement, within the context of an explicit and agreed-on educational philosophy, are quite extensive.

DISTRICT OFFICE AND SCHOOLS

Districts vary, as we have indicated, in the extent of school-level autonomy. Some give schools a lot of leeway to establish their own educational philosophy and programs, while others give less. While there is much autonomy for schools in this district, it exists under the close surveillance of the superintendent. Thus, one of his main initiatives under decentralization was to replace the eighteen principals who had retired since 1970 with APs from within the district, usually of his choice and then ratified by the CSB and parents. They were often chosen, not only because of their professional qualifications, but also because their educational philosophy was similar to his. This practice left him vulnerable to charges of "in-breeding," however, and that has become an issue in the Hispanic protest of recent years.

The district's schools are autonomous, then, within this context. The superintendent does delegate authority to principals, but it takes place only after he has influenced their selection. His subsequent style of monitoring and technical assistance is then a "collegial" rather than "bureaucratic authority" one, with principals and teachers treated as fellow professionals. Within this context, the district office functions as a service agency, and its monitoring and evaluation are nonbureaucratic in style.

The emphasis is much more on how the superintendent can help principals than on controlling them. They are usually informed in advance of impending visits by the superintendent, and he and his staff never use any formal checklists or other such procedures for evaluating what is going on. This was so much the case that one of the dissenting members of the previous CSB (1977–80) complained vigorously that the superintendent's visits to schools were often made with considerable notice and that there were not enough formal evaluations of schools and principals. As the superintendent explained: "I feel we should mainly be a service agency. All our evaluation is supportive. 'How can we help?' is the question we keep asking."

Nothing of significance goes on in the schools, however, despite this delegation, that the superintendent isn't aware of—and very quickly. He and his staff are in the schools all the time; he meets with groups of principals and teachers regularly; and through his "open-door" policy he encourages them to see him when they have problems.

The technical assistance from the district office to the schools is quite extensive, covering matters of curriculum, staff training, and assistance on community relations matters. "This is a close-knit district," explained one principal. "There is much help on curriculum and staff training." Another reported: "The superintendent spends a tremendous amount of time in the field. He visits every school and gives much moral support and recognition to teachers. That is an important source of the high morale of staff in this district."

DISTRICT OFFICE AND PROFESSIONAL STAFF

All that we have said indicates the strong support the superintendent in this district gives to his professional staff. The professionals are a key constituency in the consensus that had been developed over the years under decentralization. In addition to all the staff training, the superintendent has established close personal relationships with the professionals. Teachers and principals are encouraged to develop new programs. They are often singled out for special praise at public meetings, and they are treated with much dignity. For example, when many teachers were excessed out of the district during the fiscal cutbacks, the superintendent spoke with each one individually, to try to cushion the blow and to provide personal support. Moreover, the superintendent protects district educators from being intimidated by any board member making unannounced visits or evaluations. He has come down very hard, in that regard, on dissident CSB members who might pay such visits to schools. And, from the point of view of teachers, principals, and district office staff, this district is one of the most ideal places in the city in which to work. They feel wanted there.

This close relationship carries over to the educators' organizations as well—the UFT and the Council of Supervisory Associations (CSA). District reps from both groups have served in that capacity in the district for many years; and their public statements on critical policy issues are invariably supportive of the superintendent's positions. As the UFT rep explained: "A good district is one where teachers can do the job properly, where they feel they have support, especially support from the superintendent and CSB. This district office is very helpful to teachers. The superintendent goes out of his way to praise teachers when they have done a good job. He and his staff help the schools all the time. There are in-service courses, and people like to teach here." A school rep explained: "The superintendent has a good relationship with the UFT. He is an educator and you can really talk to him. He has real respect for the professional. You feel he is on your side. He visits schools regularly to keep up with what is going on." The principals' association rep expressed the same sentiments. "We are friends and colleagues," he reported about his relation with the superintendent. "He is open, accessible, listens, and acts on suggestions."

DISTRICT OFFICE AND COMMUNITY

One of the hallmarks of this district has been its extensive network of parent and community organizations, many of which had worked in collaboration with the superintendent's office and in support of the schools long before decentralization. The superintendent and his staff have extended and developed this network much further.

There are several components of the superintendent's community relations strategy, including (1) monthly and year-end public reports on how the district is doing; (2) school and districtwide parent curriculum committees; (3) student organizations; (4) the superintendent's open-door policy; and (5) the district's community relations office.

The monthly and year-end public reports by the superintendent are true "events," attesting to his charismatic personality. They invariably involve extensive audiovisual presentations, with films and still slides of students involved in programs; and they are presented with much fanfare, humor, and expressions of caring about students and involved educators. He rekindled through these performances his strong community support, thus maintaining his leadership position.

Parent-curriculum committees are organized around the development of new programs and curriculum bulletins, and they get parents' support, even when they make few substantive contributions. "These parent-curriculum committees are a vehicle for the principal to explain school programs to parents," related a district office staffperson, "so that we have the parents with us in what we do."

As for student organizations, they are active in schools throughout the district, and student suggestions on curriculum and administrative matters are often taken into account. This information helps indicate to the superintendents which schools have student unrest and why. It has been used to develop new programs and to "cool out" potential insurgence that might undercut the district's legitimacy and disrupt educational programs.

Parent and student involvement are then further reinforced by the superintendent's open-door policy. People with grievances not worked out at the school level are encouraged to see the superintendent about them, and they are made to feel comfortable, given his informal style. A district staffperson explained: "That open-door policy is real. You can walk in anytime. Our kids walked right in and talked with the superintendent about gym equipment, maintenance problems in the buildings, and so on. I ask you where else can kids just walk into a superintendent's office like parents and get such a reception? And you better believe that the word spread out through the district that this is happening."

One of the best indicators of the superintendent's style in relation to district constituencies has been his community relations, parent outreach office. It has maintained and expanded the community network that the superintendent and his staff have put together. "We are active in building a lay leadership cadre," explained a staffperson. "We work to keep PA presidents and others active as leadership people, even after their kids graduate. We have a network of roughly 300 people, many of them old-timers, in addition to people whose kids are still in the schools. A key person in this network, the head of the parent associations, is black. In fact, the PA presidents now are predominantly black and Hispanic."

Community involvement includes many program linkages as well with schools of education, with parks and cultural agencies where many science programs are conducted, with Lincoln Center for music programs, and with various artists' groups. Since the superintendent's educational philosophy focuses so much on nonclassroom experiences, these program linkages with outside agencies are an important aspect of the district's activities.

Cracks in the Consensus

Having thus indicated the many community linkages the district established, one might seem hard pressed to find problems, but they have existed. No community conflicts of any note existed before 1977. Since then, however, a small dissenting group has attempted to increase its power base and has been challenging the way the district has been run. That group consisted of several CSB members, depending on the issue, and they have been joined by militant Hispanic educators, one now on the CSB and the others from outside. This emerging coalition has raised a series of questions that they hope may become the focus for an insurgent, protest politics in the near future, to change the district's operations. The issues include: (1) the unrepresentative nature of the CSB; (2) the tendency of past boards to delegate much policy authority to the superintendent; (3) the perceived homogeneity of the district office and supervisory staff, particularly the limited numbers of Hispanics; (4) the assumed closed decision-making process in the district; (5) its limited commitment to bilingual programs; and (6) miscellaneous other aspects of the superintendent's style.

Such criticism must be interpreted in the context of the ethnic changes this district has experienced since decentralization began. It now has a Hispanic enrollment of close to 55%, and that there is only one Hispanic principal and minimal Hispanic representation in the district office and on the CSB have been important factors in the increasing protest. By 1979 and 1980, for the first time since decentralization, several CSB meetings were marked by public demonstrations from this Hispanic leadership.

A critical incident that became the immediate focus of this political action was the replacement of a retiring principal in a predominantly

Hispanic school. One board member pushed for the appointment of a Hispanic principal, while the superintendent and the other eight CSB members decided to appoint an AP in the district to the position, that person being white. The issue soon became a cause célèbre among Hispanic educators and leaders from outside the district. They staged many lively protests in the district office at monthly CSB public meetings, and they tried to gain the support of the chancellor and a Hispanic central board member. The latter member sent angry notes to the superintendent and the CSB, indicating his extreme dissatisfaction with their failure to appoint a Hispanic. The group kept emphasizing that this district had a nonrepresentative board that handled the issue in a very insensitive way, that the appointment reflected the superintendent's promotion-from-within policy excluding Hispanics in the past, that it represented a lack of commitment to a strong bilingual education program, and that it typified the closed decision-making process within the district.

Basically, the protest focused on "affirmative action" issues rather than on the quality of education and professional leadership in the district. There were also complaints about the district's bilingual programs, however, and that is a concern for Hispanic educators who have used the district as a vehicle for their citywide efforts to enhance bilingual education.

In actual fact, the predominantly Hispanic schools in the district contain numerous enrichment and alternative programs, designed to enhance the learning experiences of students there; and even in the school where all the protest took place, there are many such programs.

The response of both the CSB and the superintendent was to reassert their old policies that had been so effective in the past in developing good programs, while continuing to try to attract able minority educators, including Hispanics, who share their educational philosophy. That philosophy does not include a commitment to maintenance programs in bilingual education (which they regard as separatist, parochial, and educationally unsound). Thus, the controversy may broaden in the future from one focused primarily on affirmative action to one over the nature of bilingual education as well.

Given the vast network of support that the district has developed, both among parent and community groups and among educators, the insurgents will face a long struggle to take control. Moreover, since the coa-

104   110 LIVINGSTON STREET REVISITED

lition they are seeking to replace are themselves a liberal group who are committed to ethnic succession, although at a different pace from the one the insurgents prefer, it will not be easy to get them out.

The insurgents have, however, been successful in electing a new CSB in 1980 that is markedly different from any of its predecessors. A majority of its members are now committed to taking on more of a policy role. They delegate much less to the superintendent and professional staff than was ever the case before. And they are much more supportive of the insurgents' positions.

Beyond that, the superintendent retired in June 1981, at a time when it became clear that he could no longer run the district with the authority and power that he had before. His successor is the former deputy superintendent, a longtime colleague, indicating that the power had not shifted that much. However, the new superintendent will have to be much more responsive to the demands of this more active CSB than he and others in the old coalition might like. And, depending on how he and his colleagues react, this district's ethnic succession politics may be either a stormy one or it may proceed in a more orderly fashion.

Indicators of Student and District Performance

As already indicated, this is one of the most rapidly changing districts in the city. It went from 27.2% poor Hispanic in 1970 to 50.8% in 1978, and the number is higher now. Correspondingly, many of its high achieving white middle-class students no longer attend public schools there and many have, of course, moved out. Considering the fact that Hispanic students have among the lowest reading scores of any ethnic group in the city, the best that the district might do under decentralization is to keep the anticipated declines in reading scores at a minimum. It has in fact done that, having had almost no change during the period of 1971–79.[5] In three grades (2, 3, and 6) reading scores slipped slightly, and in three others (4, 5, and 9) there were actually small gains. (See Table 5.1).

Given the population changes in the district, these scores indicate some considerable proficiency in teaching reading, particularly in the junior high schools. Apparently, some of the experimental programs we described are working well.

TABLE 5.1

District D
Reading Scores 1971–79

Grade	1971	1979	Change (−)
Two	2.7	2.6	(−0.1)
Three	3.5	3.4	(−0.1)
Four	4.4	4.5	0.1
Five	5.5	5.6	0.1
Six	6.6	6.4	(−0.2)
Seven	6.6	7.1	0.5
Eight	7.3	8.2	0.9
Nine	9.0	9.2	0.2

Compared to the citywide trend during that time, however, this district did not keep up. Given its much greater ethnic and socioeconomic change in enrollment, that is not surprising. The comparison between the district and citywide experience is shown in Table 5.2.

The district did better, however, in its math scores. It was a little behind the citywide average in 1971 (5.4 score for fifth graders in the district, compared with 5.7 citywide) and narrowed the gap by 1978 to a point where they were almost the same (5.7 for the district, 5.8 citywide).[6]

On average daily attendance, the district has declined slightly relative to the city, but it still has a better record. Thus, the district declined from

TABLE 5.2

Changes in Reading Scores 1971–79

Grade	District D	Citywide	Difference Between District D and All Schools (+/−)
Two	(−0.1)	-0-	(−0.1)
Three	(−0.1)	0.1	(−0.2)
Four	0.1	0.6	(−0.5)
Five	0.1	0.7	(−0.6)
Six	(−0.2)	0.6	(−0.8)
Seven	0.5	1.0	(−0.5)
Eight	0.9	1.1	(−0.2)
Nine	0.2	1.1	(−0.9)

85.9 in 1970 to 84.6 in 1978, compared with a citywide figure of 81.1 in 1970 and 82.8 in 1978.[7]

Given the housing deterioration and the vast in-migration of poor Hispanics into the southern areas of the district, one might expect such changes to be reflected in patterns of vandalism. That has not been the case on two of our three indicators, though it has been on a third. Thus, unlawful entries have decreased from 109 in 1971 to 90 in 1978; and fires have gone down from 6 to 2 during that period. Considering the fact that there were 19 in 1973, a year of much in-migration, the drop since then has been marked. The number of broken glass panes, by contrast, has gone way up, from 7200 to almost 13,000. So there is no clear pattern.[8]

The district's record on staff integration bears particular note, since that has been a focus of the protest politics described in the chapter.[9] Black educators have fared considerably better than Hispanics. The number of black principals, for example, increased from 1 to 4 (4.2% to 12.5%) and of assistant principals from 1.8% to 7.3% during the period from 1971 to 1978. For Hispanics, by contrast, there were no principalships and only 1 assistant principal in each year. There are, however, increases in the proportion of Hispanic teachers, from 1% to 8.5%, reflecting the increased numbers of bilingual programs. Black teachers, meanwhile, increased from 2.1% to 7.7%. And for the professional and administrative staff in its entirety, the increase in blacks has been from 2.5% to 13.2%, and that for Hispanics from 1.2% to 12.8%.

Two main factors contributed to this limited incorporation of Hispanics into supervisory positions and to the generally slow pace of ethnic integration among the district's staff. One has been the district's stable teaching environment. The other has been its policy of filling principalships and other positions primarily from existing staff within the district. The stable, supportive teaching environment contributed to a remarkably low turnover rate relative to other districts in teaching and supervisory positions. In instances where there were openings, a major criterion used in staff selection was the emphasis placed on experience within the district and on the staff person's sharing the superintendent's educational philosophy.

In addition, the Board of Education's policy of allowing school staff to serve in districts where they live has also contributed to this stable staffing pattern. Though experiencing rapid demographic change, this district still has a large number of New York City public school educators who live there, and many have continued serving in its schools. Many others, moreover, live in adjacent white middle-class areas.

District D, then, has generally held its own in a period of marked population change. The many model education programs it has initiated, under strong professional leadership, seem to have helped stabilize student performance. If the district can work out its legitimacy problems vis à vis Hispanic leaders, it may well establish itself as an exemplary minority district that shows how open education may work in poor as well as middle-class areas.

6

A Successfully Stabilized Poor Black District: District E

Our next district, exercising many initiatives allowed under decentralization, and with a predominantly poor black enrollment, is one that has also developed promising approaches to curriculum and instruction. Although markedly different from either the alternative and bilingual programs of District B or the humanistic, open education approach of District D, its more traditional style has contributed to significant improvements in student performance.

District E, starting from a situation of extremely factional politics, little community legitimacy for the schools, and poor education, developed sufficient political consensus early in its history to recruit a black superintendent from outside the city. This consensus represented an instance where a predominantly black community, having gone through its ethnic succession experience before decentralization, had established its own community leaders and political infrastructure and achieved enough social peace to allow its superintendent an opportunity to develop a new educational improvement strategy.

The superintendent, given a mandate to stabilize the schools and to improve the quality of education, moved forcefully to pursue a strategy based on a production management approach and a traditional, structured curriculum. This involved setting explicit goals in the form of learning objectives; standardizing the curriculum for all district schools; making regular performance audits of schools; conducting periodic testing to measure results; and raising teacher expectations. The approach reflects the superintendent's strong centralizing style in the face of a deteriorating political and educational setting; and it has resulted in a stable and steadily improving district in an impressively short period of time. Having accomplished all these things and having kept the district on such an even keel politically, the superintendent has moved recently to a more decentralized, participative style and to developing more school-initiated programs, while still maintaining a strong district office presence in the schools.

Demography, Neighborhoods, District Characteristics

This district is located in the civic, cultural, commercial, and intellectual center of one of New York's outer boroughs and contains within it several colleges and universities, many cultural institutions, and some large community development agencies. Although the district is predominantly lower income and black, its residential areas are ethnically diverse, ranging from upper-middle-class white enclaves to neighborhoods containing middle- and lower-income blacks.

The district contains a population of roughly 200,000, with whites accounting for 35%, blacks another 60%, and Hispanics the rest.[1] The middle class and particularly the whites, however, have all but abandoned the public schools. Close to 80% of the public school students are black; another 18% are Hispanic; and no more than 2% are white.[2] Many white residents send their children to private or parochial schools that are located near their homes. Middle-class blacks as well have clamored to get into these schools, wanting "better" education than they feel is available in the public schools. The middle-class and white withdrawal are most pronounced at the junior high level, with many local residents even sending their children to schools in a different borough.

The enrollment of the district has declined substantially since decentralization, much like that in most other districts, from 25,633 in 1970 to 17,754 in 1979.[3] This decline has, in turn, contributed to a decline in school building utilization, from 98% in 1970 to 70% in 1979.[4]

An important characteristic of this district, affecting its politics, is the nature of its boundaries. The district includes only segments of several distinct subcommunities, including roughly one third of a predominantly white middle-class "brownstone" neighborhood; almost all of another one;

and half of a large black poverty area. District lines are obviously important in determining who will control the CSB. In this case, the inclusion of white middle-class areas with poor black and Hispanic ones meant that blacks would not have the control that their numbers in the public schools might have indicated. They constituted only two of the nine CSB members in 1970, and although the number went up to a controlling majority of five in 1973, it remained at that level in 1977, before increasing to seven in 1980.[5] CSBs have thus underrepresented the district's minority populations for most of its history under decentralization.

Major zoning controversies concerning an elementary school in a white middle-class area reflect some of the district's racial conflicts, having consumed an inordinate amount of the CSB's and the superintendent's time since decentralization began. Although this is only one of 22 schools in the district, it has taken on tremendous importance as one of the last remaining white middle-class schools. After an unsuccessful desegregation plan with a neighboring black school, parents in this one have lobbied for a K–8 program so their children would not have to travel outside to junior high. Since 50% of the students in the school are now black, having been bused in from outside, this plan's proponents argue that it would stabilize a desegregated school rather than maintain a segregated one. Some CSB members representing this school have tried to get support from their black colleagues by proposing a similar K–8 school in a poor black area. Many blacks in the district nevertheless defined this K–8 proposal as a last-ditch attempt by whites to retain control of "their" school, and they opposed it for that reason. The proposal finally passed in 1980, however, and it has reflected and, in turn, contributed to racial animosities within the district.

Political History

When decentralization became a contested issue in the 1960s and early 1970s, the political situation in this district was much like it was in Ocean Hill-Brownsville. There was considerable black-white confrontation in the schools and district office; and there were physical attacks on white teachers and principals, reflecting a very turbulent politics. CSB meetings were characterized by many such confrontations, and for the initial years of decentralization they were constantly interrupted by angry community activists who questioned the legitimacy of the CSB to set policy for the district.

Racial tensions were so marked that even those white educators who had publicly supported decentralization reported their fear while attending these meetings. One recounted: "I would leave these meetings constantly asking myself: 'Did you say anything wrong that might possibly be construed as racist, that might lead to harassing visits to your school?' I never knew whether my tires might be slashed, and I even feared for my physical safety as I left the building."

Confrontation between white educators and community activists often took place in schools as well. Small groups of militant black activists visited schools on a regular basis, questioning and sometimes harassing principals and teachers. The white principal quoted above, widely known in the district as committed to community control, recounted his experiences: "The militants used to come to my school regularly, telling me that this was *their* school. I told them that they had the wrong guy, that I was their friend, and that they should move on to other schools where there might be a *real* problem of staff not being sensitive enough to community concerns. They kept coming back, though, for quite a while."

In brief, this was a black poverty-area district where the legitimacy of the public schools was in serious question. The staff and the CSB were overwhelmingly white, and the goal of community activists, reflecting the politics of the area and the times, was to have many more black educators running the schools. They had more than ample evidence that these schools were not educating the students. In 1971, for example, only 18% of the district's students were reading at or above grade level, and many teachers and principals had low expectations of how much their students could learn.[6] These educators had all but given up, often running their schools as little more than custodial operations. Conditions of poverty and poor student preparedness obviously contributed to this situation, but the educators' limited capacity to cope, notwithstanding the difficult task they faced, only exacerbated the situation.

The hostility between the district's schools and the community thus ran very high. The schools were seen as alien, outpost institutions, run by and for outsiders, rather than as community ones. Communication, trust, and working relations between educators and students and between schools and the wider community had often completely broken down, and in the early 1970s decentralization was not seen as much of a solution either.

Moreover, the fact that one upper-middle-class enclave, accounting for only 5% of the district's enrollment, has nevertheless selected five CSB members, all of them white, to the first CSB, did not ease the situation. This came about because the middle class voted in greater numbers than the blacks, overcoming the numerical majority of the latter. Also, some black leaders encouraged their constituency to boycott the first election as a protest against what they regarded as a decentralization law that had granted limited powers to the CSBs.

A turning point for the district was the election in 1973 of five blacks to the CSB, at least two of whom became active in the selection of a new superintendent.[7] A former teacher and educational consultant in California, he was unknown to most board members. One of the new black members, however, successfully secured the necessary votes for this superintendent's appointment. And, over the next couple of years, that board member mediated between the new superintendent and the board, giving him much legitimacy in a disbelieving and politically unstable community.

The procedures the CSB followed in selecting the superintendent also helped to establish his credibility as well as to calm down the district. "We really did a thorough job in bringing in parents and community groups," reported a CSB member active in this period. "Nobody could easily say they weren't consulted. It may have been one of the best things we did."

When the superintendent arrived, while there had been some quieting down of community conflict, most of the conditions that had existed at the start of decentralization still did. Reading, math scores, and attendance were still low; there remained much tumult in the junior highs; the CSB was quite factionalized; and no leadership group existed to handle these problems. "This was still an angry community when I arrived," reports the superintendent in retrospect, "and I had some people come into my office, pushing their way past my secretary, saying who is this guy from out of town who was going to try to exploit these kids for his own interests. They even threatened me physically."

In addition, the teachers' union was very active in the district. It had elected several people to the board in 1973, and they voted as a bloc. They were opposed to the new appointment. "They weren't in favor of our candidate," explained one CSB member who supported him. "He was from outside the city, and they always had problems with outsiders they weren't sure they could control. They held up the appointment for several months."

Over time, somewhat slowly at first because of factionalism on the CSB and in the community and because of the many educational problems in the district, this superintendent built his strength as the leading figure there. He established a competent district office staff; and although board members did not agree on the competence of all members of his staff, or on his tendency to take on more and more authority, he not only moved into a position of leadership but began to produce increasingly positive results, which by 1980 showed this to be one of the most effective districts in the city.

CSBs and the Superintendent: A History of Improving Relations

Despite the fact that the superintendent remained in office since early 1974 and initiated many programs that improved the performance of students markedly over what it was when he arrived, his relationships with his CSB have been uneven. Virtually all his boards have indicated a high regard for him as an educator and administrator, acknowledging the many improvements under his leadership. At the same time, he has been in periodic conflict with them over the issue of who should run the district.

From the superintendent's point of view, the district needed strong leadership that he felt he had to provide, lest there be a continuation of the poor-quality education and the community anger and frustration that had existed when he arrived. He thus took on both administrative and, to some extent, policy powers, much to the CSB's chagrin.

What exists in this district is simply a reflection of superintendent-CSB conflicts that we found elsewhere, though with the usual embellishments that reflect the particular personalities involved. The superintendent saw the CSB as periodically encroaching on his administrative authority. They saw him, in turn, as moving unilaterally. For example, he made many decisions on programs, staffing, and budget that they regarded as policy matters and hence as being within their jurisdiction. They complained that he often informed them too late for them to provide any input, and some felt that this reflected his style of treating them as his subordinates who should take direction from him instead of the other way around.

It was this relationship, then—reflecting conflicts common to many districts—that constituted one of the main internal strains in the district. Such conflicts seem to be endemic to the way decentralization has been established in New York and will probably require legislative and procedural reforms if decentralization is to work better in the future. Fortunately for this district, the conflicts did not seem to have much of an effect on the schools, at least as judged by the evidence of effective new programs and improved student performance by the end of the 1970s. There have been other districts, perhaps including District C to some extent, where that has not been the case, however.

The conflict might have been minimized had the superintendent communicated more with his board prior to making key decisions, and had he responded more flexibly to board criticisms and inquiries in relation to particular issues. Instead, board members saw him as having an exaggerated concern for maintaining his professional autonomy and as interpreting CSB inquiries and criticisms as threats to that.

In brief, this is an example of a strong superintendent and a weak CSB district in which the superintendent has been effective despite conflicts with his CSB over his and the board's role. Yet, the board keeps renewing his contract, and the schools keep getting better. And, over the years, the relationship seems to have improved. Moreover, the superintendent has been able to shield the professional staff from any repercussions the conflict might have.

Centralized District Management in Political Turbulence

The story of this district, then, is one of how an active, aggressive superintendent took advantage of his authority and of the divisional autonomy allowed a community school district under decentralization in ways that were not possible under the old system. His leadership qualities enabled him to do many things under decentralization that would probably not have taken place otherwise. Indeed, he would not likely have been chosen under the old centralized system where only "insiders" who had moved up the ranks within the bureaucracy were appointed to such superintendent positions. Or, if he were chosen, as an exceptional case where they let an outsider in, he might well have decided not to come, had he known anything in advance about the system, since it would not have permitted him to take the initiatives that he did.

The management style he pursued initially was one of strong leadership and control, rather than of reliance on managing by consensus or on participative management. He was thus more of what has come to be called a Theory X rather than a Theory Y manager, although his style is much more complex and subtle than what is usually implied by those terms.[8]

The situation confronting the superintendent when he arrived in fact required the strong central leadership he provided. As already indicated, the schools were not functioning and many parents and community groups were very agitated about this; yet no individual or coalition had assumed leadership. Moreover, some of the key constituencies that a paricipative management style would have indicated should be consulted were too much a part of the problem to provide constructive early input (e.g., the teachers' union and principals' association).

CURRICULUM STYLE

Reflecting his own educational philosophy and responding to what he saw as the needs of poor black and Hispanic students, this superintendent played an active role in restructuring education there. It would be more accurate to say that he moved, not so much toward a restructuring, as toward imposing a structure where very little, if any, had existed before.

At the time he began his reform program, many principals and teachers were unable to cope with the classroom situations they faced. A common tactic of teachers was to lower their aspirations as to what might be taught, rationalize doing so by pointing to the limited preparation of the students, and end up running custodial classrooms. Outstanding teachers always existed, but the more typical approach was to have low expectations as to what the students might learn. Moreover, given the political turmoil, there was not much educational planning going on either. This combination of limited expectations and a catch-as-catch-can curriculum undoubtedly had a devastatingly negative impact on student learning, reinforcing the negative conditions that produced it in the first place.

Building on preliminary efforts by his predecessor, this superintendent embarked on an ambitious strategy for improving education in the district. In contrast to the open education approach in District D and the many alternative programs in District B, the strategy here was a more traditional and managerial one, combining: (1) *a behaviorist, goal-conscious, production management approach to curriculum*, standardizing it and making it much more uniform throughout the district; (2) *an emphasis on skills training*, "back to basics," and having more structure in the curriculum; reinforced through (3) *an increasingly elaborated set of management controls and supports*, including an extensive system of tests in every major subject (measuring student *and* teacher performance), unannounced *audits* of every school, and a program of *technical assistance and in-service training* for "marginal" teachers to help improve their performance.

These approaches were all part of a single strategy that had particular relevance for the needs of this poverty-area black district. And it had rarely, if ever, been followed in the systematic, districtwide fashion in which he pursued it.

The entire strategy hinged on the development of curriculum learning objectives (CLOs), under district office leadership. In the language of behavioral psychology that the superintendent often used, the CLOs were a series of explicit statements about *terminal behaviors* required of all students. That term referred to the content (concepts, principles, facts) of various subjects (e.g., math, science, history). The strategy was formulated in the context of the superintendent's and his staff's observations that there was virtually no uniformity in the district's curriculum. As in all poverty-area districts, the amount of mobility among schools was very high; and for a student to move from one school to another was almost like moving to another country, so poorly articulated was the curriculum.

Teachers working under such conditions of high pupil mobility and of having many students with learning problems tended to cope either by lowering their expectations and running custodial schools, as already described, or by "doing their own thing."[9] There was often nothing wrong with the latter, except that it left the students with no common core of knowledge. As the superintendent recalled: "I noticed, for example, that a subject like social studies was not taught in any uniform way. One teacher might have just returned from a summer in Israel, and she taught a great section on that. But some other teacher had just returned from Africa, and she taught that. They were teaching good material, but they were doing their own thing. And we have to make certain that our kids were exposed to a whole scope and sequence of materials."

The way to reverse the nonfunctional coping strategies of teachers, the superintendent suggested, was to institute some form of *educational planning* with *uniform standards*. He and his staff did this through using the Board of Education's curriculum guides. They took these materials on minimal curriculum standards and on the scope and sequence for each subject for grades K–9, and they translated them into a set of *behavioral objectives*. Thus, all schools would have the same curriculum and at any given time during the school year, all fifth grade classes would have to be covering a particular portion of each subject. The schools were not discouraged from doing more than that, but at least there were *minimal standards*. And the district office staff met with every principal and with teachers to inform them of the strategy and get the program under way.

Curriculum integration is also a goal. "We now have done a lot to integrate the work for any given time period for general subjects—science, social studies, English, etcetera," reports the superintendent. "If a class is working on a particular subject in science, we have the spelling, the social studies, and math all geared into that. So students will not write compositions in English in isolation from what is going on in other subjects."

There was much more to the strategy than just establishing learning objectives, however. They were reinforced by several management control and support procedures. One was an extensive program of *testing* in each major subject, usually several times a year. The tests reminded students and educators that the learning objectives had to be followed, and the results indicated the extent to which students had mastered the basic skills and subject matter specified in those objectives. Not only were the tests given on a regular basis, but the results were posted to make visible how well the learning objectives were being carried out. They were used as a measure of both student performance and of that of teachers. But individual classes were not identified publicly. "We were more concerned with the school as a whole," reported a headquarters staffperson. "We never singled out teachers or classes for praise or condemnation."

In addition, the superintendent conducted *audits* of every school in the district. He and his staff made unannounced visits to schools requiring that they be in a state of "constant readiness," lest they be observed on a "bad day." The group met with principals and APs at the beginning of the school day. Roughly six classrooms were then assigned to each member of the visiting group. They typically spent twenty minutes or so in each classroom, making the usual kinds of observations: inspecting bulleting boards and assessing the preparedness of the teacher and the extent to which lesson plans were made up and followed. In addition, the visitors made similar judgments on a schoolwide basis—observing student behavior in corridors, just outside the building, in the cafeteria, and other places.

The group then reconvened around noon, again in the principal's office, and reported on what they found. Nothing was put in writing, and the superintendent emphasized that he was aware of the limited sample of activity he and his group had taken and that their observations were meant as suggestive only of remedial actions that might be taken. In every instance, the superintendent indicated that he and his district staff were available to help the school in taking corrective actions. And he often followed up to see if problems were being actively dealt with. Thus, some schools might be given a second audit later in the year.

Needless to say, the teachers' union has not been enthusiastic about this auditing program, which its representatives see as limiting teacher automony. Moreover, union reps often recall how teachers used to be subject to arbitrary treatment by principals, before collective bargaining limited that. They saw the audits as reverting to such preunion conditions. The superintendent emphasized that the audits were insitituted, not as a punitive device, but rather as a *technical assistance* one, to help teachers and supervisors in locating problems and in pursuing corrective actions.

One follow-up activity in this regard is the superintendent's *marginal teacher program*. He asked school supervisors to make a list of teachers whose performance was not what it should have been and who, therefore, need assistance. He and his staff then made up a similar list, and there turned out to be a very high correspondence between the two. Both parties (district staff and principals) then made up a final list where there was such agreement, and the district office staff provided further training for such teachers. Each staffperson in the district office was assigned several teachers. That person would sit down with the teacher and discuss the teacher's strengths and weaknesses in a nonthreatening way. The teacher would then develop a corrective strategy under the staffperson's direction. It might involve direct instruction in classroom management skills by the staffperson, an in-service training program in the district or in education courses at a university; or it might involve transferring the teacher to another school within that district or even to another district. All this took place as a technical assistance strategy and *not* as a way of coercing or threatening teachers. In fact, it is one of the most extensive staff development programs we found in any district.

More Decentralized Approaches. Over the past couple of years, after having established some uniformity and structure to the curriculum, the superintendent has initiated several other new strategies for improving education. All relate to the broader goals of enhancing staff development, increasing parent participation, encouraging more school-based planning, making more and better use of nonschool agencies within the district, and making the public schools more attractive to the middle class. The district now has a teacher learning center in the district office at which the superintendent and his staff conduct workshops for classroom teachers on a wide variety of subjects, such as teaching writing skills, preparing students in test taking, using computerized instruction techniques, and refining learning objectives. Several of these meetings have been well attended, indicating the strong interest that teachers in the district have in such assistance. There is also a *Teacher Corps* project in an elementary, a junior high, and a high school, conducted in collaboration with a large university that includes a series of staff development (pre- and inservice) activities, with materials made available in resource rooms in each school. The district plans to include many more schools in the near future.

In addition, there is a cluster of activities run in collaboration with the *New York Urban Coalition*. One involves extensive school development efforts in which teams representing the key constituencies—for example, parents, teachers, administrators, other staff, community representatives, and students—develop a comprehensive plan and individual programs for the school. Another involves developing a broad resource network of agencies and institutions in the district (business, labor, education, government, community service agencies) that then, in turn, help the schools develop programs.

Still another recent effort is something the district calls A *Vertical Incentive program* focused on curriculum and organizational improvements in the district's elementary schools. It involves setting up a K–3 and grades 4–6 mini-school in each of the elementary schools, allowing for much participation by teachers and parents in developing new curricula that are meant to reflect the particular needs of students as well as skills and philosophic preferences of teachers.

One of the most significant of all the initiatives the superintendent has pursued is at the *junior high school level.* In this district, as in so many others, parents sending their children to public schools opt out after the elementary grades. They send them to private school or to a public junior high in a middle-class area—or they move out of the city.

The inferior quality of the junior highs became such a big issue in the 1970s that there were strong pressures on the CSB to adopt a policy of accepting waivers for students to attend junior highs in another district. In fact, this waiver policy simply formalized what parents had already been doing without asking permission. Even minority members of the CSB voted for the waiver.

The superintendent objected strongly to the policy, since it meant accepting the middle class's abandonment of the district. He got enough votes to eliminate this policy in the late 1970s, with the promise that he would work to upgrade junior highs in the district. And many of his educational improvement efforts have been concentrated on this level. They include (1) two new, alternative junior highs, functioning much like mini-schools, with an enriched curriculum and extensive teacher involvement in developing it; and (2) the development of new programs in traditional junior highs as well, in the arts, science, the basic skills, and careers. Both approaches have helped prepare students for entrance into the city's elite, specialized high schools, and the district's admissions have increased from 70 in 1973 to more than 300 in 1980.

In brief, several initiatives have been taken in this district to improve education. It would be wrong, however, to conclude that the first part of the strategy—namely the learning objectives and various management supports and controls that have accompanied them—was implemented without some resistance by the educators. There was early resistance both from teachers and principals. This conflict between the divisional interest of the district office and teachers and principals seems to have been a function of (1) the way the learning objectives were introduced, and (2) the lack of fit between program demands and the educators' view of themselves as independent "professionals."

Initially, the superintendent introduced the learning objectives without prior consultation from principals and teachers. Given the district's situation, that strategy made sense. The district was in a state of crisis, and there was a need for bold initiatives. Had the superintendent begun the program on the basis of much consultation with the educators, it might never have got off the ground. Instead, he simply announced that it would go into effect, although after the first year the educators' views were increasingly solicited on how the program might be improved.

It was not only the style of implementation that was at issue for the educators. There was also the incompatibility between the learning objectives approach and the orientations of some principals and teachers as "professionals." These educators felt that the learning objectives limited their flexibility in the classroom, thereby hampering their efforts to reach low-achieving students. As one teacher representative noted: "You are told where and when to teach, not just what to teach. It is a frame-by-frame procedure. This rigidity stifles the creativity of teachers." Another reported: "There is no room left for the imagination and creativity of teachers with the learning objectives. Teachers are frustrated by the fact that they are supposed to be teaching according to a very controlled and rigid timetable." While not all teacher reps felt this way, it was at least a prevailing view among many.

In actual fact, the learning objectives only set minimum standards. While they did specify the scope and sequence for each subject and provided time frames for different topics, they did not dictate styles of instruction, nor did they necessarily prevent teachers from going beyond minimum standards. The district office acknowledged that teachers with very low-achieving classes might have to omit some of the learning objectives or modify the timetable, in collaboration with their principals. In some schools, principals were loath to allow that, so that in this sense the teachers reps' concerns were justified. At the many schools where there was early support, however, this was not a problem.

Since this was a strategy to upgrade supervision and not just classroom teaching, several principals felt threatened also. They saw it as implying that they were not doing the job they might have been doing. The problem was exacerbated by some principals' resentment that a headquarters staffperson without a principal's license would be visiting their school to monitor how the learning objectives were being implemented. One such principal regarded it as a professional insult.

DISTRICT OFFICE AND PROFESSIONAL STAFF

Relations between the superintendent and his professional staff in the schools have generally been quite supportive, despite these problems, especially in recent years as he has begun many programs to increase school-based planning and to expand professional development opportunities for teachers to include the superintendent's forums and workshops. Moreover, teachers are encouraged to work in the district office after school and in the summer on refining the learning objectives, and the extent of teacher involvement in curriculum development seems to be quite widespread and increasing. Also, the big decline of violence in this district's schools, reflecting its improved programs and an increasing district perception that the schools have become more a community institution, have made teaching there more attractive than it was in the early 1970s.

Yet, some union representatives retain negative feelings about the district. Historically, this was a district with much hostility between the teachers' union and community activists. Even though the political climate of the district has changed markedly in recent years, residues from the earlier period still remain, as union representatives stay alert for possible district programs like the learning objectives that might encroach on teacher rights.

The other source of teacher resentment was appointments to district office staff positions. Several were based, not on seniority, but on merit, as the superintendent brought in his own people to direct or coordinate programs. He selected several white as well as minority educators, so the union could not justifiably criticize him on racial grounds. But some union representatives did resent the fact that "experienced" teachers were not as likely to get these positions as others with less seniority who the superintendent knew or who had come to his attention.

On balance, then, the superintendent's relations with the union are not as close as they are in other districts. He does meet with union representatives on a regular basis, and they make numerous suggestions about educational programs, many of which he incorporates. At the same time, his management style has not involved consulting with the union in advance on new programs. And in a district where the union had traditionally been in conflict with community activists, his style is not as reassuring as teachers would like. Yet, the fact that classroom conditions have improved and that teachers are included increasingly in curriculum development and given much technical assistance from the district office, makes it unlikely that those union representatives who are critical of some district policies will get strong support from the rank and file.

As for the principals, the superintendent has the same kind of relationship with them as with teachers. He meets periodically with their association, but he has not included it as a coparticipant in the development of such programs as the learning objectives. He told his principals that he intended them to carry out the learning objectives program. He did suggest at one point that the principals themselves audit the schools, but they understandably rejected the idea, feeling that it was too sensitive a task to evaluate one's peers in that fashion. He also informed them that he did not want them speaking up at open community school board meetings, asking for more resources for their schools. In this connection, they were expected to meet privately with him to work out such problems. "Principals used to come in with parents at public CSB meetings," a top district official explained, "and complained about not having enough staff in their schools. He told them he didn't want that anymore, and he put an end to it." What this did was to help create a more stable administrative as well as political climate that then made it possible to engage in the educational planning necessary to get needed programs under way.

The implicit trade-off for the principals was that the superintendent would defend them in public, where their school had become a target of community protest, provided he felt they were doing the best job they could. And there were situations where he did that, again trying to work out school problems with them in private.

The superintendent has, in addition, established a visitation program for principals and APs, as a technique of professional development that further enables him to diagnose and correct school problems. Each principal is periodically assigned to a different school, often for as long as two weeks, during which time the principal stays away completely from his or her home school. The school selected for the visit is not chosen on a random basis, but rather in terms of providing a particular kind of learning experience that the superintendent feels the principal may need. As the superintendent reported: "I had one situation where a principal told me he had to run three lunch shifts. I told him he was in the food business too much and should get back into education more, because he was taking valuable teacher staff time to monitor the cafeteria. So I purposely sent him to a school where they only had one lunch period, and I never told him the reason for the assignment. It turned out that he got the message, and within two days after he was back, he had changed his three shifts to one."

An important benefit of this exchange program is that the superintendent gets to find out a lot about a school a principal has vacated, since a district office staffperson is assigned to run that school. This information is sometimes a valuable aid in enabling the superintendent to provide further assistance to the school.

DISTRICT OFFICE AND COMMUNITY

As in many poverty-area districts, parent participation in this one has been limited. There are PAs in each school and a presidents' council (PA presidents) districtwide, but they have not been that consistently active until the last year or so. They have been involved in matters of principal selection and tenure and sometimes in curriculum, but that involvement has been sporadic. Indeed, participation was so limited in the mid-1970s that several previously active CSB members declined to run again. They cited their keen disappointment that there was no parent constituency to relate to.

The superintendent was generally responsive to parent concerns in the first few years of his service (1974–77), but he did not make any significant efforts to get them involved more. He was busy building a staff and trying to stabilize the schools so that he could develop new programs.

The CSB was also responsive to parent complaints, but it was not a particularly open body. In fact, it held closed executive sessions, in violation of the state Sunshine Law requiring all meetings of public bodies be open to the public. Moreover, the board has continued this practice even when its staff and others in the district have pointed out its illegality.

Actually, parent participation has waxed and waned over the years. When decentralization began it was quite strong, mostly as a carryover from the activism centering on the issue of community control. Militant protests over the selection, tenure, and competence of principals; over the adequacy of schools; and over the unrepresentativeness of the CSB were common. During the period of the superintendent's selection (late 1973), parent protests became more institutionalized in various screening committees, and that quieted down much of the militancy.

Over time, other developments, some positive and some negative, also limited parent participation. There were more minority staff in the schools and district office, and that was noticed. And the schools started getting better. On a more negative note, economic conditions may have contributed to the limited parent participation, as they probably did in other minority districts. Parents had less time for such civic activity in a period of increasing economic hardship. Also, the city's fiscal crisis was clearly affecting the schools, and parents could see that there would be fewer services than before. The prospects for reversing that situation seemed hopeless to parents who felt pressed by other concerns.

Parent participation in this district has increased significantly over the past couple of years, however. New leadership emerged in the presidents' council; several school-based programs got under way; and the superintendent has reached out increasingly to parents, through such means as his superintendent's forum where he invites them to meet with him monthly to discuss school matters.

Yet, one must be careful not to take too simplistic a view of parent participation. Limited public participation need not indicate that education is proceeding poorly. In fact, it may indicate that many past problems are being handled better, to a point where parents no longer feel a need to protest. Moreover, there may be a form of indirect parent participation in this district that may well be quite productive. The district has to some extent tried to develop more of a partnership between the school and the home, in which parents support the learning process through ensuring that books are taken home, that homework is done, that children attend school, and so forth. That is an important form of parent participation that provides a needed partnership in the actual learning process. Such forms of parent participation exist as a matter of course in many middle-class homes, and an active effort to extend them to poor minority families may well constitute a productive strategy for improving student performance. Our study suggests that decentralization facilitates the establishment of such linkages much more than the old centralized system did by attracting superintendents, district office staff, and principals who are more community-oriented than their predecessors were.

Conclusions

To summarize, in this district we have a case where an "outsider" black superintendent in a predominantly black, poverty-area district took many productive initiatives under decentralization that genuinely improved education. He took on much administrative and policy authority, having moved into a vacuum of leadership that existed because of a divided and relatively inactive CSB. The many programs he initiated constitute an impressive array of improvement efforts. Moreover, the superintendent not only initiated these new programs; he was also quite active on follow-up and implementation. He closely monitored how programs were carried out and made changes as new information on program results became available.

The superintendent's approach to innovation seems to have gone through two stages. The first, exemplified by the learning objectives strategy, reflected mainly a top-down, centralist style in which he made the key program and policy decisions and then explained them to school staff. The second, much more pronounced over the past year or so, has been a more bottom-up, participative mode. Several programs have been developed at the school level, with the planning taking place there, mostly by educators, and sometimes in collaboration with parents. Even the learning objectives program now includes much input from teachers and principals as they feed back information to the superintendent on how things are working out. This second phase has, in turn, deepened the superintendent's base of support. That was demonstrated most dramatically at a CSB meeting in early 1981 in which several hundred parents charged the CSB with stalling on the renewal of the superintendent's contract. His contract has been renewed, and the superintendent has clearly established himself and his programs in this district, which has emerged as one of the most effective of the minority ones under decentralization.

Indicators of Student and District Performance

Having considered the main curriculum initiatives the superintendent in this district has exercised, one would expect that they should be having some impact, and they have. At every grade level there has been an improvement in reading scores during decentralization. Table 6.1 shows

TABLE 6.1

District E
Reading Scores for 1971 and 1979

Grade	1971	1979	Change (+/−)
Two	2.4	2.7	0.3
Three	2.8	3.4	0.6
Four	3.5	4.6	1.1
Five	4.2	5.5	1.3
Six	4.8	6.3	1.5
Seven	4.8	6.6	1.8
Eight	5.5	7.6	2.1
Nine	6.2	8.0	1.8

the scores in 1971 and 1979, with the net gain for each grade level.[10] All 9 grades improved, with the largest gains occurring among the highest grades that had been furthest behind. Like District B, described earlier, District E has outperformed the city as a whole in this regard. A comparison between citywide gains and District E ones is shown in Table 6.2. At every grade level, District E did better than the city as a whole.

The gains shown for District E are similar to those made in District B. Both had roughly the same scores in 1971, and both have improved to the same extent, though with quite different curriculum and administrative styles.

Moreover, the same arguments against alternative explanations, other than decentralization, apply to District E as they did to District B. There has been no change in the socioeconomic level of the pupils that would account for the improvement. In fact, there is probably a greater proportion of poorer children in District E now than there was in 1971. And regression artifacts do not seem to be a plausible explanation, since the gains have occurred year by year. In any case, the pupils in District E were reading better in 1979 than they were nine years earlier, and it

TABLE 6.2

Changes in Reading Scores (1971–79)

Grade	District E	Citywide	Difference Between District E & All Schools (+/−)
Two	0.3	-0-	0.3
Three	0.6	0.1	0.5
Four	1.1	0.6	0.5
Five	1.3	0.7	0.6
Six	1.5	0.6	0.9
Seven	1.8	1.0	0.8
Eight	2.1	1.1	1.0
Nine	1.8	1.1	0.7

appears that this improvement was due to decentralization. More specifically, it was probably due, at least in part, to the educational and staff development programs described in this chapter, as well as to the administrative initiatives of the superintendent.

These gains, unlike those in District B, are reflected quite dramatically in math scores as well.[11] Thus, the gap between District E math scores for fifth graders and the citywide scores has narrowed considerably from 1971 to 1978. In 1971 the District E score was 4.4, compared with 5.4 citywide, while in 1978, the difference was 5.4 for the district and 5.9 for the city.

Attendance data show the same pattern of improvement, relative to citywide trends.[12] In 1971 the citywide figure was 83.6% average daily attendance, compared with 84.6% for the district. By contrast, in 1979 the citywide figure had gone up to 84.2%, while that for the district had increased to 87.0%. Again, many of the educational program initiatives in the district probably had much to do with the improvements.

District E has put a great deal of effort into preparing its students for admission to the city's specialized high schools, and that effort seems to have paid off.[13] In one junior high school, for example, all eighth grade students are trained intensively in test-taking techniques as well as in subject matter relative to the test for Brooklyn Tech, and then all are *required* to take it. Trends in the number of District E students gaining admission there show the results. In 1973, 48 were admitted, and 119 were admitted in 1980. These improvements held for the other specialized high schools as well, although the numbers were not nearly as large. The number admitted to the Bronx High School of Science went up from none to 3 during that period, from 5 to 6 for Stuyvesant High School, from 10 to 19 for the High School of Music and Art, and from none to 2 for the High School of Performing Arts. Considering the fact that this district has lost so many middle-class students, these increases are an indicator that its improvement efforts have begun to pay off. Moreover, considering the chaos that existed in this district's schools in the late 1960s, and through the early years of decentralization, we may well conclude that it is an exemplary case, along with District B, of a minority district where decentralization has contributed to promising gains in school and student performance.

Trends in vandalism rates are also significant in assessing this district's performance under decentralization.[14] As we indicated in our earlier discussion, the schools in this district were a focus of much community resentment in the 1960s and early 1970s. Fires, false alarms, and violence were quite common, and this was one of the more difficult districts in which to carry on an orderly educational program, let alone embark on improvement efforts. Since 1971, however, those problems seem to have diminished quite substantially. From 1971 to 1978, the annual number of reported broken glass panes fell from 6,000 to 3,500, unlawful entries from 170 to 80, and fires from 5 to 2. The district's schools are now regarded much more than before as communty agencies, as institutions in which local residents have much more of a stake and pride than before, and some of that may well be the result of changes we have described under decentralization.

We suspect that part of the improvement in this regard relates to trends in staffing patterns within the district, mainly an increase in proportion of minority staff. From 1971 to 1978, blacks have increased from 40.9% to 63.6% of the principals; from 20.5% to 34.9% of the teachers; and from 21.9% to 51.8% of all professional staff within the district.[15] And the same trend holds for Hispanics, though the numbers are smaller (remembering, of course, that this is a predominantly black district). For Hispanics, this representation among teachers has increased from 1.7% to 5.5%, most of them in bilingual programs, and for the professional staff in its entirety, from 1.8% to 6.6%. As we indicated in this chapter, under decentralization this district has developed an increasing cadre of black middle-class professionals. Many of them grew up there and attended its public schools; they are thus able to relate well to its students. Their employment in increasing numbers is probably a further contributing factor to the political stabilization there as well as to program improvement.

In brief, along with District B, District E constitutes an exemplary case of what improvements are possible under decentralization. Many problems obviously remain, and decentralization has not been a panacea for all the ills besetting these districts. But relative to where they were before—as well as, we suspect, to many other inner-city minority districts in New York and elsewhere—these districts show significant improvement over the past decade. Such changes probably cannot be attributed to chance events and are more likely to have resulted from the many staffing, program, and administrative initiatives pursued under decentralization and, more specifically, from the management styles of these superintendents.

7

A Recently Stabilized Poor Black District: District F

District F represents a formerly integrated community that experienced considerable ethnic succession through the mid-1970s. When decentralization began, a coalition of white liberals strongly committed to integration and moderate blacks emerged as the leadership group. They appointed a new, white liberal superintendent and ran the CSB, establishing a situation of early political stability. But that stability was short-lived, as the white exodus of the 1950s and 1960s continued and as more blacks moved in.

By 1975 black community organizations and political leadership had gained enough power to overthrow the old coalition. The new CSB that was elected that year reflected these new interests, whose leaders wanted to run the district themselves rather than share power with any remaining white leadership or black moderates. After a few years of much political unrest and factionalism, accompanying the shift in power, the district has now settled down. The factions have coalesced, and the CSB and the superintendent are now free to direct their energies to educational improvement efforts rather than to turf struggles.

The scenario here, then, is one of early social peace and political leadership that could not survive the ethnic succession that the district was experiencing, followed by the emergence of a new leadership group that reflected more accurately the demographic changes that had taken place. A reasonable prediction for this district is that it may well emerge with an increasingly effective public school system, now that it has worked out many of its political problems.

Demography, Neighborhoods, District Characteristics

District F, located in an outer borough, encompasses poor, lower-middle-income, and middle-income minority communities. These communities are predominantly residential, composed of a mix of high-rise apartments, brownstones, row and townhouses, and single-family homes.

The district contained a diverse mix of Jewish, black, Irish, and Italian residents during the 1940s and 1950s. Beginning in the mid-1950s and increasing over the next two decades, the whites moved out to more middle-class areas of the city and to the suburbs. The only significant exception has been the settlement of Hasidic and Russian Jews in one part of the district. That area remains the center of New York City's growing Orthodox Jewish populations, and it contains the headquarters of the Labavitch, powerful Orthodox group in the city. But even in the years just preceding decentralization, many whites still resided in the district. As an active CSB member who had lived in the district for many years described his neighborhood: "In 1969 we still had an overwhelmingly white *residential* population, with an overwhelmingly black *student* population."

The ethnic succession has been a north to south flow, and it had been quite rapid. Many blocks have experienced the familiar pattern of white flight and panic selling, brought on by blockbusting real estate agents. Moreover, the impact of the ethnic sccession has spread to adjacent districts to the south.

All these demographic changes have had a big impact on district politics, though there was the usual "lag" period when outnumbered longer-term white residents still retained power. Thus, when decentralization began, there were still many whites active in community affairs. Many were executives, small businessmen, or professionals; they had grown up in the community; and they had children in the public schools. Moreover, they were strongly committed to public education for their children and to living in integrated neighborhoods, and they saw decentralization as an opportunity for them to bring the schools closer to the community. This remaining white middle class, in fact, elected a majority to the first two CSBs.

In the early years of decentralization, this was one of the few districts with a growing enrollment. In fact, it was the only one in its borough that increased in enrollment from 1970 to 1975, having gone up from 25,737 to 26,997 during that time.[1] Since then, it has declined a bit, but the district has had an overcrowding problem until quite recently. Thus, in 1978 it had a utilization rate of 112%, one of the highest in the city.[2] It has had 3 new schools since then; and that, along with an enrollment decline, has brought the rate down.

As for the backgrounds of students, the district's predominately black enrollment went from 74.0% in 1970 to 86.0% in 1980. Meanwhile, Hispanics dropped from 15.0% to 11.4%, while whites had all but completely left, declining from 9.3%, representing that middle-class group just discussed, to 0.7%. This has emerged as one of the main black districts in the city.[3]

Moreover, because of its size, it has the largest middle-class *and* poor black enrollment of any district. While it has over 50% of its students from welfare families—classified as families receiving aid to families with dependent children (AFDC)—that is well below the proportion on welfare in the city's other black districts.[4] The remaining black students are from working- and middle-class families, although a majority of that group has enrolled its children in private and parochial schools. Attracting them back has become a priority for the present CSB.

Political History

The district has gone through three stages since decentralization began in 1970, with a different CSB and superintendent in each. The first had as its dominant coalition a white liberal group who constituted a majority on the CSB, working closely with black moderates, the whites having the support of Orthodox Jewish groups, the Catholic church, the UFT, and remaining civic and parent groups. This was a strong board that nevertheless delegated much authority to a new and effective white liberal superintendent whom it appointed, and who was strongly committed, like the boards, both to educational improvement efforts and to orderly ethnic succession among the staff.

A second, transitional stage (1975–77) was one in which emerging black political organizations, antipoverty agencies, and parent groups moved into power, displacing the older coalition. It was a period marked by much turbulence in which "representational" concerns superseded "educational" ones, as these new groups pressed for more blacks on the CSB and more affirmative action in staffing. Rather than have the older coalition act as their surrogates and impose its own definitions of orderly ethnic succession, these black groups took the initiative themselves. Soon blacks became the majority on the board, with two or three whites remaining, but in a distinctly secondary role. This was a period of much turmoil, in which the legitimacy of both the CSB and its superintendent were increasingly challenged. The superintendent during this time was a professionally and administratively oriented black woman who had been her predecessor's deputy. After a series of conflicts with her CBS, this superintendent was ousted, with a majority of board members objecting to her style of professional dominance.

The third and most recent stage (since 1977) is one of political consolidation. The CSB has a black majority and is led by a very strong president. Their concerns have become "educational" ones, after having successfully recruited a black male educator from outside. He and the board have initiated an educational approach similar to that in District E, involving a standardized curriculum, although the approach is significantly more collaborative and has the CSB playing a more active role.

The first CSB was composed of six whites and three blacks.[5] Almost all of them were professionals or parents. Thus, it included an attorney, a physician, a black Methodist minister, a junior high school teacher, a college librarian, an executive, a bookkeeper, and a counselor in a narcotics control program. They worked incredibly long hours to establish district policy and procedures and to secure a strong professional staff. As a leading board member recalled: "Our school board loved to meet. We met every night of the week. We would have met Saturday and Sunday if it weren't for the fact that ministers and rabbis had to devote time to their religious organizations. Our nightly meetings started at eight and ran past midnight. It's incredible that for five years I spent at least four hours a day on school board activities."

One of the CSB's first major actions was to replace its incumbent, predecentralization superintendent. He wanted to stay, but, like several of his superintendent colleagues who had also served before decentralization, he was both unwilling and unable to accept an increasing role for his community school board and for parents and community leaders.

Board members characterized him as "paternalistic," "inflexible," and not open to "innovative programs." A board member explained: "It was almost pathetic. He looked down on us and treated us as if we were little children that had to be tolerated."

The superintendent the CSB chose was an able educator and administrator who had a very good reputation as a principal in a poverty-area school, having restored order there and built up an excellent educational program. And he was to become an oustanding superintendent in the district for the next four and one half years in which he served there. He was the first "new" superintendent to be appointed under decentralization, and this gave the CSB a strong sense of accomplishment as well as the reputation of intending to spearhead many reforms. "We were the only CSB at the time to displace an incumbent superintendent," reported one of the board members, "and this sent tremors through the district [among the professional staff]. People perceived us as a renegade board, that we were in power to clean house and take off on uncharted paths. All of us were deeply involved in the community and got our civic consciousness through the civil rights movement, and by being on the school board we actually had an opportunity to develop new policies and make our presence felt."

Following up immediately on such a commitment, the CSB assigned each of its members as a liaison to various schools. This enabled them to review programs and evaluate school staff, both of which they regarded as basic to the success of decentralization.

When the new superintendent took hold, however, the board became less involved in district administration. It realized the importance of having a professional educator run the district. As his administrative skills and educational leadership became increasingly apparent, the CSB limited its role to that of policymaker. The superintendent then developed his own extensive outreach strategy, as he and his staff set up a program to visit all schools in the district, observe teachers at first hand, and relate to active parent association members.

This first CSB was also committed to achieving a more balanced ethnic representation. When one vacancy soon developed, as an elected board member was judged ineligible to serve owing to his employment in another city agency, the CSB filled it with a black woman. Still later, it chose another black to fill a vacancy. "So this was a majority white board," explained one of its members, "that chose to make itself a majority black board." Yet, many new black leaders in the district regarded the first CSB's strategy of orderly ethnic succession as not at all what they wanted, since it implied for them too slow a process, which they wanted to speed up considerably—and with blacks whom *they* rather than this established power group chose.

By 1973 the district had undergone significant changes in both population and politics, both of which affected the composition and outlook of succeeding boards. Emerging black leaders in antipoverty agencies and the political organizations soon became well enough organized to exert increasing pressure on the CSB and the superintendent. Some of these activists disrupted CSB meetings, with their demands for more parent participation, more appointments of blacks, and more "community control" of the schools.

Concurrent with this developing activism among blacks was a reduction of involvement by both Catholic and Jewish parochial school groups, as they found that the CSB had limited discretion in granting funds to their institutions. Meanwhile, many more whites had moved out, completing a pattern of ethnic succession that had been under way since the 1950s. In some instances, they were spurred on by "blockbusting" real estate agents, whose areas changed from white to black ownership in a matter of months. By 1973 most of the remaining white middle class had left, with the exception of one concentrated settlement of Orthodox Jews.

A key figure in this changed balance of power was a state senator who ran a powerful Democratic club in the area. He was elected to the 1973 CSB and pushed it to appoint more blacks as teachers, principals, and district office staff. He also helped to replace white activist parents and professionals on the CSB with blacks. He and other black leaders no longer wanted either white liberals or less community-control-oriented blacks as surrogate representatives of their community. And, from the perspective of the latter two groups, this marked the beginning of the CSB's and the district's decline. One of the white liberals who felt this change keenly explained: "The second school board marked the emergence of local politicians and people who were interested in building a power base."

A contrasting view was that they reflected the legitimate interests of emerging black groups for much more representation on the CSB and professional staff. Rather than representing a *decline* in the district, they were simply a change toward more affirmative action and ethnic represenation. And, rather than constituting a shift in emphasis from educational to patronage concerns, they reflected a new kind of politics. Indeed, advocates of this view resent the implication that when blacks gain greater power, education is suddenly seen as more political, as though schools are run in accordance with "higher," nonpolitical goals when white groups are dominant.

As an example of this new politics, the district's main black antipoverty agency group began to be much more openly critical of the CSB for not giving blacks more power and accessibility to district decision making. One of its leaders characterized the first CSB somewhat negatively as "provincial and professionally oriented." The label of being "professionally oriented" was applied in this instance in a highly pejorative sense.

A critical feature of the new situation was the priority black leaders gave to using state and federal funds to secure more positions for blacks and increased black control over district decisions. School board meetings soon became marked by increasingly contentious confrontations, as the still active coalition of whites and moderate blacks from the first board fought back against community control advocates.

All these events had a big impact on the superintendent who resigned in late 1974, after being offered a high administrative position at headquarters. The board's factionalism and the increasing power of its new, community-control-oriented members had made it increasingly difficult for either him or the board to function with the effectiveness that they had before.

The new coalition on the CSB had not completely won out, however, and the board followed the first superintendent's recommendation of his deputy to be his successor. In appointing this person, a black woman whom he recruited to the district, the 1973 CSB thereby committed itself to continue having the district run by a strong professional.

That commitment was short-lived, however, with the election of a new CSB in 1975 that did not have a single incumbent from the first board. This marked the end of the white liberal–moderate black coalition, and it was the beginning of the end for the new superintendent. She tried to run the district as a strong administrator and educator in her own right, and that did not set well with her board. From her point of view, the

CSB wanted to be involved with day-to-day administration in ways that it did not know how to do and had no businesss doing. From the board's point of view, she tried too hard to run the district herself, being unwilling to give the board an important role. One board member recalled: "When we started on the CSB [1977], whatever information I wanted I had to fight for. She gave us a hard time." A parent activist who later became a CSB member explained: "She was completely uncooperative. She wouldn't tell us anything. She wanted to run the district and set all policies."

One of her problems was her objection to what she regarded as antipoverty agency and clubhouse politics intruding in district affairs. "I built up the parent constituency to counterbalance the poverty agencies," she explained.

A typical situation reflecting the CSB's increasing pressure on the superintendent was its continued demands at evening meetings that she put together information that would be made available to the board the next morning. This pressure continued through the end of 1978, when she left to take an administrative position at the Board of Education headquarters. "The board would ask me to provide information which would require me to work all night long to get it out the next day," she explained. "When I handed them the information, the CSB members wouldn't spend the time to read it. They set up committees, but the CSB reps did not show up for meetings or do any work. When I submitted a budget or proposal for the CSB to review, it would take weeks for them to get to it."

The departure of this black superintendent and the rise to power of a new CSB president in 1978 mark the beginning of the power consolidation stage in District F. This president is a highly articulate, educated, self-made black who had been a writer and now runs a profitable business in construction and community development. Having the strong support of a black elected official, who had maintained his own power position in the district, the president has been effective in coalescing the board and giving it a coherent direction and sense of purpose. "He is an expert at the art of compromise," explained a CSB member.

The president was largely responsible for the board's bringing in a new superintendent from outside the city. That person, a black male educator from the West Coast, began serving in January 1979.

This most recent CSB, in collaboration with its superintendent, has moved the district in several important new directions. It has brought about a new political stability that has established a more favorable climate for educational planning and improvement activities. It has developed a close working relationship with the teachers' union, and it has redirected the board's priorities back to "educational" issues and away from "representational" ones.

The new stability has seemed largely a function of the CSB president's and superintendent's leadership and of the fact that ethnic succession had largely run its course. There had been some serious factional conflicts on the board when this president was first elected by his colleagues, but that is no longer the case. Now that black communiy control advocates have gained the power they had fought so hard for, the politics of the district has calmed down considerably.

In addition, the CSB president has been effective in gaining the support of the teachers' union. He has brought the union into district decision making, and he has moved to protect teachers from undue monitoring and surveillance by CSB members. The fact that the district's black leadership had coalesced around a strong CSB president who, in turn, had the support of a powerful state senator and his Democratic club, probably helped in this new alliance, since the union had a single group it could relate to, knowing also that the CSB president, its leader, controlled the group's actions vis-à-vis teachers.

A different interpretation of the collaborative relationship between the UFT and the CSB comes from a member of the district's black leadership. "Rather than say that the CSB has been particularly supportive of the UFT," explained one such leader, "it is more accurate to say that the CSB demonstrated it wants control and has gained UFT respect. Over the past three years, there has been a working relation, rather than a hard-and-fast confrontation. Yes, the CSB president has championed the needs of teachers in programs on student discipline and teacher training. Yes, the relationship is one of cooperativeness and mutual respect. Yes, there are few contractual violations, but you shouldn't give the impression of more UFT power and CSB subservience to the UFT than is actually the case."

The other main development has been the increasing initiative taken by the CSB and the superintendent in establishing educational policies and programs. The president has been very active, for example, in pushing the board to articulate clear educational priorities. It is establishing districtwide curriculum objectives in all the main subjects to ensure uniformity among schools. It has set up school-based and districtwide curriculum committees composed of the superintendent, district office staff, principals, teachers, and parents to further standardize programs. It is developing a program to evaluate teachers and upgrade their quality. It has a major program for specialized junior high schools, with each oriented toward a particular career or curriculum area. It has begun developing more programs in black history and culture, including an annual districtwide educational conference featuring keynote speakers, and funded by corporations, foundations, and community agencies. And it has also begun trying to bring parents into greater involvement in district affairs.

All these educational improvement activities reflect the district's positive resolution of the many political conflicts that existed in its turbulent transitional period. Power had finally shifted to a new black leadership group. The CSB, having reached its goal of ethnic representation, could turn its attention more to education. Being more secure politically, its members felt freer to delegate more administrative authority to a superintendent with whom it maintained a much more productive and collaborative relation than did the previous board with its superintendent. And this present superintendent could begin to exercise educational initiatives that his predecessor could exercise only with great difficulty. In brief, many of the prerequisites for district effectiveness that existed in other districts that had successfully developed productive new programs have now emerged in this one.

Superintendent's Management Style

Unlike the superintendents in other districts of our study, this one has been in New York City only a relatively short time, having been appointed, as already indicated, in January 1979. Community school districts have a complex politics that limits a superintendent's capacity to have any significant leadership role until he or she adapts to those conditions and then establishes a political base. One of those conditions, in the case of this superintendent, is a very strong CSB and board president. And it simply takes time to establish one's authority in such an agency. While the board did renew the superintendent's contract in the spring of 1981, the discussion that follows on his management style must be seen in the context of his limited period of service as of this writing.

CURRICULUM STYLE

District F does not have any single educational philosophy that guides its curriculum activities. None of its three superintendents has imposed one on the district, and the present superintendent describes himself as "eclectic." He is interested mainly in results and does not have any particular preference for one style over another.

There has been one consistent line of curriculum approach since decentralization began, however, and that has been to standardize it and make it more uniform. The first superintendent, for example, relied heavily on the central board's curriculum materials and worked on improving instructional efficiency within that standard curriculum, rather than experimenting much with new programs. His successor followed that tradition, and the present superintendent has done likewise.

There is also much emphasis in this district on basic skills instruction: in reading, writing, oral expression, math, and the like. At the same time, there is at least a strong expression of interest on the part of the superintendent in developing student skills in critical thinking and problem solving, and in the arts.

Actually, the district has a fairly wide range of specialized programs. It has, for example, several magnet schools, zoned for the entire district. One is in bilingual education, and there are others in open education and the performing and communications arts. Furthermore, much curriculum planning is now under way for the junior highs at the initiative of the CSB, which wants to establish a series of specialized schools as related to different careers. The ones it has talked about include maritime and marine biology, health and the medical professions, aviation and aerospace, the arts and communications, and a junior high school specializing in science. The district has been particularly interested in getting more of its students into the city's many high schools that specialize in these areas; hence its present commitment to try to specialize its junior highs along similar lines. All of this is still in the early planning stage as of this writing.

One important mechanism that the district has developed and that may play a significant role in future program development is its curriculum committees. Organized in each school and districtwide, they provide the potential for improved planning at both levels. Moreover, they constitute a vehicle for the district office knowing more about what is going on in individual schools. "Curriculum committees are an excellent feedback for me," explained the superintendent. " 'If you don't speak up,' I tell them, 'you will have to take the consequences of our making policy from the district office in a vacuum.' "

The district's other main curriculum initiative relates to black culture. One such effort is its annual conference series in which a major black leader appears as a keynote speaker. It also has similar such programs in schools. "We are working to create a sense of tradition among our students," explained the CSB president. "Many kids are not aware of their own history and culture. It will be the policy of the district to force our kids to learn and to have pride in themselves and in their culture."

In summary, there is a fair amount of curriculum activity that seems to have increased in recent years. Much of it reflects these general themes of standardizing the curriculum, providing specialized magnet schools, and emphasizing black culture.

These activities have been undertaken through a collaborative effort by the superintendent and the CSB. The superintendent has been responsible for formulating many of the programs—for example, the curriculum committees and black culture projects—and for their implementation. But, unlike in most other districts, the CSB and particularly its chairman have played an active role.

DISTRICT OFFICE AND SCHOOLS

Under the first two superintendents, there was much monitoring and technical assistance, the two roles a district office would have to play for decentralization to go well. Both superintendents could almost be characterized as a single administration, with the second following through consistently on styles and strategies initiated by the first. Curriculum coordinators were always out in the field. In fact, the first superintendent forced them out and evaluated their performance only according to what they did in the schools, not in the district office. Each superintendent personally evaluated all principals, all new teachers, and all probationary and unsatisfactory teachers. Although superintendents in some other districts are out in the field a lot, also, the field emphasis of these two was quite marked. And it may well have contributed to the improved level of performance in the schools, whose reading scores were close to the highest of any poor black district in the city.

Field visits have been less of a priority of the most recent superintendent, who has played much more of a role as conceptualizer, strategy formulator, and central office policy analyst than his predecessors. He spends a considerable amount of time, for example, getting proposals written to secure more outside funding. In the years just before he arrived, there had been so much conflict within the district—between the CSB and the superintendent and within the CSB itself—that it had not effectively mobilized itself to write proposals and successfully secure funds.

The present superintendent and his staff are moving to rectify that, but given the district office cutbacks in the fiscal crisis, there aren't enough of them to concentrate on that and still maintain the kind of monitoring and technical assistance field operation that had existed before. Several principals expressed a high degree of concern about this. "The first two superintendents used to visit the schools a lot," one of them explained. "He doesn't come around." Another reported: "He has had minimal involvement in the schools."

Some of these perceptions reflect the fact that old-line principals resent an "outsider" with no experience in the New York City system and no ties to its professional associations having been appointed as superintendent in their district. And, to the extent that this new superintendent spends less time than his predecessors in the schools, that only reinforces the alienation and hostility.

The feedback the superintendent does have is through the school-based curriculum committees and through his staff who visit schools. He makes his own visits as well, though his style is not as field-oriented as that of his predecessors.

To conclude, the district office has somewhat less of a direct, monitoring relation to the schools than it had in the past. At the same time, there remains continued contact, despite the perception of several principals that that is not the case. Their perception is important, however, in indicating a generalized feeling of alienation that some of these principals have about developments in the district since decentralization. Their views are often couched in racial terms, and we would assume that the replacement of these principals over the next several years by others—including some blacks, who are more sympathetic to the affirmative action goals of the CSB and the superintendent—would probably alleviate the feelings that shaped the perceptions.

As for how much autonomy the schools have, the situation in this district is one of much decentralization to the school level, particularly through the curriculum committees. Each school determines its own curriculum, subject to general standards developed by the district office. This practice has been reinforced by the present superintendent's eclecticism as an educator and by his participative management style. The curriculum committees thus fit his style. As he explained: "My style is indirect. Unless you give people an opportunity to buy into and develop a stake of ownership, there will not be good implementation. I can be directive, but on big policy and program issues, that is not the way you get good implementation. I have set up curriculum committees that include a cross section of principals, teachers, students, and paraprofessionals in each school. I am building a consensus through these committees."

DISTRICT OFFICE AND PROFESSIONAL STAFF

The main pattern during the past year or two has been one of political peace and collaboration in relations between the district and its professional associations, reflecting a general development within the district. The result has been that the district and the union are able to work in some harmony on such sensitive issues as what to do with teachers rated as unsatisfactory. The CSB and the superintendent have pursued a policy of fairness to such teachers, not just pushing them out and having it on their record for the future.

At the same time, the district is quite firm in getting teachers out who have not performed in the classroom and are not amenable to help through in-service training and other forms of assistance. It has thus spent a lot of time in training principals to document charges against such teachers, and its experienced deputy holds monthly conferences on it. The union, on its side, fights hard to represent its members, but its officials understand and respect the position taken by the district. As the superintendent explained: "The UFT understands that in this district we have a good relation with them, but if we get to the table, we mean business. We don't come to the table unless we have a strong case, and the union knows it."

DISTRICT OFFICE AND COMMUNITY

One of the main priorities the present CSB has is to bring parents back into district and school affairs. That is very difficult to do in a poor community, with so much pupil mobility, and in hard times when parents have to work more than before. In the 1979–80 school year, the CSB embarked on an interesting new experiment. It required the parents to pick up their children's report cards on open school day, to be followed up by a visit with the teacher. The general count was that roughly 18,000 parents came in, the largest number by far that had ever visited schools for one event. Allowing for some exaggeration in the numbers, the turnout was quite impressive.

This program, developed largely at the initiative of the CSB president, was meant as a first step only in improving parent involvement. Pursuing the program took much effort because there was considerable resistance by parents who did not like being "coerced" into such an activity and who resented having to be involved like that. As the president reported: "I feel that if parents don't make the sacrifice to come to school to find out how their child is doing, then how can you expect them to raise their kids? I am trying to find a way, through using a carrot-and-stick technique, to get parents involved more continuously over the year in parent association activities."

An annual districtwide conference and the various competitions that the district has been conducting constitute further strategies for stimulating parent involvement. Both have a central theme of black accomplishments and opportunities in America, something that may attract more people. For example, the theme of the 1980 meeting was "black education beyond *Bakke*," involving an examination of the potential impact of the *Bakke* decision on opportunities for blacks in professional schools.

This constitutes imaginative programming, and it may attract more middle-class parents back into the schools. The curriculum committees that have been set up move in the same direction. The CSB president summarized the philosophy behind these efforts. "One thing I've found is that in terms of decentralization," he said, "you just can't leave the public schools to the poor, because the poor aren't able to come out in the numbers that are necessary. When you leave the public schools to the poor, that is when the special-interest groups take control. And the only way that we can get around that is to involve the minority middle-class parents who are able and concerned about their children to come to our schools, and to work for the schools and for their kids."

Conclusions

This is a district, then, that has gone through much turmoil under decentralization but has nevertheless emerged with considerable potential. Under its strong CSB leadership and with an able superintendent who works well with the board, it has developed some approaches to improving programs and linkages between school and the home that may become models for the future. To repeat a theme that was discussed in analyses of other districts, these innovations seem to be a direct result of decentralization and have not been nearly as prevalent under the old centralized system. Boards and superintendents did not have the flexibility to develop the kinds of productive, black-culture-centered programs, for example, that this district has begun to develop, as a way of increasing parental involvement and of linking the schools more to the home. Before decentralization, such efforts would have had to be cleared through headquarters, with the possibility that some central staff, unfamiliar with the district's situation, might veto them or, at best, delay their implementation. Or they would have to be acceptable to the superintendent who, in this district, rarely, if ever, left his office during the school day, and didn't have much of a relationship with the community.

Notwithstanding all the politics and the problems that this district had in its turbulent "transition" period, it has thus emerged as a productive example of what decentralization may bring about. Its recent strategies are important to publicize and examine in greater depth, to show how they might be applied to other situations.

Indicators of Student and District Performance

We have described this predominantly black district as having gone through several distinct stages: a first through 1974 under a white superintendent and his integrated CSB; a second transition period, from 1975 to 1978, under a black female superintendent when blacks were coming

TABLE 7.1

District F
Reading Scores for 1971 and 1979

Grade	1971	1979	Change (+/−)
Two	2.5	2.7	0.2
Three	3.1	3.6	0.5
Four	3.8	4.6	0.8
Five	4.6	5.6	1.0
Six	5.2	6.4	1.2
Seven	5.3	6.7	1.4
Eight	6.2	8.1	1.9
Nine	8.0	9.7	1.7

into power; and a third, consolidation stage under a black male superintendent, with a strong black majority board.

The question is whether these trends have had much impact on student performance, particularly in view of the fact that the student population has not changed greatly since 1971.[6] At about that time, 75.9% of the public school students were black, 14.8% Hispanic, and 7.8% white. In 1978 blacks were 85.5%, Hispanics 12.0%, and whites 1.1%. Most of the district's ethnic changes had thus taken place before decentralization, and the decentralization years simply represented the completion of a transformation from before.

As Table 7.1 indicates, the district's reading scores have improved during the period of decentralization for every grade, with greater improvements in the upper grades.[7] In 1971 District F's reading scores were behind the averages for the city as a whole. Since then, the district has closed that gap. That is, the improvement in reading scores in the district was greater than that for the city as a whole. Table 7.2 points up that trend.

An important qualification should be made, however, in this regard; namely that most (though not all) of the improvement in this district occurred before 1975. By the time the first superintendent left, this was

TABLE 7.2

Changes in Reading Scores (1971–79)

Grade	District F	Citywide	Differences Between District F & All Schools (+/−)
Two	0.2	-0-	0.2
Three	0.5	0.1	0.4
Four	0.8	0.6	0.2
Five	1.0	0.7	0.3
Six	1.2	0.6	0.6
Seven	1.4	1.0	0.4
Eight	1.9	1.1	0.8
Nine	1.7	1.1	0.6

one of the highest-achieving black districts in the city. It may just be starting to regain its momentum, now that it has passed through the difficult transition period.

There is no similarly clear trend in math scores.[8] The district scored at 0.4 of a grade level behind the city in 1971; and it was 0.5 behind in 1978. District scores seem to fluctuate in a way similar to those of the city as a whole.

As for attendance, the district has declined from 86.7% average daily attendance in 1970 to 85.3% in 1977.[9] Meanwhile, the citywide attendance figure has increased from 81.1% in 1970 to 82.8% in 1978.

Vandalism data show little trend, except on unlawful entries.[10] From 1971 to 1978, the annual number of reported broken glass panes decreased slightly from around 4,700 to just 4,000. And there were only 2 fires in 1971 and the same number in 1978. Unlawful entries, on the other hand, went up from 114 in 1971 to nearly 200 in 1978, indicating that the schools had become a target in that respect.

A fairly significant change has begun to appear in the district's staffing patterns since decentralization, although it is not as marked as in some minority districts.[11] Blacks increased from 10.7% to 33.8% of the total professional staff, and Hispanics from 0.8% to 3.5%. For the Hispanics the change was almost entirely at the teacher level, with only 1 Hispanic principal and no APs in service in 1978. For blacks, on the other hand, the increase was across the board. Principals went up from 17.7% to 33.3%; APs from 6.8% to 22.6%; and teachers from 10.7% to 17.1%. Over 60.0% of the remaining principals are white, and for some of them, as our interviews indicated, serving in such a changed district with many more black students and staff is a more difficult assignment than they had faced many years before.

A basic question one must ask in regard to this district is whether it can regain its former momentum, now that is has gone through the difficult throes of its ethnic transition. For the last couple of years, it has stabilized politically under an able black superintendent and an active CSB. It remains to be seen whether this political stabilization will be reflected in student performance.

8

A Showcase White Middle-Class District Effectively Managing Rapid Ethnic Succession: District G

Ethnic succession is invariably an unsettling experience, but in some cases it is handled much better than in others. District G is one of those cases. Located in a transitional area of an outer borough, it has undergone major demographic changes since decentralization began, from an atypically affluent, white area to a very diverse one. The main changes include a marked exodus of upper-middle-class Jewish families to suburban counties; a modest influx of middle-income Catholics, blacks, Orthodox Jews, Chinese, Greeks, and Hispanics; and a very large influx of poor blacks.

The district in experiencing this change has found ways to adapt in a manner that has continued to maintain stable communities and social peace. It has also sustained a high standard of educational performance throughout its elementary and junior high schools.

Local leadership has been the main reason for the district's success in adapting. Since decentralization began, it has had a series of CSBs that have played a major policymaking role and have been widely recognized as among the strongest and most effective in the city. A highly educated, affluent, and professional group compared with their counterparts in other districts, many board members were active in citywide politics as well as in the district; and that has contributed to their power, reflecting among other things their outside career and organizational interests (religious, political, labor). This was, then, a cosmopolitan rather than a locally oriented board that got much of its power from its outside affiliations.

The experience and maturity of this board were reflected in its choice of a superintendent who, by dint of his long and successful tenure (he has served since 1972), has been recognized by his peers as the senior community superintendent of the entire New York City system. His effective leadership has also been central to the district's performance. Recognizing the district's diversity and its rapid demographic change, he fashioned an approach that fit those conditions. It led him to refrain from imposing any single educational philosophy or strategy on the district. This approach resulted in much diversity of programs in different schools, providing them with a needed flexibility and with local option. He essentially extended decentralization to the school level, then, permitting a customizing of curriculum and school improvement efforts to local needs, which often related to broader social concerns of neighborhood stabilization and to retaining the white middle class.

At the same time, he and his board provided strong central leadership as well. They have maintained a districtwide emphasis on basic skills training, plus enrichment programs for higher-achieving students. They have established a desegregation program that has been accepted by local residents and that has achieved good results.

This chapter explores how the superintendent and the CSB maintained political stability and high-quality education in the face of such rapid ethnic succession. Their effective coping strategies reflected a recognition that for these goals to be attained, the schools had to become an organic part of their community in ways that both reflected community values and supported community development activities.

Demography, Neighborhoods, District Characteristics

When decentralization began, this was one of the most affluent districts in the city, encompassing elegant homes and a few remaining estates in the center, high-rise apartment buildings along the main north to south arteries, and a mix of expensive and more moderately priced homes in other areas. Observers of the New York City schools often referred to it as the "Golden Gate" district because of its past affluence. Many experienced teachers and principals looked forward to serving there, particularly in their latter years, since students came in with few of the social problems and learning difficulties that are so prevalent in poverty areas.

As community school districts go, this one is about average in size, having an enrollment of roughly 25,000 students in 1979–80.[1] This constitutes a decline of about 4,000 since 1970, that decline reflecting the district's aging population and the departure of many middle-class residents. The decline has been particularly noticeable in the sparsely populated white areas in the south and east where utilization rates in some schools went as low as 60.0% and 70.0%. Even for the district as a whole, utilization rates went down from 86.0% to 81.7% from 1970 to 1975, despite the overcrowding in northern-area schools with their new black population.[2]

Changes in pupil composition have been even more dramatic than those in total enrollment. Since 1970 whites have dropped from 81.9% to just under 50.0%, while blacks are now close to 50.0%.[3] Moreover, changes in the socioeconomic status of students have accompanied these ethnic ones. Those from AFDC families increased from 7.8% in 1971 to roughly 25.0% now, and the number keeps going up.[4]

The large influx of poor blacks, increasing rapidly since the early 1970s, has fundamentally altered the character of the district. It has resulted from several concurrent developments: vacancy decontrol in high-rise apartment buildings, leading to an increasing subdivision of apartments and to increasing numbers in each unit; the Welfare Department's relocating of displaced welfare families to the area, sometimes reportedly "bribing" landlords to take more of them; and the construction of low-income projects in the north central part of the district.

By the mid-1970s the district suddenly had many poor blacks who immediately placed heavy demands on the public schools and other service delivery agencies and whose presence frightened many white middle-class residents into leaving. Whereas before 1973, blacks attending district schools were mainly bused in under open enrollment, they were now an *indigenous* black population for whom it had to provide schooling. Other minority groups had also moved in—Chinese, Greeks, Hispanics—but their numbers were insignificant compared with those of the blacks. Because of that huge black influx and the white exodus, *neighborhood stabilization* became a major issue. Moreover, this was not merely a racial matter, since middle-class blacks had moved in also, many of them New

York City civil servants with a strong interest in not having schools become like those in the black poverty areas from which they had just moved.

As one might expect, the classic condition of transitional inner-city districts soon emerged here. There was an immediate overcrowding of schools in areas where the blacks had concentrated, while a few miles to the south and east, in areas with an aging white population, the schools were vastly underutilized.

The other important demographic change was the increasing numbers of Catholic families who had moved into formerly all-Jewish neighborhoods. The Catholics tended to be less affluent and less liberal in outlook than their Jewish predecessors. Despite the fact that many of them sent their children to parochial schools, many used the public schools as well.

Ethnic Succession

The educational "power structure" of the district had been mainly Jewish in the years preceding decentralization, reflecting both the population who lived and went to public school there and those who served as educators. District informants estimate that as many as 8,000 to 10,000 New York City public school educators live in the district, making it a major UFT and CSA stronghold in the city and affecting its politics. Supervisors and district office administrators have been almost exclusively Jewish, as are the majority of teachers, the main reason being the central board's traditional policy of appointing people to schools in districts where they live. As the district's population and public school enrollment changed, this old power structure came under increasing challenge; and with decentralization, Catholics gained representation, both in parent associations and in professional educator ranks as well.

More generally, several kinds of interest-group conflicts emerged, including religious, racial, and geographic ones. These differences reflect ethnic succession, the relative responsiveness of the district office to different areas (e.g., the northern-area schools versus those in the south), and some fundamental conflicts of values. Much of the politics of the district reflects the way in which these interest-group differences have been managed.

The main groups include a Catholic lay organization; Orthodox Jewish organizations, parent associations, the teachers' union and principals' associations, political clubs, and community development corporations. The latter represent civic groups trying to stabilize their neighborhoods in areas undergoing demographic change. These groups have been active in proposing slates of candidates for CSB elections, in staffing decisions, in pressing the district for particular educational programs, and in actually developing programs on their own. Blacks are the only constituency not organized; they are just beginning to get themselves together, through churches and parent associations.

EARLY ETHNIC DIFFERENCES

When decentralization began, the parent leadership in the district, supported by many district educators, did not want Catholics as CSB members. These public school parents and educators were strong advocates of a separation of church and state and felt that no Catholic CSB member could easily set aside religious interests on matters relating to the potential non–public school use of public school funds and facilities. A big issue was the after-school use of public schools for recreational and educational programs for *all* youth in the community, regardless of whether they went to public school or not. Public school parents favored curtailing such community programs where there was a forced choice between them and public school ones in a period of fiscal cutbacks.

Catholics who had been members of the local school board before decentralization, as well as those who had not, tried to run on parent slates and were turned down. They felt so disfranchised that one of their group, a district leader in the southern part of the district, formed a Catholic lay organization with its own slate. They made a conscious choice to never run more than four candidates and therefore never have a Catholic majority on the board; and, in the 1970 election and in each succeeding one, they have successfully elected their four candidates. Decentralization thus opened up this district's public schools to a broader religious and ethnic representation than before.

Two main interests, then, were a Catholic group who gained in power under decentralization and a predominantly Jewish group who were very influential at the start of decentralization and gradually experienced a waning of their power. The two groups differed on a wide range of policy and program issues, including the selection of a superintendent and other staff, curriculum, tracking policies, and instructional styles. The conservative group, by far the vast majority, favors a more traditional and structured curriculum with an emphasis on basic skills instruction done in conventional ways—through drilling and rote learning—and with the educators in a controlling mode, encouraging orderly, compliant, rule-following behavior by students. They also prefer homogeneous classes based on ability grouping, and they place a high priority on special programs for advanced, high-achieving students as well as for low-achieving ones. By contrast, the liberal parents favor open education, ungraded and heterogeneous classrooms, and such "progressive" approaches as "hands-on" and "experience-based" learning.

It would be incorrect to attribute this difference in values to religious background alone, however, since many Jewish residents had similarly conservative values as the Catholics, particularly those in the southern part of the district. There were thus geographic and perhaps class differences as well that differentiated these groups from one another, with liberal activist parents tending to be a much more affluent, upper-middle-class group than the more conservative ones. The big split in the district, then, was between a liberal and a conservative group, with these groups tending to reflect differences in background, with the qualifications just mentioned.

There was also a split along geographic lines. The northern area of the district had become predominantly black after 1973, and it had one set of interests, relating to the need for relief from overcrowding, for additional resources for low-achieving students, and perhaps for a desegregation program that would enable some black students to get an education in less crowded schools. The center of the district was in rapid transition, and many of its middle-class residents, white and black, were deeply concerned with stabilizing their neighborhoods. Finally, the geographically dispersed southern and southeastern part of the district, almost exclusively white and containing both young families with school-age children and many middle-aged and elderly residents, was concerned about the district's rezoning its schools to bus in poor blacks from the north. Their fears were the usual ones of white middle-class residents in such areas of what might happen to their schools and neighborhood if blacks came in—that the quality of education would decline, that crime in the schools would increase, that property values would go down, and that their community might lose its middle class.

The CSB and the superintendent had to balance off all these interests, and one of the big problems in doing that was that the board's membership was typically overbalanced in favor of the south and center as opposed to the north. The north had many more poor blacks, and they tended to vote in lesser numbers than white middle-class people residing elsewhere. Liberal parent informants were often quick to note that the north was consistently shortchanged because of this imbalanced representation.

Political History

Since decentralization began, this district has had a series of active CSBs that have always included four Catholics, one Orthodox Jew, four others usually supported by the UFT, parent groups, and political clubs. Parent leaders have been conspicuously absent, with never more than one or two serving at any given time. The vast majority of CSB members have represented other organizational interests (religious, political, labor), although they have been responsive to parent concerns. This has been more of a "power-broker" board than many. One of its members, for example, has been very active in labor and citywide educational politics, and another became the chancellor of the New York City schools. Moreover, there has only been one black member through the entire decentralization experience, and that person was appointed to fill a vacancy rather than elected.

The CSB has other characteristics as well that made it one of the strongest and most activist in the city. It has been a highly educated, affluent, professional group, relative to its counterparts in other districts. The first board, elected in 1970, for example, included three attorneys and several educators. Only one of its nine members was not a college graduate.

Still another characteristic of this CSB has been its clear conception of its role. Until 1977, when the CSB became less active and less assertive of its power, though even to some degree since then, it has made it very clear to the superintendent that the board makes policy and that the superintendent serves at its pleasure.

This assertion of CSB power gained strong affirmation through its series of strong presidents, particularly one who became the New York City Board of Education chancellor. Although board members had different points of view on other matters, they maintained a general consensus on this one. Since 1977, with the CSB president's departure, this board, like many others throughout the city, has not continued to play quite so strong a role. It still oversees the superintendent and requires that he run the district in line with its many policies, but it gives him more autonomy and flexibility than its predecessors did.

It is worth describing how the first board functioned, since it set a tone for later ones, and since it reflected so much the hopes of many that seem to have been dashed in recent years. Its members were quite missionarylike in their zeal to make decentralization work for their community.

A missionary-oriented member described their orientation well: "We were like the founding fathers and a mother [one female board member]. We were very productive. We quickly formed our committees and made our bylaws. We expended a phenomenal amount of energy. A tremendous excitement was generated. We were proud of ourselves. Every public meeting was a big show, and there was much excitement surrounding them. You could see history being written."

One of this board's first decisions was to select a superintendent. Like several other middle-class districts, the board in this one opted to reappoint the incumbent. It soon became apparent, however, that this old-line superintendent could not function well under a newly decentralized system in which he was accountable to an elected CSB and had to be responsive to board and community pressures. He was a strong believer in professional power, and that was incompatible with the position taken by the CSB and by many parent and community groups. Not surprisingly, the superintendent and his CSB soon developed irreconcilable differences over how the district should be run. On the matter of the superintendent's authority, he cosistently refused to comply with the CSB'S demands that he be accountable to them for his actions and that he develop procedures for evaluating his professional staff. By the end of the first year, the CSB was already looking around for a successor.

A critical incident during the term of the first CSB illustrates well the forces operating in the district as they affect both how policy decisions are made and their substance. It involved the selection of a new superintendent to replace the incumbent.

After much preliminary screening of candidates, the choice narrowed down to three, two of whom were acceptable to a narrowly based liberal parent coalition, with the third the overwhelming choice of the CSB reflecting the preferences of more conservative constituencies. Although parent leaders made field visits and did interviews with the candidates, at the CSB's invitation and in the company of individual board members, the CSB itself made the final decision. It announced the decision at a stormy public meeting in which parents made angry protests and completely disrupted the proceedings on several occasions. These parents perceive, in retrospect, that the CSB had made its decision before the screening of the final three candidates, making a mockery of the extensive parent participation that was seemingly involved.

The person selected differed from the other two candidates in fundamental respects, further reflecting the values of the CSB and its constituencies. He was somewhat *traditional* in educational philosophy, though flexible and tolerant of other points of view, while the other two endorsed *progressive* approaches like open education and ungraded and heterogeneous classes. He *did not enunciate any explicit or particular educational philosophy* in public meetings or interviews just prior to his appointment, while both of them had an explicit philosophy that they did express. He had *the support of many established organizations in the district*—for example, political clubs and the church—that support having been mobilized by CSB members, while they were relative *unknowns* to such organizations. Coming from outside the district, he might have been a relative unknown as well, but the CSB had done much preliminary work in paving the way for this appointment. Moreover, he had more *administrative experience* than they, having been the superintendent of a poverty-area district elsewhere in the borough, while neither of them had ever served in that capacity. Also, he was a *Catholic* of Italian origin, while his competitors were both *Jewish*. Given the concern among CSB members and some power groups in the district with opening up positions to ethnic groups other than Jews—in a word, given their commitment to ethnic succession—the fact that he was of this background, in addition to having those other characteristics, was certainly in his favor.

In brief, this superintendent had many background characteristics, skills, and orientations that the CSB valued, while his opponents did not. He was, in that sense, a person whose background and outlook *fit* the district's values as this CSB interpreted them.

One of the main characteristics of this CSB is that despite its members' differences in background, constituency, and philosophy, its decisions were often made with a broad district perspective in mind. That has been so in its handling of such policy issues as desegregation, the monitoring and evaluation of staff, and curriculum.

Another example of this perspective is the CSB's active involvement in appointing Christian principals. The Catholic members and one former CSB president, in particular, felt that the district's staff should be more representative of the community. They ultimately prevailed on the issue. As a CSB member explained: "Our district was totally Jewish at one time in its supervisory and administrative staff. That is not good." One result of this view has been the district's appointment of four Christian principals under decentralization, three Italian males and one Irish female.

The CSB and the Superintendent

It should be obvious from our extensive description of this strong CSB that it would want to maintain much control over its superintendent, making certain that he followed district policy. And yet the superintendent it chose was a strong personality in his own right. The fact that he has stayed for nine years and has consistently been given long renewal contracts indicates that the relationship has worked out satisfactorily for both parties. He has been willing to let the board play a dominant policy role, while on its side the board has willingly delegated to him broad administrative powers.

Despite the general harmony between the superintendent and the CSB and the productive relationship that usually prevailed, there was a series of conflicts between them over the years that reflected an underlying difference in outlook. The difference had to do with his style of managing the professionals. As the senior superintendent of the system, he had come up through the ranks as a teacher and principal, had been active in the professional associations, and identified with the educators and their problems. He felt that one got the highest performance out of them when they were treated as colleagues and as professionals.

Several board members had quite a different outlook. They felt that the professionals required strong supervision and were not always convinced that he was supplying it. As one of the more active CSB members noted: "He is too tolerant of some principals. He backs his professionals no matter how good their teaching quality is." Another stated: "His only fault is that he does not interfere enough with principals to get them to work harder."

One critical incident illustrates in extreme form the conflict that existed. At a private meeting of the CSB and the superintendent where the matter of his contract renewal was to be discussed, the school board president laid out a list of criticisms of the superintendent's performance, largely along the line of his lack of strong leadership in pressing the educators toward better performance. His list of particulars included criticisms that the superintendent had not given enough staff supervision, had not evaluated principals firmly enough, did not have enough of a district office presence in the schools, and was therefore not leading the district as the CSB president felt is should be led. There was much commotion at the meeting, and the discussion ended with the president's proposal that the superintendent himself write an ad for the press, indicating that the district was considering applications for the superintendency, the understanding being that the superintendent would also be a candidate. Ironically, in the 5 to 4 vote favoring the proposal, the four who voted against were all Jewish members of the board, supporting their Christian superintendent. The ad was placed, but very few candidates applied for the job. As the weeks went on, it became increasingly clear that the superintendent was the only candidate, and he was given another three-year contract.

A general consensus among board members was that this was a largely symbolic act by a very strong CSB president to reassert the CSB's authority and to reaffirm to the superintendent that the board and not he ran the district. As one CSB member supporting the superintendent reported: "There was never any real challenge by the board about his continuing as superintendent. His record speaks for itself. What the board wanted to show was that he was accountable to it. He sometimes lost sight that he serves at our pleasure."

Since that time, there has never been any serious question on the CSB's side about the superintendent's overall performance or contract renewal, but there have been recurrent differences between them on similar types of issues. There have been conflicts over such matters as his not consulting with the board in advance on a decision to give a principal tenure; on his use of outside consultants from among his professional colleagues in universities; on his holding daytime meetings with the principals, thereby taking them out of their schools; and on his tendency at times, from the board's perspective, to communicate decisions only after he has made them.

We have seen versions of this conflict in many districts, reflecting as they do the typical differences that often exist between superintendents and boards. And the fact that this superintendent kept getting his contract renewed and has worked productively with his various boards indicates that the conflicts were not severe in this instance. They seem mainly a result of a *strong board* and a *strong superintendent* trying to collaborate. Most of the time they do, and when they do not, matters tend to get worked out. A major issue in our analysis relates to how he has run the district, and it is to the matter of his management style that we now turn.

Superintendent's Management Style

The same kind of congruence or goodness of fit between the superintendent's style and the values and needs of the community that existed in Districts B and E, both minority areas, existed in this transitional but still predominantly white middle-class district. Its superintendent is an *experienced professional* in a district where many educators reside and where parents, teachers, principals, and CSB members are very vocal about educational matters. He is a *competent administrator and an astute politician* in a district that contains many diverse interest groups whose competing demands had to be balanced and whose strong CSBs, which liked to control things, had to be handled. He has a somewhat *traditional educational philosophy* that matches the conservative values of a majority of the district's parents. Yet he is *flexible* enough to endorse those more "progressive" programs of open education and heterogeneous classes that existed in liberal pockets within the district. And he has considerable *interpersonal skills and a civility* that people in the district value. As even one of his strongest critics from the CSB noted: "He is definitely a caring, considerate, warm human being, though from my point of view, he is no leader."

A CURRICULUM STYLE ADAPTED TO DIVERSITY AND DEMOGRAPHIC CHANGE

Unlike some districts whose superintendents had an explicit educational philosophy that they imposed to a large extent on the schools, the superintendent in District G often went out of his way not to impose any single point of view. He and his staff did press for programs for gifted and talented students, in an effort to retain and attract back the middle class. Even in this case, however, the district office initiative was in response to a strongly expressed need from white middle-class parents for "advanced" programs and reflected a districtwide concern with maintaining an ethnic and economic balance.

Thus, though his personal preference was for more traditional approaches, emphasizing basic skills and structured approaches to learning, the superintendent supported whatever programs the schools worked out, provided they got results. As he explained: "My philosophy is that if we are truly decentralized, I am not about to mandate from the district office an education philosophy. So long as the schools reflect the needs of their communities, so long as they have results, and so long as good education goes on, I don't interfere."

One of the district's principals summarized this situation well: "In this district, we do not have an overriding educational philosophy. It is the responsibility of each principal in every school to develop their own programs more or less underneath the broad district objectives. It is recognized that every school in the district is unique and that the principals working in conjunction with their teaching staff and the parents associations are pretty much in a position to determine what is best for them."

A visit to schools in the district reflects its diversity. Several schools in the more liberal areas of the north and center tend to have more "progressive" and less "traditional" approaches. Some, for example, with liberal parents and progressive principals, have gone into open education programs.

By contrast, most schools in the conservative areas to the south and east have quite traditional programs. Their classrooms tend to be run in more structured ways, with an emphasis on order, teacher control, and a traditional subject matter. Yet, one of the showcase schools in the south now has open-classroom-type programs as well, having formerly been a very traditional school that parents in the area no longer preferred.

The district office does more on curriculum, however, than just support local option, despite the fact that it has few curriculum coordinators left as a result of the citywide budget cuts. It has secured state funding for extensive pre-K programs, through an assemblyman from the district. It has secured a federally funded ESAA grant of more than $2 million in support of its broad desegregation programs. It has four magnet schools with programs for high-achieving students, through grants for the gifted and talented. It has many media programs that the superintendent has provided for individual schools. It has an ecology center in the district office and ecology programs at a nearby national park, both of which may well be among the most unique and sophisticated programs of their kind anywhere in the nation. It has many retired and elderly residents working with its students as tutors. It has poets, writers, dramatists, and other artists in district schools. It has developed a diagnostic-prescriptive reading program with a computerized management information system that has data on students' reading skills and weaknesses and on the particular resources available for reading instruction in every school and in the district office (textbooks, audiovisual materials, etc.). This program has been used in the district's strong push on reading, as a support for teachers and schools.

A central aspect of the district's curriculum relates to retaining its middle class in a period of sudden and rapid transition and to stabilizing those neighborhoods that have begun to tip. The district office, in collaboration with individual schools, has done many things to stem the middle-class exodus. Pre-K programs, programs for the gifted and talented in magnet schools and others, extensive reading programs, and classes for high-achieving students have been initiated, as well as such other enrichment programs as those in ecology, the humanities, science, and the like.

A few years ago, the district lost up to 50 middle-class students to a neighboring district, as a result of the latter's new experimental programs; and in the last year or so, those students have returned in response to the district's new programs. There are also individual schools, some even in the north, that are attracting back white middle-class students through their magnet programs, after it looked like they would become virtually wholly minority student schools. These programs reflect the district's concern with maintaining *quality* education for advanced middle-class students while pursuing *equality*-oriented programs for poor minority students. The programs may well have stabilized the district much more than would otherwise have been the case.

A Local Desegregation Program That Works. Perhaps the most significant of these efforts has been the district's desegregation program. It has involved the busing of roughly 2,000 minority students from overcrowded schools in the north to underutilized ones in the south. In relation to this program, *zoning* has been by far the most contested issue the district has faced, with over 80% of public discussion at school board meetings focusing directly on it.

The program started as a particular solution to the overcrowding of one northern-area school, and it later extended to several others. The first technique involved the use of *frozen zoning*, whereby new minority students in the school's area would be rezoned to southern-area schools. *Capping* was also involved, whereby receiving schools were to receive only a limited percent of incoming minority students, thereby minimizing the likelihood of political resistance, and of tipping, that starting at 5% and eventually rising to 15% as the numbers of bused-in students increased.

Viewed in comparison with adjacent districts that faced many of the same demographic changes, this one developed a much more *proactive* approach than most. Although some liberal and northern-area parents regarded the program as piecemeal, it may well be a model for other inner-city districts facing similar circumstances. Indeed, the CSB and the superintendent went out of their way to anticipate many problems and to avoid the *reactive* strategy that so many other school districts follow.

Several ingredients made this a successful effort, combining astute district leadership with community involvement. There was extensive parent and community participation. The bused-in students were dispersed across many receiving schools, rather than concentrated in one or a few. The district secured large federal grants through ESAA to provide services in the receiving schools, both for minority students and for indigenous students needing help. Considerable planning took place, and there was much bargaining and political persuasion exercised by the CSB and the superintendent.

Needless to say, many parents in the receiving schools were apprehensive about what might happen with the black students coming in—about academic standards and safety within the school, about relationships between black and white students, and the like. The district assuaged many of these fears by offering programs for indigenous white students (as the legislation provided) and by indicating to the parents the many costs of their not accepting the program, not the least of which was that their underutilized school might be closed, given the city's fiscal problems. As one CSB member explained: "The biggest job is to sell busing to the white parents. We tell them: 'Accept minorities or have your schools closed.' We also use the extra federal dollars as a carrot." Thus, a combination of sensitivity to white parent concerns and the astute exercise of influence have made desegregation more acceptable in receiving schools.

Like most busing programs, the main burden for travel in this one was on minority students. And some of their parents were quite apprehensive about what the experience would be like for their children, traveling long distances to a strange new school and neighborhood. Once they saw the schools to which their children were traveling, however, both the physical plant and the quality of the neighborhood and educational programs, their concerns in most instances were allayed.

This case has broad implications, as a locally initiated desegregation plan under decentralization that went considerably better than had the centrally mandated plans of the past. Indeed, it was out of the failure of past desegregation efforts mandated from central that the demand arose in black communities for decentralization. At the time, opponents of decentralization—teachers, principals, school headquarters—argued that it would lead to more ethnic separatism, as particular groups would work to consolidate their political power base in local districts. What went on in this district, however, is quite contrary to that prediction.

DISTRICT OFFICE AND SCHOOLS

A key to the effectiveness of this district was the superintendent's firm policy of decentralization to the local school level. He has gone out of his way to allow principals and their school constituencies to make critical decisions on curriculum, rather than have them mandated from the district office. This emphasis on school-level autonomy has served at least two functions. It has given the schools a much-needed flexibility and responsiveness. It has also protected the superintendent from getting caught in an undue amount of crossfire between opposing educational philosophies and interests.

Indeed, there have been instances over the years in which activist parents have urged the superintendent to *mandate* on a districtwide basis policies that they felt were right—for example, heterogeneous classes, open education, and so on. He always argued that mandating curriculum and classroom organization policy from the district office was contrary to the spirit of decentralization. From their perspective, he was not exercising strong leadership.

A reluctance to mandate curriculum and classroom practice from the district office may still be accompanied by an active district office presence in the schools—by way of technical assistance, staff deveolopment activity, and monitoring and evaluation. This district is hampered somewhat in these activities by having so few district office staff to engage in them.

Some curriculum support services are provided from the district office to those principals and teachers who will make use of them. The computerized management information system for reading instruction that we cited above is an example. The development of magnet schools, of programs for the gifted and talented, the media techniques, and district office curricular materials are others. And the district now has an advisory council of principals, the superintendent, and district office staff that are developing educational programs.

The superintendent has met monthly with his principals to discuss their many problems and to try to assist them where possible. Many of them feel under increasing stress as they are asked to provide more and more services from fewer and fewer resources. Many are involved in busing programs, in breakfast and lunch programs, and in special education programs, though with fewer staff, and are faced with continued parent complaints. They particularly resent the massive amounts of paperwork the district office asks them to do and the requirement that they make so many observations of their teachers. The superintendent and his staff have been trying to help them with leadership training programs and additional resources, where possible.

DISTRICT OFFICE AND PROFESSIONAL STAFF

Another factor in this district's success has been the superintendent's close, collegial relationship with his staff and their associations, which is much like that of the superintendent in District D. These districts have several things in common. Both have a large white middle-class population, have many New York City public school educators living there, and have strong local chapters of their associations. And both have superintendents with long service within the system who had come up through the ranks and had been active in these associations themselves. They are thus "insider" rather than "outsider" superintendents.

Teachers and principals *count* in these districts. The superintendent relates to them as a senior colleague, providing much support for them and indicating a considerable reluctance to evaluate and discipline them in a fashion characteristic of some parts of the private sector. For some critics of the New York City school system, it raises a basic policy question as to whether such a superintendent style is compatible with an effectively decentralized community school district. It is certainly not compatible with the management models of community control advocates or of many parent activists—which is not necessarily to say that it is "wrong."

Interestingly, the CSBs of Districts D and G took diametrically opposed positions on this. The former found its superintendent's close relations with his professionals quite commendable, while its counterpart in District G did not share those sentiments at all.

The view of several CSB members was that the superintendent had not pushed his professional staff hard enough, that he had not been critical enough in his evaluations, that he had not transferred out or retired teachers and principals who were not amenable to further training and yet were unable to perform. As a CSB member stated: "He backs his professionals no matter how good their teaching quality is. He works well with the UFT. He does them many favors, but he never collects on them on important issues, like getting rid of poor teachers." What this board member and others were saying was that the superintendent was too easy on the professional staff. These board members felt that, as a former teacher and principal, the superintendent identified too closely with his colleagues and did not exercise the authority of his office enough. Some board members felt that he informally consulted in advance with the teachers' union or school supervisors on important decisions before doing so with his board.

The superintendent, on his side, felt that these complaints reflected a lack of understanding of how one effectively manages professionals. As he explained: "Board members have asked: 'How come there are not critical things written on your evaluations of principals and teachers?' I act instead, and these board members don't understand the procedure. As for our principals, many have become shell-shocked. Everything is coming at them at once. We have 1,600 to 1,800 bused-in kids, and with a lack of funds we have no guidance staff. The CSB don't treat the professionals like professionals. I told the board: 'You want them to be professionals, and yet you treat them like babies.' "

There existed, then, a difference in approach and in philosophy between the superintendent and some CSB members over how to manage the professionals. The CSB members wanted more *bureaucratic authority* exercised by the superintendent. They wanted him to make more forceful evaluations and take more corrective actions in cases of low-level performance. The superintendent saw himself as *managing a professional organization*, not a bureaucratic business one, with the former requiring different attitudes and actions on his part than would be required in running a business. He was more sympathetic than the board with the professionals' problems, identified more with them, and handled cases of low-level performance in ways that maintained the professionals' dignity while taking corrective action where he felt that was warranted.

There is obviously no simple answer to this question of the most appropriate style for managing professionals in such a decentralized community school district system; the answer depends largely on how *effective* the district is. In brief, the best style is the one that *works*; the question then remains of how one defines "effectiveness." If one takes as the definition the performance of students—through reading and math scores, attendance, and so on—this district is doing quite well, having maintained its position as one of the top 3 in the city, despite its increasing percent of poor minority students. And the fact that the district *has* maintained its position may well be a result of its many new programs under decentralization—desegregation; magnet schools; Intellectually Gifted Children (IGC) and gifted and talented programs; the diagnostic, prescriptive reading program; pre-K; and the other enrichment programs already discussed. One could argue, of course, that more aggressive personnel policies might have given the district an even higher performance, and that is the CSB's position.

DISTRICT OFFICE AND COMMUNITY

This district has had a mixed experience on matters relating to parent participation. From the perspective of activist parents, the district has been unresponsive. They feel that parents have been shut out by the CSB and the superintendent, and to the extent that all CSBs in the district have followed a policy of excluding parents from decision-making authority, which they have, the parents are partly right.

On the other hand, the development of the district's desegregation programs involved much parent participation. Moreover, some schools in liberal areas have had much involvement of parents in the actual development of curriculum. They have had strong PAs who have been quite influential and whose expressed preferences have been taken into account in the selection of principals as well as in curriculum.

In fact, the superintendent's whole strategy of decentralization to the school level gave a strong voice not only to principals but also to parents. In that way, the district has provided a built-in opportunity for parent participation in decisions affecting their schools.

The one development in the district that has contributed to what parent involvement exists is the demographic changes of recent years. Many middle-class parents have been trying to upgrade their schools because of their fears that the middle class would leave—contributing not only to declining school programs and quality but to declining property values as well.

The formation in recent years of community development corporations is a prime example of this phenomenon. They have been concerned with neighborhood stabilization through upgrading the quality of housing and vital city services like education. One of these development corporations has been very involved in the schools, and it has worked to secure federal funding for a pre-K program at one elementary school to help retain its middle-class students. These development corporations have provided an avenue for some alienated parent activists to continue trying to improve the schools. As a parent explained: "The parent activists turned off by the school system are turning their energies toward the community development coporations." While the corporations are an outlet for such frustrated activists, the district office and the CSB, as the recognized legal agency for the local schools, cannot be easily bypassed.

In sum, while the CSB in this district has not supported parent participation to the degree that some activist parents would like, there are many active PAs in the district that play a role in the schools. And the fact that the superintendent has given the schools so much autonomy has provided many opportunities for parent involvement. So, while it is true that the CSB has not given many of the activists much of a hearing, it is not true that parents play a limited role in local school affairs.

DISTRICT OFFICE BUREAUCRACY

The district office staff is composed of a small, fairly cohesive group whom the superintendent has recruited and who are strongly loyal to him. This contrasts sharply with some districts where individual CSB members have exercised much influence in selecting staff, often by explicitly political criteria. The CSB members of this district deferred to the superintendent in these appointments even when they disagreed with his judgment.

He thus has a staff who work very closely with him and who are not fragmented into competing turfs as is the case in some districts. Since until recently the district has received minimal outside funding, given its middle-class population, few positions exist in the district office. By and large, then, this is a district with a limited administrative overhead staff; and that, of course, makes it difficult for the district office and the superintendent to provide the kinds of services to the schools that he would like. That is still another reason why local school autonomy makes sense for this district.

Indicators of Student and District Performance

As we indicated earlier, this district has undergone sharp changes in its pupil population in the 1970s, with white middle-class families moving out and many poor black families moving in. Under these conditions, it is difficult to assess the effects of decentralization on student performance. On balance, however, reading scores have gone up in 5 of the 8 grades.[5] These figures are shown in Table 8.1. Compared with the city as a whole, this district does not show as great an improvement. In 7 of

TABLE 8.1

District G
Reading Scores for 1971 and 1979

Grade	1971	1979	Change (+/−)
Two	3.0	3.2	0.2
Three	4.2	3.9	(−0.3)
Four	5.0	5.5	0.5
Five	6.6	6.8	0.2
Six	7.1	7.6	0.5
Seven	8.0	8.5	0.5
Eight	10.0	9.8	(−0.2)
Nine	11.4	10.5	(−0.9)

the 8 grades, citywide averages show a larger improvement than here. (See Table 8.2.)

But, as already mentioned, it is very difficult to evaluate the changes in this district, since it has undergone such a sharp change in its pupil population—particularly in the socioeconomic level of the families from which the students come. If the district were to only hold its own in terms of reading levels, that might be a significant achievement under decentralization, given these population shifts. It seems to have done that.

One significant trend over the past couple of years has been the marked increase in the district's efforts to secure outside funding.[6] Such funding has increased from $941,888 in 1975, the third-lowest in the city, along with two white middle-class Queens districts, to $1,523,971 in 1977, and it is up now to $3,398,684. While some of that increase is due simply to a changing population, some has resulted from new competitive grants

TABLE 8.2

Changes in Reading Scores (1971–79)

Grade	District G	Citywide	Difference Between District G & All Schools (+/−)
Two	0.2	-0-	0.2
Three	(−0.3)	0.1	(−0.4)
Four	0.5	0.6	(−0.1)
Five	0.2	0.7	(−0.5)
Six	0.5	0.6	(−0.1)
Seven	0.5	1.0	(−0.5)
Eight	(−0.2)	1.1	(−1.3)
Nine	(−0.9)	1.1	(−2.0)

that reflect on the aggressive, entrepreneurial efforts of its district office staff and superintendent. One example of this is its big ESAA grants for desegregation programs we described earlier. District G used such funds to provide educational services for 2,000 black students in those schools. And it brought in additional funds to provide enrichment programs for middle class students in those schools. Despite big changes in the ethnic composition of students in the schools involved, there were marked improvements in reading scores.[7] Table 8.3 summarizes those improvements. In every one of these schools, much of the improvement in reading scores came in the last couple of years after the desegregation program was put into effect.

Data on other indicators show some decline, although again the dis-

TABLE 8.3

Ethnic Changes and Reading Scores in Receiving Elementary Schools (1972–79)

	Ethnic Composition (Percent White)		Reading Scores (Percent at or Above Grade Level)	
	1972	1979	1972	1979
A	99	81.4	69	75
B	95	76.3	77	83
C	92	76.3	57	64
D	86	71.6	58	73

trict has generally held its own relative to its increased enrollment of poor minority students. Thus, in 1972 its average daily attendance was 91.1%, and that went down to 88.2% in 1979. It is still above the citywide figure of 84.2%, however, and the decline has leveled off since 1978.[8]

Vandalism rates, by contrast, do show increases reflecting the changing socioeconomic composition and neighborhoods in some parts of the district.[9] The annual number of reported broken glass panes has gone up from 5,800 in 1971 to just over 9,000 in 1978; and unlawful entries rose from 68 to 85 during that period. Fires, on the other hand, decreased from 2 to none.

These changes have not yet been accompanied by significant changes in staffing within the district, although there are some small ones.[10] There were no minority principals in 1971, and there remained none in 1978. Two of the district's 45 assistant principals (4.5%) are black, compared with none in 1971. There has been a small increase in minority teachers during this period. There were only 3 black teachers in 1971, or less than 1.0%, and that number increased to 33, or 3.0% in 1978. As for Hispanics, the number of teachers increased from 1 to 7, or from 0.01% to 6.0%. The full-time professional staff in the district increased from 3 blacks (0.2%) in 1971 to 96 (5.6%) in 1978, while Hispanics increased from 1 (0.01%) to 18 (1.0%). This district will thus be under increasing pressure from federal authorities (e.g., the U.S. Office of Civil Rights) to have more ethnic balance among its professional staff in the future, since its staffing patterns still reflect older traditions (Board of Education appointment procedures) and demographic conditions. The district has changed on its ethnic composition only since the mid-1970s, however, and it will take awhile to reflect that more in its staffing.

In brief, this is a district that experienced a big influx of poor blacks and other minorities in the early 1970s and that has, by and large, accommodated quite well in terms of its performance. Under decentralization it has been able to *adapt* to these changes in a way that has helped stabilize neighborhoods and maintain levels of student and school performance that existed before. Again, we do not believe that this capacity for responsiveness would have been nearly as strong under centralization. Our discussion in this chapter of the many curriculum and desegregation initiatives the district has taken, particularly in recent years, suggests that they have been facilitated by a decentralized system that allowed for that kind of local-level response to environmental change.

9

An Isolated Suburban White Middle-Class District—Doing What It Had Always Done: District H

Our final district provides a number of insights into the effects of size on district management. This district, covering an entire borough, has the largest enrollment of any in the city, now numbering about 35,000, spread over 48 schools.[1] Before becoming linked by a bridge to another borough in 1965, it was quite isolated from the rest of the city, resembling a rural and suburban county. Only pockets of business and slum housing could be characterized as urban.

Since 1965 the district has increasingly lost its isolation, as it has undergone a major influx of middle-income whites seeking more affordable housing in suburban communities adjacent to the city. Concurrent with this white influx there was also an in-migration of low-income blacks.

District H, unlike the others examined in this study, functioned quite autonomously prior to decentralization. It was also politically stable, with a consistent level of above average (for the city) academic performance, and it has remained that way despite the in-migration of so many new groups.

Several factors contributed to the stability, including a long tradition of cooperation among various interest groups and the appointment in 1975 of a superintendent who functioned as a broker in balancing off group interests. In achieving this stability, the superintendent and the CSB have now turned their attention to managing such a large and dispersed district more effectively. In doing so, they have moved from a functionally specialized organizational structure to a geographically decentralized one.

Demography, Neighborhoods, District Characteristics

The district's population changes since 1960 reflect the bridge's impact, with an increase from roughly 221,000 in 1960 to 378,000 in 1981.[2] Most of the new white population has settled in middle-income communities in the southern part of the district. The new blacks have settled in one concentrated area in the north. The district has, in addition, a small indigenous, middle-class black group who has lived there for several generations and maintained quite harmonious relations with whites. By contrast, the newer blacks are more of a poverty group. The district's whites are predominantly Catholic, constituting up to 75% of the total population. The vast majority of them are of Italian background, and they constitute the main ethnic group in the district. Both the superintendent and his deputy are from that group, as are many of the district educators and CSB members. A vast network of parochial schools serves this Catholic population, with over one third (roughly 20,000) of all student enrollment in these schools.

There is also a Jewish population that, though relatively small (around 5%, or 15,000), is quite influential and is also increasing. Many Orthodox (Hasidic) Jews have migrated from an adjacent borough, having brought with them their traditions and institutions intact and settled in the center of the district. Others, of Conservative or Reform persuasion, live in the north and center and have contributed to the cultural life of those areas. Jews are also spread throughout the new communities in the south, along with other white ethnic groups.

Remaining groups constitute a very small segment of the population. There are some new Hispanics, Greeks, Koreans, and Vietnamese, and a Protestant group. There are many small Protestant churches, particularly Lutheran, but white Protestants as a body are estimated at no more than 10% of the total population, perhaps less.

The student enrollment in this district's public schools is the highest in the city. It went up from just under 36,000 in 1970 to roughly 39,500 in 1975, reflecting the influx of middle-class whites and then blacks from other boroughs. It is now down to 35,000 and declining. White enrollment declined from 86.4% in 1970 to 80.1% in 1979, while Hispanics increased from 3.9% to 6.0% and blacks went from 9.2% to 11.7%.[3] The socioeconomic status of students, meanwhile, has declined slightly, reflecting these ethnic changes. The teaching staff is very experienced, with roughly 88.0% of them having had five or more years of teaching experience. Only the more affluent middle-class districts in Queens and Brooklyn have more senior teachers, reflecting the general citywide pattern of white middle-class districts having the most experienced teachers and poor minority districts having those with least experience.

A number of geographic divisions separate various racial, ethnic, and economic groups from one another. The main one is between the north and the south, with an expressway separating the two. The area north of the expressway is the most urban part of the district. An estimated 85% to 90% of the district's blacks live there, most of them in low-income projects and deteriorating slums. The concentration of so many poor blacks in this one area has created serious service delivery as well as social problems (e.g., integration, racial conflict, crime).

Immediately adjacent to this slum area, also in the north, are some upper-middle-class and more affluent residential communities. They exist on a series of hills overlooking two other boroughs and providing spectacular views of the shoreline and the harbor. The contrast between the elegant homes on top of the hills and the slums below is very dramatic.

Most of the district's wealth, as well as its cultural, governmental, educational, and commercial institutions, are concentrated in the center and the north. Governmental offices, museums, several colleges, libraries, and other cultural centers are all there, as are some middle-income apartment buildings. The northern and central parts of the district are, in that sense, the more cosmopolitan, liberal, urbanized areas, quite incongruous with the rest of the district, but there nevertheless.

The south, by contrast, is another world. Historically, it consisted of a series of small, self-contained communities—particularly in the southwest—all of them turned much more toward southern New Jersey and the past than toward New York City.

The southeastern part of the borough is the area where many of the middle-class whites, newly arrived from other boroughs, have settled. One of the area's most striking characteristics is its enormous amount of housing construction. The new residents have a strongly protectionist, territorial sense, with many "hocked up to their ears in mortgages," and "digging in to preserve 'peaceful' [a code word for all-white] neighborhoods." In some of these families, each parent may hold two to three jobs at once. For those more upwardly mobile than their neighborhors and who feel particularly threatened by increasing numbers of poor blacks living nearby and/or attending the public schools, this is just a way station for a later move to New Jersey where they hope they can "really get away from it all."

In brief, the district has two main areas: a more urban, established one in the north and center, where most of the blacks, the white liberals, and the borough's main institutions are concentrated, and a newer, more suburban one in the south, with new white ethnic migrants, fleeing from neighborhood deterioration in other boroughs. These areas coexist in a kind of uneasy truce, and there have been proposals to rezone the borough into two community school districts, corresponding to the north–south division, as we shall discuss below.

Educational Interest Groups

This district has a very organized set of constituencies, the most influential of which include unions, political clubs, parents, the Catholic church, and local colleges. The UFT has been particularly vocal and strong.

The most powerful parent body is the district's Federation of PTAs. Unlike in any other district, the Federation acts in concert with teachers, and that imposes constraints on what kinds of issues are raised and how hard parent grievances are pushed. The Federation fits with the district's culture and mentality, however, and independent parent associations have never been able to get established there. The United Parents' Association (UPA) has tried to organize in the district, but it has never been successful. One of the things that hurt its organizing effort was its being identified as an advocate of decentralization. As one informant explained: "The UPA was seen as espousers of decentralization, and in that sense as antiteacher. And the district's parents saw cooperation with the UPA as hurting collaboration with teachers. All this took place in the late 1960s and early 1970s."

The UPA and independent parent associations, then, tended to be defined by many district residents as a New York City-oriented, liberal, antiestablishment group. Some people even regarded them as radicals. The Federation, by contrast, was a conservative local body that did not want to evaluate or criticize teachers. It reflected the district's respect for authority, in this instance, professional authority, that some of the newcomers were beginning to question. But those newcomers were not that much of a voice when the UPA tried to organize, and they have not pressed since then to set up independent parent associations.

There are also political clubs, both Republican and Democratic, that represent particular areas of the district. They endorse slates of CSB candidates, and they push for particular staff appointments—for principals, APs, and district office positions. Much of this activity in regard to jobs goes on sub rosa in all districts, but here it is even more covert than elsewhere. There is endless talk and rumor about how particular CSB members are subject to political pressures regarding appointments of people for principalships. But district residents are extremely reluctant to discuss these matters, particularly with outsiders.

The Catholic church is another powerful institution in the district. Even though there is only one CSB member explicitly identified as a Catholic slate person, the church's presence alone exerts a profound impact on the district. The parochial schools are a major competitor with the public ones. Beyond that, parochial schools use many of the same buses as the public schools.

Political History

Long before decentralization came to the New York City schools through legislation, this district's schools were informally quite decentralized, reflecting its physical isolation from the rest of the city. A watershed year in this regard was 1960 when the central Board of Education appointed its first "outsider" superintendent. An experienced junior high school educator within the New York City system, he eventually gained acceptance.

District residents and educators differ markedly in their assessments of his administration. Some activist parent and civic leaders remember him as a traditional educator and administrator who did an adequate job but was neither "innovative" in the sense of developing that many new programs nor responsive to parent input.

By contrast, several district educators, a number of whom he appointed, as well as conservative residents, have a much more positive view. As one such educator noted: "He was a classic product, a very unusual man. Brilliant, knowledgeable, and saw horizons far greater than anyone these days dares to see. He made significant changes in the district. He brought in the Bureau of Child Guidance, psychiatric consultation, and special education. He cooperated with all segments of the population and was very creative about using various community resources."

Both assessments have some validity. From the perspective of liberal activists, a distinct minority in the district, this superintendent was much like other traditional, Board of Education administrators. Certainly, he did not provide the educational leadership these activists had hoped for. On the other hand, he did appoint several new curriculum directors and principals and did initiate new programs.

The decentralization that this superintendent had established was not the kind, however, that many decentralization advocates wanted, as that issued emerged in other parts of the city. His style of decentralization maintained *professional* dominance. While it did upgrade the staff and curriculum and linked the schools to other agencies, those positive developments never involved a sharing of authority between himself and outside lay groups. He was a "new-style" educator in the 1960s in his approach to involving community agencies, but he was very much an "old-style" superintendent in his unwillingness later on to allow an elected lay board or parent groups to encroach on what he regarded as his "professional" educational prerogatives in decisions on staffing and programs. His seeming acceptance of low academic achievement among poor and minority students were out of time with the goals of community control advocates. As a result, he was to come into increasing conflict with his CSB under decentralization and not experience the same community support during his last few years as superintendent that he had before. Before getting to that, it is important to understand how the district reacted to decentralization.

Much like residents of other white middle-class districts, those in this one were wary of decentralization. One informant summarized the situation quite well: "People here don't like change of any kind. They have tremendous respect for authority and unthinking adherence to it. They have an overwhelming loyalty to existing institutions, regardless of how they are working. They feel it is unseemly to criticize public officials. And they didn't want to get involved in problems of the city." One of New York City's biggest problems, which some district residents felt they would be dragged into under decentralization, related to issues of race. For them, decentralization was a strategy designed to increase the power of blacks, and white residents of the district clearly did not want that. It was only after decentralization began and they saw the possibility of improving education for their own communities as well as for poor minority ones that white middle-class groups in this district and in others redefined the strategy as more than just for blacks alone.

There were other conditions in this district that further contributed to its early resistance to decentralization. Like other white ethnic areas, its residents included union members, civil servants, and New York City educators, most of whom regarded decentralization as a distinct threat. This district's PTA was reluctant to support a strategy that might pit parents and teachers against one another. And the teachers' union, a strong force in the PTA, was vehemently opposed to decentralization.

Nevertheless, decentralization did come to the district as it did everywhere else in New York City, and one of the first big issues for the newly elected CSB was to select a superintendent. There was a small group of liberal parent activists, most of them from the northern part of the area, who wanted to replace the incumbent with a new, outside superintendent who would provide leadership for raising educational standards and be more amenable to CSB and parent input in district decisions.

This group did not have enough power to prevail in that decision, however; and after much delay, the CSB reappointed the incumbent superintendent. Although he stayed on for four more years, his relations with the CSB and with activist parents were strained. He tried to run the district as he had before, reserving to himself many decisions on curriculum, staffing, and budget that he regarded as educational ones. The CSB, on its side, regarded those decisions as matters of policy and within its prerogative, and it pressed him to share authority and make educational changes. He kept resisting, and the continued encounters wore down both parties.

The experience of this superintendent and his CSB thus recapitulates a similar one of other old-line superintendents and their boards throughout the city, except that he stayed on much longer than they did. It was an increasingly difficult period of service, however, and the superintendent's resignation was a welcome relief for all parties.

In 1973 the CSB undertook an extensive search for his successor, and contrary to what one would expect, it selected an outsider who had been a superintendent in a small New Jersey community. What was more surprising was the fact that all three of the final candidates were from outside, indicating how much this CSB was determined to depart from tradition.

The new outsider superintendent served for two years, from 1974 to 1976, and, in retrospect, it is amazing that he lasted that long. He started with no constituency, and he made little effort to build one. Teachers, principals, and other educators undermined him, and it soon became apparent that he was unable to provide much leadership.

By 1976, then, the CSB selected still another superintendent, and he has been there ever since. An educator who had lived and served in the district, he had been a deputy superintendent there and had many of the political and interpersonal skills that his predecessor lacked. He represents still another of those district superintendents under decentralization who reflect so much the backgrounds, values, and styles of the community. Although not a native, he had lived and served in the district a long time and was therefore very knowledgeable about its traditions, its politics, and the workings of its schools. As a former community and public relations staffperson in this district, he was skilled at dealing with its many educational interest groups. And he was a Catholic of Italian origins, which further legitimated him as one of the district's "own."

KEY ISSUES

Several key issues keep emerging in this district, most of them having little to do with decentralization, though decentralization should give the district more flexibility in dealing with them. One set relates to the district's *size* and *geographic spread*. As the largest district in the city, it has been extremely difficult to manage from a single office. The sheer logistics of district office staff getting out to all the schools constitutes one problem. And the absence of any kind of rationally laid out network of roads and transportation routes constitutes another.

The district's topography (physical layout) has a lot to do with its poor transportation system. Large, irregular hills run through the center; and many areas, particularly in the south and west, are very low-lying and contain extensive marshland. Building an efficient network of roads through these areas would be difficult and expensive. The result has been that transportation of students has been a very complex operation, with long, irregular bus routes.

On the matter of the district's size and its manageability, there has been much discussion over the years about breaking it up into two separate north and south districts, with the expressway as the dividing line. Arguments for redistricting were that it would make the new smaller districts less bureaucratic and more open to parent and community participation, thereby lessening the insulation of the local boards and district office professionals, increasing their accountability to the public, permitting the district office to provide more technical assistance and monitoring of individual schools, helping to bring in more money—thus improving education.

Compelling arguments were made against redistricting as well, however, and the opposition always prevailed. It argued that as two districts the borough would be divided along racial and ethnic lines, thereby making integration even more difficult than it already was and increasing racial animosities; that transportation, which was already difficult, could become even more so; and that the borough might get less funding than before.

There were some informal political agendas on both sides that were not mentioned in these public discussions. Those opposing the change saw their power base threatened by redistricting, while those who were for the change saw it as a way of increasing their power. In general, the groups who supported the change were minority parents and white liberals from the north who felt disfranchised and who felt that their area would be given better treatment with its own separate district. In addition, a small number of district office staff and CSB members saw administrative benefits resulting from such a change.

In 1975 redistricting was such a big issue that the CSB set up a special task force to look into the problem. The final CSB vote was 7 to 2 against it. The small coalition of minorities and liberals had not been strong enough to carry the day. And those groups against it included the parent federation; the UFT and CSA; most of the district office professionals; and, of course, seven of the nine CSB members.

The problems that redistricting was designed to address did not disappear, however, and since 1976 when he was appointed, the superintendent and his staff have continued to find it difficult to administer the district as a single entity. Finally, in the summer of 1979, the superintendent proposed a new plan, maintaining a single district office but dividing the district into three geographic areas, each to be supervised by one administrator who would, in turn, report to the superintendent.

Another issue is *integration*. Outside observers as well as enlightened local residents are concerned about the future of race relations in the district for all the reasons indicated earlier. Many whites came there in part to get away from deteriorating neighborhoods. And they then found that poor blacks were also moving there, many of them relocating from neighborhoods from which these whites had fled. In recent years the borough has experienced continued conflicts between the two groups, and the schools were one arena where those conflicts were expressed.

There are at least two points of view within the district as to how well it had handled integration and race problems. One, espoused by the superintendent, many of his professional staff, CSB members, and some parents, is that the district has done a good job in the face of a difficult situation. The superintendent, for example, maintains that he made many zoning decisions before schools located near new, low-income housing projects become solidified as all-black schools. As he noted, in defending his administrative actions: "I designed the zoning here to limit segregation. There were many steps taken to integrate blacks and whites. We have some intermediate schools that are examples of the best in integration. One of them has 60 percent blacks, and its programs are so good that many whites have wanted to get into them. Had one big series of projects been maintained as integrated housing the way we wanted, this would not have been the problem it is."

Many district residents and some central board staff, by contrast, have a different view. They note, for example, that 2 elementary schools have a 70% black enrollment, though the total district enrollment of blacks is under 12%. They also report that some black students are zoned long distances into segregated black schools, even when there are predominantly white or integrated schools nearer where they live. As one central board staff person noted: "This district is not addressing the race issue like it should. There are other districts that do the same thing, but the way they are managing it now, they will have a falling-dominoes situation, where schools will become all-black. They don't understand where they are historically, and they don't engage in the long-range planning. Some of it is not their fault, with the building of those low-income projects all in one area, but they are going to be in deep trouble if they don't address the integration problem better than they have."

The actual situation is somewhere between the two conflicting perceptions, though it is probably closer to the latter. From the perspective of central board staff who have a broad, comparative view of how districts are doing on the integration issue, this one has not distinguished itself.

In recent years, and related to the race issue, *declining enrollments* have been a source of great concern to public school administrators and CSB members. Total enrollment is now down to 35,000, the lowest it has been since decentralization, and down from a high of over 40,000 in 1975. Declining birthrates, the area's aging population, and an out-migration of younger families are three important reasons. Many new residents, for example, have children of high school or college age. Another reason for the decline may be the desire on the part of public school parents to protect their children from what they perceive as racial problems of the public schools. This is borne out by data on trends in parochial school enrollments in the district. Since 1975 public school enrollment has decreased by more than 5,000 students, while that in Catholic schools in the district has remained stable, at roughly 15,000 for elementary and junior high levels. This pattern reflects a national trend, but public school officials and parent groups in this district view it with much concern. They fear that it may be interpreted as reflecting a declining confidence in public education in the district.

At any rate, there is competition between the two systems. Catholic schools at all levels do have waiting lists, and public school supporters are often defensive about their declining enrollment. A recent development is for parochial schools to attract high-achieving black students, many of whose parents are as anxious to get their children out of the public schools as are the whites.

This move to the parochial schools, however, is not just one of avoidance. Many of these schools have excellent programs, in addition to having fewer racial problems than do public schools. And what is quite noticeable to all district residents is the high academic achievements of parochial high school graduates. Each year the daily newspaper publishes information on the college admissions, scholarships, and other prizes of graduating seniors from the district's high schools, and in recent years a preponderance of these have gone to Catholic high school graduates.

One significant advantage that Catholic schools have over public ones is their K–8 grade organization, which parents see as more beneficial for the safety of their children and for maintaining authority and discipline than the geographically distant junior high and intermediate schools of the public system. Students in the latter must often travel away from their neighborhood to these schools, and that has been a concern not only in New York but in inner cities throughout the nation. Indeed, the public schools in this district, as in others, plan to experiment with some K–8 schools to retain many students who would otherwise leave and to attract back those who have left, and the district may well move more extensively in this direction in the future.

It should also be noted that the relation of the public and parochial schools in this district is not just a competitive one. There is much cooperation on common programs as well, far beyond anything that exists elsewhere in New York City, as we shall discuss in a later section.

Managing a Large, Diversified District

This district's stability is largely a function of the superintendent's style. His main skills are those of balancing the demands of the district's many constituencies, of working harmoniously with his CSB, and of delegating effectively to his district office staff and to principals. Recognizing the professional standing of the principals and the district's geography, he has given principals much autonomy in the running of their schools. At the same time, he has established a strong district office presence by requiring that minimal standards are met and by working through his staff to maintain districtwide programs.

By and large, however, he is much more of a *facilitator* than a *dy-*

namic leader, and that seems to be the style that this diverse, conservative district desires. As one parent observer noted: "He gives the principals a peaceful environment, and it is up to them to run their schools. It permits more diversity to emerge. He has been successful because he gave the district what it wanted. He is a facilitator, not an innovating leader." Decentralization could thus produce innovative, "new-style" superintendents such as those of Districts B and E; or, as in this case, it could produce ones who served a district's desire for a stable political and administrative climate.

CURRICULUM STYLE

In comparing the district's various schools, then, what stands out most is their diversity. Some have open education programs, while many are more traditional. Much like District G, this one allows individual principals to develop their own educational philosophy and programs, as long as minimal standards are met, and as long as the parents support them.

One of the district's strengths has been its principals and district office curriculum specialists. Its science and math coordinators, for example, were among the most imaginative in the city. They developed many programs that they made available to the schools, played an active technical assistance role, and were successful in securing state and federal funding. In science, for example, there were programs that combined science and reading, there were science fairs, and there were experientially based, hands-on programs that were all developed by the district's creative science coordinator, who was widely recognized as such both inside and outside the district. And he worked with many outside cultural and recreational agencies in running these programs.

The math coordinator and his programs were of the same high quality. In fact, one of his remedial math programs was so well regarded in Washington that the district received Title I and then Title III grants to disseminate it all over the country. Some parents complain that this coordinator has spent too much time on the national dissemination of the program and too little in schools within the district, but it is clear that he has provided it with some excellent programs.

Principals in the district have also done exciting and productive things. One such principal, for example, devised a highly individualized open education program in 1979, with strong community agency linkages. Parents were initially resistant, but he soon won them over, and in two years he increased student attendance from 79% to 90%. He was somewhat of a rebel who was allowed to "do his thing" after he secured parent support, and there have been others throughout the district who have been equally effective.

As for the district office's role, it has exercised educational program initiatives even in the face of fiscal cutbacks. These initiatives include, in addition to the math and science programs already mentioned, those for gifted and talented students, various other enrichment programs—such as districtwide instrumental music programs, a diagnostic reading center, a brochure and training for parents on how to work with their children to improve their school performance, and some significant administrative improvements. Two such improvements include the increasing use of the computer to program classes and instruction and a reorganization of the district to facilitate a closer monitoring of schools and more adherence to minimum curriculum standards.

There are different perceptions as to how innovative the superintendent and district office have been on curriculum. One view, held by liberal parents, by curriculum coordinators appointed in previous administrations and whose jobs have been eliminated under the recent reorganization, and by other district educators, is that this superintendent has been much more of a "caretaker" than an "innovator." As one former coordinator reported: "There is no district educational philosophy and no curriculum leadership by the superintendent or CSB. Educational philosophy has emerged at the individual school level. Curriculum has been neglected in this district because administrative and political responsibilities consume the superintendent's time."

By contrast, other district educators point to the district office initiatives listed above as reflecting a much more activist superintendent and district office presence than the critics acknowledge. As one central staffperson explained, in defending the record: "The programs here since 1976 have been very good. Many people at the central board have cited us for our programs. They have become models for the rest of the city. And they have been put together under the most adverse circumstances, with the budget crisis. Headquarters has been amazed at what we have done with the limited amount of money at our disposal—enrichment programs, math and science programs, the gifted programs, instrumental music programs in all our schools, a diagnostic reading center, a computer program. We have done a lot here and have been very innovative."

A Multiagency Model Program. One of the most significant educational programs in the district, developed outside the district office, though with its involvement, is a consortium of over 100 agencies, serving youth and adults from kindergarten through graduate school and including parochial, private, and public schools as well as colleges. Begun in 1974, it has been funded by several foundations (Carnegie, Ford, and Hazen) as well as by such participating agencies as the New York City Board of Education, the district office, the Board of Higher Education, the archdiocese, and local colleges. It has many different kinds of programs, for both advanced and low-achieving students—for example, a diagnostic reading center at one college; a college course program for junior high, intermediate, and high school students; a learning exchange of many different courses taught by community members in offices, homes, and schools all over the borough; a classroom assistant, teacher training program; math and English skills centers; and curriculm development efforts to better articulate educational programs in the district from kindergarten through college.

The consortium is a nonprofit corporation whose board includes top officials from the central Board of Education, the district, the archdiocese, the colleges, and the teachers' union. It is an extraordinary program in terms of its multiagency participation, its broad scope of activities, and its target students. Its able director has forged a cooperative program that has public and parochial school officials working together. That is quite an attainment, since there is so much competition between them as well.

DISTRICT OFFICE AND THE SCHOOLS

Given this district's size and geographic spread, the amount of contact between the district office and the schools has been somewhat limited. The present superintendent has given the schools much more autonomy than did his predecessors. In addition, the district has fewer central office staff as a result of the budget cuts. And it was never easy to cover so many schools over such a wide area to begin with.

In recognition of these problems, and to promote more district office leadership on curriculum and instruction, the superintendent reorganized the district in the summer of 1979 into a new, tripartite structure. It was to be managed by three supervising principals, each responsible for a different geographic area. The three areas were delineated so that the main ethnic groups in the district would be represented in each. And the supervisory principals would be responsible for monitoring curriculum and instruction practices, training and evaluating staff, developing new curriculum materials, helping make the curriculum more uniform throughout the district, and improving communications between the district office and the schools. Since each supervisory principal is responsible for only one third of the schools in the district, it would now be possible for the district office to provide much more direct supervision than before.

One of the main features of the reorganization is that it has eliminated the district office coordinators, whose functions are now taken over by the new supervising principals, with the coordinators being reassigned to particular schools as principals. Needless to say, many coordinators were unhappy about that change, which they assert was made without their having been consulted. These coordinators and some parents expressed much concern that the coordinators' expertise would no longer be available on the districtwide basis that it was before, but only for the schools to which they had been assigned.

The superintendent, however, had a different view, as he justified the change: "All those science programs that existed before exist today, and that coordinator is not here. These things still go on. And in many schools, they never saw those coordinators. The schools saw them only once a year."

It is difficult to assess how the reorganization has affected the district, just based on two years' experience. Interviews with principals, a group originally opposed to the change, elicited a range of responses. Those who were positive commented on the increased contact they had with the district office, through visits from the supervising principal; and they regarded the contacts as supportive. Those who were negative complained about the supervisors' attempts to standardize the curriculum through issuing impersonal directives, rather than visiting each school to see what its individual problems were.

It is likely that this change the district has undergone from a *functionally specialized organization*, with district office curriculum experts providing assistance to schools, to a *geographically decentralized one*, with district office generalists supervising schools, has probably had results similar to what takes place in business organizations that undergo such changes. There is a lightening of the administrative, "fire-fighting" load on the top executive. There may also be some increasing uniformity in the product (e.g., the curriculum). At the same time, there is probably a sacrifice or diminution of professionalism as the specialists from the old structure are reassigned, since the generalist administrators who take their place have much less expertise in those fields. And there may be a lessening of flexibility for individual schools as the new generalist administrators (supervisors) attempt to fit them into a particular mold.

There is no question that the district's size has made it difficult to manage from one central office. The reorganization was an attempt to establish a new structure that would facilitate improved management. That structure must be understood in the context of the district's declining budgets, its superintendents' perennial problems of managing a district of this size and geographic dispersion, and the particular concerns of the present superintendent with gaining greater control over district administration.

The biggest changes the reorganization effected were in the relation of the district office to the principals. The latter are now more closely supervised than they were. And they have a new administrative layer (the supervising principals) between them and the superintendent. They objected initially to the change largely for these reasons, but they still have access to the superintendent when necessary.

DISTRICT OFFICE AND COMMUNITY

This district is a close-knit community in which public officials are subjected to much pressure from citizens for improved services. In the case of the schools, that pressure is reinforced by the high visibility given to school issues by the daily newspaper and by the importance of schools to so many local residents. The new ones, in particular, have become quite vocal in their demands for better schools, or at least the kinds of schools that they deem "better." The result has been that the superintendent and the CSB take parent complaints very seriously. The CSB and the superintendent are sometimes characterized as taking parent complaints so seriously that they may react to them in a way that undermines the professionals.

Decentralization in a close-knit district like this one requires that public officials be highly responsive. Ironically, although the district has at times been overresponsive to parent grievances in what may sometimes be unproductive ways, the CSB has not functioned in that open a fashion. Despite the state's Sunshine Law, requiring that all board meetings be open to the public, it continues to hold meetings in secret and does not divulge to the public either the times of those meetings or their substance. This practice is not unique to District H, which is merely recapitulating what has taken place in several others, but it is particularly interesting in light of the district's overresponsiveness in other respects.

On the more positive side, the PTAs are very active, and even though parents do not constitute a formal, separate body, they do play a strong role in the district on various committees and through the district's responses to their complaints. Also, the Federation of PTAs has been successful in having some of its candidates elected to the CSB.

DISTRICT OFFICE BUREAUCRACY

As for the organization of the district office, a few patterns stand out. One is the very significant role played by the deputy superintendent. He takes care of all matters relating to business and administration and does that very well and expeditiously. He has been particularly active in developing a computerized information system to help in generating reports on the fiscal and educational picture of the district. In addition, as a native to the district and as an astute administrator and political analyst in his own right, he provides the superintendent with strong back-up assistance in making nonroutine strategy decisions as well as in day-to-day management.

Another feature of the district office is its small staff, relative to many minority districts. One reason for its small staff size is that until quite recently it did not have that many large, federally funded programs, because it did not have enough of a poor minority student population to warrant them. The coordinators had been successful in securing outside grants, but they were generally for small, delimited programs that did not require much staffing.

Since the superintendent's style is to have decisions made through a consensus, and in committees and task forces, there is much coordination within the district office. Relations are quite informal, and few if any separate, fragmented turfs exist, now that most of the coordinator positions have been eliminated.

Indicators of Student and District Performance

Historically, this has been one of the highest-achieving districts in the city. Having high reading scores relative to other New York City districts, however, may not indicate academic excellence. As one community leader reflected: "We just have fewer very low scores rather than many very high ones."

The district has had a large white middle-class student population, and the numbers have not changed appreciably since decentralization. Thus, in 1970–71, 9.2% were black, 3.9% Hispanic, and 86.4% white. In 1978 the numbers were not that different: 11.1% black, 5.8% Hispanic, and 81.2% white.[4] A district would be expected to have high reading scores with that kind of student population, and that is in fact what has occurred. (See Table 9.1.) In 1971 almost all grades in the district were reading above the average for the city as a whole. And after eight years, they have increased that lead. In other words, District H has outperformed the city as a whole.[5] Table 9.2 indicates these trends.

District H may thus be the exception to the rule that it is extremely difficult for districts reading above grade level to improve their performance even further. This district appears to present a paradox. A superintendent who has had more of a mediating than program development style is nevertheless presiding over a district whose students have done very well in reading in the past and continue to do well. Part of the explanation is probably the students themselves, and part may well be some of the curriculum coordinators, principals, and teachers.

Trends in math scores are roughly the same as those in reading.[6] The

TABLE 9.1

District H
Reading Scores for 1971 and 1979

Grade	1971	1979	Change (+/−)
Two	2.7	3.4	0.7
Three	3.6	4.3	0.7
Four	4.6	5.9	1.3
Five	6.0	7.0	1.0
Six	6.7	7.8	1.1
Seven	7.4	8.9	1.5
Eight	8.7	10.0	1.3
Nine	9.8	10.0	1.2

TABLE 9.2

Changes in Reading Scores (1971–79)

Grade	District H	Citywide	Differences Between District H & All Schools (+/−)
Two	0.7	-0-	0.7
Three	0.7	0.1	0.6
Four	1.3	0.6	0.7
Five	1.0	0.7	0.3
Six	1.1	0.6	0.5
Seven	1.5	1.0	0.5
Eight	1.3	1.1	0.2
Nine	1.2	1.1	0.1

district was nearly a grade ahead of the citywide scores in 1971 (6.2 for the district and 5.4 for the city), and it widened that gap slightly by 1978 (5.9 for the city and 6.9 for the district).

Attendance rates in the district have also been high, but they have been declining since decentralization, and the gap between the district and the city has begun to narrow.[7] Thus, in 1970 the average daily attendance was 91.1%, while the number was down somewhat to 89.2% in 1978. That is still above the citywide average, which has gone from 81.1% to 82.8% during that time.

One significant change in District H that may possibly be a harbinger of things to come is its rates of vandalism.[8] Crime is way up in the borough over the past decade, and so too is vandalism in the schools. Thus, broken glass panes have increased from 5,900 in 1971 to 7,500 in 1978. Fires have increased from 2 to 5 in those years. And unlawful entries rose from 58 to 118 during that period. Informal social controls that used to operate so effectively in such a traditional area seem to be breaking down somewhat.

As for staff changes, there has been little overall increase in the representation of minority professionals, with the exception of black principals.[9] Those numbers have increased from one (2.3%) to five (10.6%) from 1971 to 1978. For the staff as a whole, blacks have increased only from 1.9% to 2.7% and Hispanics only from 0.4% to 1.5%. Whites are still 95.3% of the total staff. One big reason for this is the inaccessibility of the district. The trip from other boroughs is so long and time-consuming that most public school educators, like other civil servants employed there, live in the district. Since its indigenous or residential black population is still very small, and since only a small portion of that group are likely to be going into education or some other white-collar professional or business field, their numbers remain small in the school system; the same can be said for Hispanics.

In sum, this is a district quite unlike the others in New York City. It has always been decentralized to some extent, owing to its inaccessibility and to the fact that it encompasses an entire borough. It still has a predominantly white middle-class population, and although the crime rate and rates of school vandalism are increasing, its student performance remains high. Decentralization seems not to have had much impact either positively or negatively in this district. It was decentralized before and it remains so. It was relatively separate from the city before and also remains so, though to a lesser degree. If the numbers of minority students increase in the future, as seems likely, then this district's capacity to adapt will be tested for the first time. But even that increase is likely to be slow and, at least for a while, not that big. Unlike all the other districts we have studied, this one may be much more a sui generis case, from which it is very difficult to generalize or extrapolate. In many respects, this district may still be much more oriented toward areas outside the city than toward the city itself, despite over fifteen years of experience with the bridge that now connects it to one of the other boroughs.

10

Different Views of Decentralization

Interpreting the Findings: Pessimistic and Optimistic Views

There are at least two ways of viewing the New York City experience with decentralization. One is that decentralization does show promise in many districts and should be given a better chance (1) through efforts at mobilizing a stronger coalition in its support; (2) through legislative changes to give more authority to the districts and provide greater clarity as to the respective roles of headquarters and the districts; and (3) through changes in the districts themselves, that is, in procedures for selecting CSB members, in the drawing of district lines, in the training programs for the CSB members that have been so limited thus far, and in the mechanisms for interdistrict dissemination of effective educational practice that have also been quite limited.

A second view is that decentralization has not worked or, at best, has been accompanied by only marginal improvements in student performance that may well be due to other factors, such as programs initiated by the central board to improve reading and math skills. Our position, based on eight case studies, on information about other districts, and on aggregate statistical data, coincides much more with the first view.

Student Performance Under Decentralization

When decentralization was first proposed for New York City, many predictions were made about its possible consequences. The proponents believed that it would be beneficial—that through community involvement in the schools, pupils' performance would improve. The critics believed that decentralization would have harmful effects—that it would lead to disorganization and even chaos, and that pupils' performance would suffer. What actually happened?

As measured by reading scores, pupils' performance under decentralization has improved. This conclusion is based on examination of citywide reading scores for grades 2 through 9, from 1971 to 1981.[1] The net change in their performance is shown in Table 10.1. As the table shows,

TABLE 10.1

Reading Scores for 1971 and 1981

Grade	1971	1981	Change (+)
Two	2.8	2.9	0.1
Three	3.5	4.0	0.5
Four	4.3	5.0	0.7
Five	5.2	6.3	1.1
Six	6.2	7.1	0.9
Seven	6.5	7.8	1.3
Eight	7.5	9.0	1.5
Nine	8.6	9.8	1.2

there was improvement in all 9 grades. Thus, the critics who predicted harmful consequences, at least on this particular measure of effectiveness, were wrong, and the proponents appear to be right.

There are, of course, other possible explanations for the improvement in reading scores besides decentralization. For example, it could result from selective migration in and out of the city—from an influx of students from higher socioeconomic families and an out-migration of students from lower socioeconomic families. But, in New York City, just the opposite has occurred during the period of decentralization. The number of poor families has not decreased since 1971, and middle- and upper-middle-class families have continued to abandon the public schools by moving to the suburbs or by enrolling their children in private and parochial schools. In short, selective migration is not a plausible alternative explanation of the improvement in reading scores.

Another possible explanation is that the school system has changed its reading tests during this period. It did, indeed, change the tests several times from 1971 to 1981. Our conclusion, however, is not affected by these changes. In the years 1971 to 1981, pupils' performance in the districts as compared with the citywide averages improved. Thus, a change in the reading test does not account for the improvement during the period of decentralization.[2]

Given the limitations of these data, one might still want to be skeptical. But even the most conservative conclusion could be that decentralization did not harm the children, and this evidence suggests that it benefited them.

A Model on Prerequisites for District Effectiveness

One useful way to summarize what we have found, at least from a public policy point of view, is to develop an empirically derived model of the prerequisites for district effectiveness.

The model abstracts from the eight case studies done in connection with this research. It summarizes the essential forces that bear on district performance. It does not describe any single district, since the positive elements are present only in varying degrees in any particular case.[3] Moreover, we have purposely not undertaken to rank the districts in terms of degrees of effectiveness, since that task is too complex and ambiguous to have much meaning. For one thing, effectiveness is, at best, a multidimensional concept; it is difficult, if not impossible, to make judgments as to which dimension is more important.[4] We have made mention of *bottom-line* and *process* indicators, and sorting out their significance is beyond the scope of this study. In addition, many of the causal or situational variables are also multidimensional and subject to only varying degrees of control at the district level. So, rather than describing how the districts differ on all these dimensions, we begin instead by developing this model. Table 10.2 contains the main elements of the model, which essentially includes the key variables in our study.

It is thus possible to delineate many of the factors that contribute to or reflect district effectiveness. One of the most important factors seems to be the presence of a "strong" superintendent. We mean by the term "strong" at least two things: (1) the superintendent has much formal au-

TABLE 10.2

Prerequisites for District Effectiveness

More Effective	Less Effective
1. COMMUNITY POLITICS	
(a) *Relatively stabilized*	*Turbulent*
No major leadership struggles within and across interest groups	Leadership conflict
No major disruptions of CSB meetings	CSB meetings chaotic
CSB and district have much legitimacy within the community	Community distrust of CSB and district
Schools relatively free of violence	Much unrest in schools
(b) *Education-oriented leadership in power*	*Political interests in power*
Parents, civic-minded groups prevail rather than political clubs, churches, and antipoverty agencies	Political clubs
2. COMMUNITY SCHOOL BOARD	
(a) Quite *cohesive*; a majority coalition	Very factionalized
(b) *Clear role definition* and priorities	No clear sense about its role
(c) *Assumes policy role and delegates much administrative authority to superintendent*	*Does not assume policy role* and deeply involved in administration
(d) *Much role consensus with superintendent* on his and their authority	*Little role consensus with superintendent*
(e) *Strong chairperson* with political base and skills to develop a consensus	No strong chairperson
(f) *Power in hands of parent and civic-minded, profession-oriented people*	*Power held by politically oriented members*, aspiring politicians, "power brokers" representing narrow group interests
(g) *Little or no CSB involvement in "patronage"* appointments of staff	
(h) *CSB members spend much time on board activity*, active committees, good attendance at meetings	*Much CSB involvement in handing out jobs* Committees meet rarely, if ever; attendance at CSB sporadic
3. SUPERINTENDENT	
(a) Has much administrative and even some "policy" authority	Little authority
(b) Takes many curriculum and administrative initiatives	Takes few such initiatives; sometimes too busy in political turf struggles with CSB

More Effective	*Less Effective*

A STRONG SUPERINTENDENT — A WEAK SUPERINTENDENT

- (bi) Developed cohesive cadre of district office staff, working closely with superintendent — Does not control all district office staff, some of them holdovers and/or loyal to others—e.g., CSB members, political groups
- (bii) Has achieved much *administrative stability*, both in continuity of staff and in their support of superintendent's programs — Much less administrative stability; conflicting philosophies and loyalties among staff
- (biii) *Has evolved one or a few broad program directions* — No clear, coherent program directions
- (biv) *Programs fit community needs* — Less fit of programs to community needs
- (bv) *Much staff development activity* — Minimal staff development
- (bvi) *Collaboration, working relations with teachers' and supervisors' unions* — Arm's-length or adversarial relations
- (bvii) *Many program linkages with outside agencies*—e.g., universities, cultural agencies, employers, other districts, parks — Minimal program linkages
- (bviii) *Much parent participation activity* that the superintendent has initiated in formal and informal programs — Minimal parent participation programs
- (bix) *Much initiative and success in securing outside, state and federally funded programs* — Minimal initiative and success in this
- (bx) *Developed strong productivity orientation*—much effective monitoring and evaluation and program change based on that — Minimal monitoring and program change based on it

4. BOTTOM-LINE, PERFORMANCE MEASURES
   - (a) Reading scores improved and/or held their own, relative to citywide trend — Reading scores declined
   - (b) Math scores same as above — Math scores declined
   - (c) Attendance same as above — Attendance declined
   - (d) Placement in specialized high schools same as above — Placement declined
   - (e) Vandalism stabilized and/or declined — Vandalism increased

thority to run the district in ways that he or she deems appropriate; and (2) the superintendent uses that authority to take many initiatives to improve education in the district. It is possible to have the first without the second, though not the other way around. That is, without a base and some legitimacy, no superintendent would be able to provide much leadership, a condition that exists in some community districts in New York City.

The first condition helps insulate the superintendent from undue political pressures, either from board members or from community groups—for patronage appointments, for favored treatment in budget decisions, and the like. In these cases, the CSB established a wall, protecting the superintendent so that he could run the district. The superintendent is still held accountable for student and district performance, but there is minimal interference in day-to-day administration. Moreover, the superintendent may have some broad policymaking powers as well—as, for example, in establishing an educational philosophy for the district and setting up programs and administrative procedures for implementation.

In some instances, the superintendent may have aggressively seized such formal authority and had it institutionalized. This is most likely to happen when the CSB is inactive, weak, and/or divided and puts up only token resistance.

The second condition involves the superintendent taking many initiatives over and above having such formal authority; (1) in curriculum and instruction (educational); (2) in administration (managerial); and (3) in mobilizing constituency support (political)—all of which may contribute to educational improvements.

Our general argument is that whether a superintendent is "strong" or "weak" thus has many dimensions. And the more the above-listed ones are present (see the bi–bx categories in Table 10.2), the stronger is the superintendent and the more effective is the district.

Management Style

At the same time, not all "strong" superintendents need have the same management styles or must behave in the same ways. Thus, there is more than one way to run an effective district, and one of the positive effects of decentralization has been that it has facilitated such a diversity of management types, as the case studies indicate. On curriculum, for example, superintendents in some districts that maintained or improved their reading scores had a very explicit educational philosophy that they imposed on the schools, while those in other districts that had a similar performance did not. Thus, the superintendent in one district had what he and his staff referred to as a humanistic, open education philosophy that they articulated endlessly for the general public *and* their school staff and CSB, while one in another had a very traditional, structured, "back-to-basics" approach, emphasizing a uniformly standardized curriculum, basic skills instruction in conventional classrooms, and the like. The difference between these two districts in curriculum style could hardly have been greater. The first favored a "learning-through-doing," highly individualized and affective approach to learning; the other one emphasized a "production management," Frederick Taylor-like style, with much formalization, standardization, and uniformity, including a variety of controls over teacher and student behavior, such as audits, tests, in-service training for "marginal" teachers, and so on. Neither was necessarily "better" than the other. Rather, they were simply different, and those differences were a function, not only of the superintendent's values, but of the situation. In each case, they fit the educational needs and learning styles of students—of affluent, middle-class whites in one case and of poor, low-achieving blacks in the other; and of educators attuned to open education approaches in the one, as opposed to educators who had not yet established uniform, minimal standards in the other.

Yet, we studied two other districts that had held their own in reading scores where there was no explicit educational philosophy that the superintendent and his staff imposed on schools. In a white middle-class district in one of the outer boroughs, while the superintendent had a somewhat traditional philosophy himself—supporting traditional classroom and more structured approaches to learning, both of which matched the values of his many conservative, middle-class constituencies—he accepted and even supported those open classroom schools where they were preferred by the principal and parents. In fact, he even appointed an active advocate of open education as principal to one of those schools, much to the amazement of both the principal and the parents. In this instance, orchestrating a diversity of curriculum styles became the superintendent's strategy, matching the diversity of the population groups that the district served. At the same time, since retaining and attracting back the white middle class was a major concern, the superintendent developed a series of curriculum approaches—magnet schools, pre-K programs, and programs for the gifted and talented—that, in turn, matched the preferences of that population group.

One could make the same point about there being no one best way as related to other management style considerations. For example, with regard to decentralizing to the local school level, one superintendent has exercised strong central leadership and imposed a uniform curriculum on the schools, leaving little room for local option. By contrast, supporting school-level autonomy is a key feature of another superintendent's management style. Both styles have been effective.

The most effective management style is thus the one that seems to most fit the situation of the district being managed.[5] Several situational factors are particularly important. One is the learning styles of students and the values of their parents. Liberal, white middle-class communities, for example, may prefer open education and less structured classrooms, whereas poor black areas or conservative white ethnic communities may prefer and need a more traditional and structured approach. A second factor is the extent of diversity of communities within a district. The more diverse they are, the better it may be for the superintendent to refrain from mandating curriculum and to decentralize those decisions instead to the local school level, allowing curriculum preferences to bubble up from the principal, teachers, and parents. Still a third factor is the extent of demographic change within a district. The more the change, the more flexible the superintendent should probably be in providing autonomy for individual schools and in allowing them to determine their curriculum and staffing, including the selection of the principal.

At the same time, despite management style differences, effective districts may have certain features in common, as related to the superintendent's position and behavior. As indicated above, the CSB must delegate more formal authority to the superintendent, concentrate itself on setting broad policy, and attain agreement with the superintendent on their respective spheres of authority (role consensus). Beyond that, the superintendent needs the following: a strong political base in the community; a well-trained business manager; a strong deputy and an upper-middle-management cadre of curriculum directors; a satisfactory working relationship with teachers and principals; good monitoring to facilitate program changes; an active staff development program; professional proposal writers; and a strong administrator of funded programs to secure outside monies. Furthermore, he needs to have state and federally funded programs integrated with tax-levy ones so that they complement one another. In this same vein, he needs to integrate various curriculum specialists into a collaborative educational strategy, with each reinforcing the others' programs. He needs to handle headquarters, through effective negotiation for needed resources and district autonomy, and/or through creative noncompliance with headquarters policies that frees the district from having to negotiate continuously with central staff. And he needs to develop a network of relations with district-based and outside agencies for collaborative programs and with elected officials to help in securing city and outside funds.

This rather formidable list constitutes what might be called an organizational and behavioral profile of what is required to run an effective district in a decentralized system like New York City's. It applies, with appropriate modifications, to any district. We developed it in large part as a composite of the strengths of all the districts and superintendents we studied. Some are stronger on some dimensions than others, with the assumption being that effective districts will be stronger on more of them than less effective districts. In that sense, this is an ideal-type model, one that's never realized in any single case but that specifies the prerequisites for district effectiveness.

Determinants and Consequences of Management Style and Superintendent Differences

A main question of this study is when strong superintendents are most likely to emerge in districts. A number of conditions give rise to that likelihood. A key one is political stability. Those districts whose educational politics has settled down have much better prospects than do politically unstable districts. In the latter instance, the CSB is likely to be quite factionalized, and its membership is usually unstable with frequent changes in ethnic, economic, and geographic representation, which are often a reflection of districtwide population changes. Those changes in CSB membership are often associated, in turn, with changing board preferences for superintendents or, at best, with considerable political conflict between the CSB and the superintendent. The latter spend a good deal of time in struggling to secure a mandate for key decisions (policy and administrative), while many board members constrain him by being deeply involved in administration (e.g., patronage) to solidify their political base. In these situations, having to secure the five necessary votes of a nine-member board for many administrative actions becomes a major problem of the superintendent. It keeps deflecting his resources from other tasks, such as developing and implementing effective programs, developing staff, and trying to secure outside funding. These districts have typically had many superintendents since decentralization began.[6]

Politically stable districts, on the other hand, often have less turnover among superintendents, and the ones who serve there are given much authority. They are thus likely to remain in office for a long enough time to provide the continuity in educational philosophy and staff that is so necessary to develop effective programs, and they are given the flexibility to do so.[7]

The question remains as to why some districts are more stable politically than others. At least two factors seem to contribute to such stability. One of the most important is the existence of a strong leader on the CSB, usually as its chairperson, with the political base and skills necessary to mobilize the consensus needed within the CSB to insulate the superintendent. Such a leader may be effective in coalescing board and community factions through political trade-offs (e.g., providing jobs in antipoverty agencies or other community organizations). Such effectiveness limits militant groups from staging protests that might interfere with the development and implementation of potentially effective programs. We cited examples of such leaders in several of the case studies.[8]

Having an infrastructure of established parent and community organizations also helps considerably in maintaining political stability. It existed before decentralization in many middle-class districts, and they were able to adapt easily to the change, just grafting it onto a preexisting structure while peacefully absorbing newly emerging groups.[9] Indeed, one of the ironies of decentralization has been that it worked more smoothly at first in the very middle-class districts where there was so much initial resistance to it. These were districts where many New York City educators lived, as did civil servants from other local government agencies who feared that it might soon spread to their agency as well.

By contrast, the poverty areas that wanted decentralization the most did not have, at least initially, the infrastructure of political and parent organizations to make it work easily. They often experienced much community conflict in the early stages of decentralization, deflecting their attention from educational matters, until there was such a settling-down process.[10] This is not at all to argue that conflict per se has always been dysfunctional for improved education. Conflict often calls the district's attention to important issues that were not adequately addressed in the past—for example, taking corrective action in cases where principals, teachers, or programs were not adequately serving students. We are referring here, however, to poorly contained, runaway conflicts that went beyond those constructive purposes, having less to do with educational improvements than with factional politics and leadership struggles among community groups.[11]

On the other hand, we have found several poverty-area districts that have moved beyond an early stage of political turbulence to one of much more social peace and stability.[12] It is therefore incorrect to say that only white middle-class areas have been in a position to benefit from decentralization. Strong superintendents, supported by a relatively stable politics, exist throughout the city, although there remains somewhat more turbulence, on balance, in poverty-area districts that came into decentralization without any preestablished community and parent organization. The most turbulence, however, now exists in districts in transition, that is, in those undergoing the most demographic change from white middle- and working-class to poor minority residents.

A critical question is how district politics and management style may affect student performance. Is it true that relatively stable communities with strong superintendents have better student performance? If so, why? What is there about politics and administration that relates to the classroom teacher and the student? After all, community politics and district administration are seemingly quite removed from the day-to-day workings of the classroom. Why wouldn't teachers just do what they thought best or were doing before, without being disturbed by such seemingly distant forces?

Our field studies suggest a number of ways that these outside forces affect the classroom. First, when political stability and its correlates—a strong superintendent and staff continuity—exist, the district is able to develop a more coherent, long-term approach to educational programming and staff development than when this is not the case. Programs can be more easily developed, tested, evaluated, and modified without constant disruption or major changes in philosophy and emphasis. The reader should note in that regard that the present superintendent in four districts that have many effective programs has served since the early 1970s, with much continuity of staff, educational philosophy, and program as well. While we would not argue that stability and continuity always positively affect student performance, that seems often to be the case, for the reasons just stated. Beyond that, superintendents in stable districts where they do have authority and a mandate to lead are much less likely to dissipate their limited resources in political struggles with their boards and can allocate more of such resources to effective problem solving.

Moreover, with some exceptions, staff morale seems better in stable than in unstable districts. There is less likelihood, for example, that teachers will want to transfer out of districts where they perceive the superintendent and district office to have the support of the CSB to pursue programs that improve education.

Results of Decentralization: Bottom-Line and Process Indicators

As we indicated in our previous discussion, the ultimate test of decentralization has to be what it does for students in classrooms. That is very difficult to assess in any clear and unambiguous way, because of all the other factors that affect such measures of student performance as reading scores. One factor is the backgrounds of students. The continued increases in the proportion of poor minority students and the corresponding decline of white middle-class students since decentralization have no doubt helped to pull the scores down. Some may argue that decentralization helped facilitate these changes, but they had been going on long before decentralization, and we found little evidence that it contributed any to the trend. Indeed, if anything, it may well have served to retain or attract back middle-class students in many districts where a concerted effort has been made to develop enriched and/or alternative programs for this group.

The other significant factor has been the city's fiscal crisis, leading to staff cutbacks, to larger class sizes, and to the shrinkage or even elimination of many programs. Judging from our observations of districts and schools, that has to have taken its toll also, probably contributing to some further departures of their middle-class students.

What is so interesting is that despite these problems, reading scores in the New York City public schools have gone up since 1970. And those in several of the districts we studied, including several in poor areas where achievement had been particularly low under the centralized system, have gone up even higher than the citywide average.

We believe that the case for or against decentralization has to be made in terms of many process criteria in addition to the bottom-line ones. Decentralization advocates argued that the attainment of *social peace;* of a *legitimacy* for the schools as a community institution; of a *fit* between the schools and the community in regard to curriculum, instructional styles, staff backgrounds and orientations, and program linkages; and of more *program innovation* and/or more *efficiency* in existing programs might well result from that change. We have found many districts that moved in this direction, including minority districts whose politics was very turbulent at the start of decentralization and whose education programs were not working well initially.

These developments have taken place more in some districts than in others, as the case studies indicate, but at least some are present in all the districts we have studied. In brief, a community school district system has come into existence in New York City as a result of decentralization. It has provided for enough social peace, local-level flexibility, and openness so that schools can be more effectively responsive and accountable to their local constituencies. And we turn now to a summary account of those developments that we take to be important indicators of some of the benefits of decentralization and that seem not to have been present to the same degree under the previous, centralized system. We base the account on four districts where we saw many of these productive developments take place to some considerable degree.

CASE #1: DISTRICT B

One Hispanic poverty-area district we studied is a very good example of what is possible under decentralization. Its CSB selected an entrepreneurial, energetic, young Hispanic male as its superintendent in 1973; and he was in many respects a "new-style" superintendent who would probably not have been appointed under the old system. He has provided much educational leadership in new program development and staffing, as well as in community development activity, as our chapter on that district indicated. He was born in the community; has taught and run programs there; and is deeply committed to its development, as are his staff. He thus represents a new, upwardly mobile, minority professional who personifies the district's most deeply held aspirations and beliefs, and whose upward mobility has in no way lessened his ties to this community. In fact, if anything, it may have deepened them, as he "returned" to the community in the early 1970s after having served in a staff position at headquarters. He has used his credentials, skills, and network of professional relations to help improve the quality of education considerably over what it had been before.

After bringing in many new staff (as teachers, program directors, principals, curriculum coordinators, proposal writers, and administrators), he facilitated the development in this district of some of the most promising programs in the city. He and his staff set up a network of 19 alternative schools, each concentrating on a particular program theme—for example, performing arts, careers, science, math, and communications. They brought in tremendous amounts of outside funds for new programs. One of these programs, involving students traveling all over the city, visiting cultural, business, and government agencies for purposes of enriching their experiences and concepts to improve reading skills, has resulted in substantial improvements in student performance and has been widely acclaimed, as have the alternative schools. The district has developed, in addition, a network of bilingual schools that is beginning to show promise. And it has many collaborative programs with community agencies—for example, a health program with a nearby hospital, an environmental education program with an adjacent district, and a tutoring program with one of the city's specialized high schools. Moreover, it has done this with a white, Hispanic, and black staff that has become one of the most integrated staffs in the city. And the district has reached a level of social peace and political stability that had not existed there before. In the early 1970s, factions within the community were in continual conflict with one another and with the schools over the quality of programs and over who would control them and benefit from them.

This district has gone a long way toward making its schools into community institutions rather than alien outposts, which is what many of them were seen as being before. And it now has large numbers of graduates who go off to the city's elite, specialized high schools and to academic private and boarding schools. Some of these graduates return to the district to express their appreciation for the preparation its schools gave them for their later academic experiences.

There have been problems in this district, which we documented in that chapter, but it constitutes a significant example of what is possible under decentralization.[13] Decentralization in this instance helped create the conditions under which an energetic, professional, and yet community-minded superintendent became the catalyst for many educational improvement activities. And those activities resulted in big improvements in reading scores, far beyond citywide improvements, and in later academic attainments of graduates. The actions of a strong political leader in the CSB who helped to recruit this superintendent and establish his authority were very important in the district's success. But it was the superintendent and his staff who developed and maintained a dynamism in this district that did not exist before decentralization.

CASE #2: DISTRICT E

A second example is a poor black district in one of the outer boroughs, whose able superintendent has also been there since the early 1970s. A black male from outside the city, he is another example of a "new-style" superintendent who also would probably not have been appointed under the old system. When the CSB selected him as superintendent, this district was in political turmoil. Bands of black youths and community activists were disrupting schools and CSB meetings. One such group had barged into his office immediately after his appointment, charging that he would be exploiting this community and its students for his own benefit. During the past several years, however, this district has reached a degree of political stability and of legitimacy that seems to be directly related to the many program and administrative improvements that he initiated.

The schools in this district were typical of those in poor minority areas. Little teaching was going on in many of the schools, as teachers and principals had low expectations of what students could learn. There was often high teacher absenteeism; students roamed the halls endlessly; and there was much violence inside the schools and much vandalism. Moreover, there was no uniform curriculum. Teachers were either running custodial operations or "doing their own thing." If a student moved from one school to another—and this happened often with the district's high mobility rate—there was little continuity in educational experience, despite the supposedly "centralized" system. Indeed, changing schools was almost like going to another country.

The superintendent has dealt proactively with these difficult problems in ways that were not possible under the old system, and he has acted on a districtwide basis. At least the things he did and the results he got had never happened in any poor black district before decentralization. He moved to standardize the curriculum through the use of explicit learning objectives, thereby establishing and maintaining minimum standards. Those changes, in turn, raised teacher expectations as to what black students from poverty backgrounds could learn.

The program was strongly supported by various administrative procedures: systematic audits of classrooms and schools by district office staff; frequent (monthly, bimonthly) testing of students; special assistance to "marginal" teachers and to principals in schools where reading scores were considerably below those of others in the district serving similar student populations; and a visitation program in which principals and assistant principals would spend a few weeks in another school to sensitize them to improving administrative and supervisory practices.

In addition, the superintendent has developed a broad-based, junior high school improvement program in an effort to retain middle-class students who had been leaving in great numbers after elementary school, as they do in other districts. It is obviously aimed as well at those who would be staying anyway. The district now has two alternative, satellite junior highs and several programs in existing ones for gifted and talented students.

The results of these many programs and administrative initiatives are quite dramatic, as reading scores have risen far beyond those citywide. The district has also developed a cadre of black professionals: principals, curriculum coordinators, and teachers, many of whom grew up in the area, live there now, and are sensitive to the needs and values of the students.

There still remain some problems in this district. Some board members, for example, periodically criticize the superintendent's strong leadership, claiming that he sometimes usurps their policymaking role. But the prevailing tone is one of improvement and a prospect of still further gains, attributable in very large part to the leadership of this superintendent, who is another product of decentralization.

Our other two examples come from districts with a much larger white middle-class population, indicating that the benefits of decentralization seem to exist in many parts of the city. Some of the same patterns described in Districts B and E hold there as well.

CASE #3: DISTRICT G

A white middle-class district in one of the city's outer boroughs illustrates still further the improvements that seem to have accompanied decentralization. There, a somewhat conservative CSB, oriented toward more traditional styles of instruction and curriculum, recruited an experienced, mainstream, and somewhat traditional superintendent in the early 1970s, and he has been there ever since. Indeed, the fit between his background, skills, and philosophy on the one side and the community's values and expressed needs on the other has been equally strong as that in the Hispanic and black districts just described.

A major development in this district since decentralization has been its increasing black student population, which now constitutes roughly 40% of its total enrollment. Many of this district's programs have been developed in the context of that change, and they have been implemented in ways that have been closely attuned to community conditions. Thus, the district has a very effective desegregation program involving the busing of close to 2,000 black students from overcrowded schools in the north to underutilized ones in the south. This has been done with strong leadership from the CSB and the superintendent, with much community participation, and with much district initiative in securing outside funding. The district secured sizable ESAA monies (for remedial programs and extra staff) to service the bused-in black students and for remediation as well to white indigenous students in receiving schools who have learning problems. In addition, the district has secured funds for enrichment programs (pre-K programs, those for gifted and talented students, and magnet schools) to prevent white middle-class flight and to attract back into the district white middle-class students who had left.

Previous studies of the school headquarters bureaucracy suggest that this district's initiatives in developing its districtwide desegregation plan are probably much greater than might ever have come from headquarters.[14] In fact, the director of the headquarters central zoning office indicates that this is one of the best desegregation programs of its kind he has ever seen.

In brief, we have in this instance an illustration of how a district desegregation and neighborhood stabilization strategy, initiated under decentralization and taking advantage of increased authority and flexibility under decentralization, may be much more effective in improving student performance than was ever possible under centralization. Thus, the district experienced a big improvement in reading scores for both the bused-in minority students and the indigenous whites; and it has held up its reading scores, in the aggregate, over the past several years, while changing from 20% to almost 40% poor minority.

A further strategy in this district, also facilitated by decentralization, and pursued in several others as well, has been to push decentralization down to the local school level, enabling principals, teachers, and parent association leaders to have a determining influence on the educational philosophy and curriculum in their schools. This superintendent and board, for example, have not mandated the curriculum and instructional styles that should prevail in the schools but have merely set general standards and policy parameters within which programs must exist. In this instance, the superintendent followed a strategy of orchestrating diversity, in recognition of differences in values and style preferences of parents throughout the district. Some preferred open education and heterogeneously grouped classes, while others preferred a traditional, more structured approach and one that grouped students by ability. Such a condition of school autonomy sometimes existed under centralization, as an aggressive principal might defy the dictates of central bureaucracy. However, there is greater likelihood of its happening under decentralization, where schools have much more flexibility and where technical assistance and support services are available in a district office not nearly as removed from the school and its problems as headquarters staff downtown.

Ultimately, it might well be desirable to push decentralization down to the local school level, as many districts like this one have already begun to do. But that may work well only under a decentralized, community school system where needed monitoring and technical assistance are located close to the school and are provided by staff intimately familiar with local school conditions.

CASE #4: DISTRICT D

Our last example is a once predominantly white middle- and upper-middle-class district in an outer borough that now has a poor Hispanic student enrollment of more than 50%. The CSB there selected a strong, forceful educator from within the district as superintendent who reflected its values, and he and his staff have developed an extraordinarily rich curriculum, with many outstanding programs. A charismatic person with interpersonal, public relations, and administrative skills, he has gathered around him a highly professional district office staff and principals who have served the district well.

One of the hallmarks of his success has been his forceful development of a humanistic, open education philosophy, emphasizing individualized approaches to instruction, and dealing with the emotional as well as intellectual development of students. That philosophy is, in turn, embodied in a vast array of educational programs in every subject area and is adapted to the needs of all ethnic and economic groups. Indeed, this district, under the superintendent's leadership, has developed one of the most professional curriculum and staff development operations we have seen. The emphasis is on informal education approaches, "hands-on" learning and on many out-of-classroom experiences that are the opposite of the approach in District E, but they have had good results in this district, as that one has had there.

Some of the exemplary programs include many collaborative efforts with outside agencies, including Lincoln Center, a local zoo and planetarium, schools of education, and a Boy Scout camp away from the city. The district has, in addition, produced impressive curriculum bulletins—in science, social studies, reading, math—that are in wide demand elsewhere. It has gone far in developing a coherent education program strategy by facilitating much collaboration among curriculum specialists in the district office, between that office and the schools, and between state-funded and federally funded programs on the one side and city-funded ones on the other. Indeed, its use of outside funds to develop innovative programs that fill important gaps in existing curricula offerings and its follow-up activity in then institutionalizing the best of those programs under city funding reflects a very creative approach.

This district, like the others, has problems, some of them serious, but it nevertheless reflects some extraordinarily productive approaches under decentralization. A close look at how these programs have developed indicates how important decentralization has been for their initiation and continued effectiveness.

While these four districts are among the "showcases," indicating how decentralization has faciliated improvements in education, they indicate only in somewhat more dramatic form processes that have taken place in many others as well. And there are some general patterns that have emerged here that seem to be a direct result of decentralization. For one thing, the schools and districts generally have a legitimacy that they clearly lacked in the 1960s, particularly in minority areas. There is a degree of political stability in relation to public education that had not existed before. Moreover, the fit between the schools and the community is much greater than it ever was. The superintendents appointed by these CSBs are clearly community-oriented. Before decentralization, headquarters-appointed superintendents were "organization types." They were oriented upward in that kind of centralized, machine bureaucracy to headquarters, rather than outward to the community, with many of them aspiring to promotions to higher headquarters positions.

The same pattern holds for principals. While the opponents of decentralization sometimes cite particular "ethnic" appointments of principals, implying that these people are not as qualified as their predecessors or as others from the civil service lists, we have noted a much greater community sensitivity and concern among the principals under decentralization. Many of these districts have seen the early retirement, both of old-line superintendents and principals, largely because they found it difficult to adapt to new demands. It had become clear to them that, under decentralization, they served at the pleasure of the CSB and were much more vulnerable than before to demands of the board and parent groups. In some cases, able educators and administrators were lost to the system, but in many more, people whose values and skills were now obsolescent were leaving a system that needed other types of leaders. On balance, with some exceptions, that has probably been a very good thing.

Perhaps most impressive of all has been the development and, in some cases the flourishing, of new educational programs and program linkages with outside agencies that seem to have been a direct result of the greater flexibility and openness of the system under decentralization. Many of these programs and linkages have been customized to the particular learning styles, values, and needs of students in ways that were not possible under the old system. Each of the districts cited above represents the development of a comprehensive curriculum strategy. In the Hispanic district, it was a combination of alternative schools, a bilingual network, and many enriched programs through federal funding. In the black district, it was the introduction of standards and uniformity, where neither existed before. In the white district experiencing a big influx of blacks, it was a neighborhood stabilization approach, with strong efforts to retain the middle class. And in the formerly white district with the Hispanic influx, it was an open education approach that then became adapted to students in Hispanic areas as well.

Each of these districts had the flexibility under decentralization to do what its superintendent and CSB thought was required to best adapt to the needs of students and the community. Centralized bureaucracies do not encourage that, and we found enough of it taking place to make us conclude that decentralization is working in many places and could work in many others, if given the needed support.

11

Epilogue

Despite the many positive developments under decentralization, there remain many unresolved problems. They relate to broader issues of district governance, district administration and programs, and headquarters-district relations. They will have to be addressed more systematically in the future if the New York City school system is to realize the potential that the best of the decentralized districts have demonstrated.

District Governance

COMMUNITY SCHOOL BOARDS

There is some question as to whether the quality of community school board members has been maintained since decentralization began in 1970. Many board members throughout the city were optimistic at that time about the prospect of improving education in their district. Although not adequately prepared for the experience, they had a sense of mission, as the first elected body that was embarked on an exciting new experiment. They tended to be very dedicated, and they spent long hours on board affairs. For many, it was almost like another full-time job.

Starting with the 1973 elections, however, there was a noticeable shift from parent-oriented and professionally oriented CSB members to those supported by the teachers' union, political clubs, parochial school groups, and antipoverty agencies. Each had a particular interest: the union in job security for teachers; political clubs and antipoverty agencies in patronage; and religious groups in maintaining their share of federal funds.[1]

The CSBs thus became more narrowly "political," in the sense of looking out for these group interests. Several became increasingly involved in district management, particularly in allocation of jobs and patronage. CSBs became, in that sense, much less like policymaking agencies and much more like additional administrative bodies that might delay the implementation of programs. What has emerged in some districts has been CSB control by local "power brokers" who represent organizational interests that do not include parents and are not oriented toward educational considerations.

Nevertheless, some dedicated people, including parents and public-interested professionals, remained on CSBs through the 1973 and 1975 elections. By 1977, however, and certainly by 1980, even they had left. Some left after becoming disillusioned when they realized how little power the CSBs had, especially when budget cuts reduced the funds available for new programs. They felt that they could be more effective elsewhere, working with citywide groups—for example, to restore budget cuts.[2]

One result of these changes in the backgrounds of CSB members has been a deterioration in CSB effectiveness. If early CSBs had an unclear definition of their role when decentralization began, later ones had an even vaguer one. Some abdicated their policy role and got deeply involved in district administration, stifling the superintendent and professional staff on matters that should not have concerned them. Most important, educational policy matters took little if any precedence for these boards, while administration and political patronage became primary interests.

The general behavior of many recent CSBs often reflects this decline. Attendance at meetings seems to have fallen off. CSB members follow through much less on committee assignments. The boards too often perform no useful *educational* (policy) or *representational* function.

Another prevailing pattern was the unrepresentative composition of the early boards. In districts that included middle-class and poverty areas, the former were vastly overrepresented, even when their children constituted a small segment of student enrollment. Fortunately, many whites on these early boards took a broader districtwide perspective in their board decisions than was originally feared.

This representational imbalance resulted from the white middle-class populations voting in greater numbers in CSB elections. And in some districts where a militant, community control group resided, activists resented the compromise decentralization law so much that they urged their communities not to vote, as a gesture of protest.

COMMUNITY SCHOOL BOARDS AND SUPERINTENDENTS

The relationship between CSBs and their superintendents has been one of considerable strain. It has worked out relatively well in several of the districts we studied, but even in these districts the conflicts have sometimes been severe. In District B, described above, its effective superintendent spent a year-long struggle with a new board that tried to curb his authority. In District E the superintendent often clashed with his board over what they regarded was his nonconsultative style. And the same conflicts have existed elsewhere. Some of this reflects what sociologist Charles Bidwell referred to as a "creative tension" between boards and their superintendents, but some tension has clearly gone beyond the point of being "creative."[3]

Superintendents throughout the city have become what one former headquarters administrator referred to as the "whipping boys" of their boards. The usual problems include misdirected actions on both sides. CSBs fail to establish broad district policies, treat the superintendent too much like a subordinate employee rather than as a professional, and become too involved in detailed administrative matters that they lack the staff or expertise to handle and that are really the superintendent's prerogative.

Superintendents contribute to the conflicts as well. Some make unilateral decisions on critical policy matters and inform the board only after the fact; they treat the board members as laypersons who do not understand the complexities of educational issues; or they flood the board with so much unsynthesized information that it is difficult even for sophisticated members to sort it out easily. These are tactics that professionals commonly use to maintain their power and autonomy.

Unless this conflict is better resolved, districts are going to have a harder time attracting able superintendents. In one district, for example, the conflict was so intense that a leading educator there who had been in line for the superintendency indicated that he wouldn't subject himself to what he referred to as the "public castration" that his superintendent had faced at the hands of that board.

DISTRICT BOUNDARIES

One of the most politicized aspects of decentralization has been the drawing of district lines. No consistent criteria have been applied citywide, except to maintain district size above a certain level. Decisions on this matter have depended mainly on whose local power base was at stake.

It would probably help in the future if school district boundaries were made to correspond as much as possible with those of other service agencies in line with reforms now under way in New York City government more generally. The schools need to collaborate with many other agencies, and having a common constituency and information base would help.[4]

In addition, some ethnically mixed districts have proved unmanageable, in large part because of their diversity. Conflicts between white middle-class and poor minority populations have made it extremely difficult to maintain the political stability needed to permit the superintendent and the CSB to manage effectively.[5] Unless the CSBs and superintendents handle these conflicts better, there seems little to be gained from having such ethnically diverse districts.

By contrast, other, ethnically homogeneous districts are now so small that they fall below the minimum size prescribed in the Decentralization law. One might argue, of course, that these districts have finally reached a small enough size to be manageable. They are, after all, still far larger than most school districts throughout the country. We have no ultimate solution, except to say that consolidation may be appropriate in some of these cases, just as redrawing district lines to limit a dysfunctional ethnic diversity may be appropriate to others.[6]

District Administration

CURRICULUM AND STAFF DEVELOPMENT

Some districts, such as the ones described above, have taken many initiatives in educational program and staff development. Others have not, however. We have already indicated what distinguishes the effective from the ineffective districts in this regard. The former have achieved some degree of social peace in connection with the schools, have recruited able superintendents, and have proceeded to insulate them from undue CSB or other outside political pressures. These superintendents have, in turn, engaged in many educational improvement activities. It should be possible to develop guidelines and more concrete strategies, based on the analyses of some of these successful districts.

MARGINAL TEACHERS AND PRINCIPALS

One of the most difficult problems that districts have to face has been what to do about marginal teachers and principals. We have seen in the case studies, for example, how principals, particularly those near retirement, were eased out of districts where the CSB, the superintendent, and/or parents did not regard their skills or orientations as matching district needs. Most of the time this led to appointments of effective principals as judged by student achievement and local constituencies' satisfaction, though sometimes it did not. It usually reflected a trend toward ethnic succession, which had been one of the original goals of decentralization, but many white principals continue to be appointed by minority-dominated boards. Few blacks, however, are appointed by white-dominated boards, except sometimes for mini-schools.

Dealing with marginal teachers is another matter, however. Experienced New York City educators estimate that up to 10% or 15% of the teachers perform "unsatisfactorily." Some can be helped through closer supervision, in-service training, and other forms of support. Others, however, some with severe psychiatric problems, cannot be helped in these ways and should be removed, both for their sake and for the sake of the children they are not serving. The cost of doing that, of bringing up teachers on "charges," going through the several-step grievance procedure, is quite prohibitive. Decentralization has not affected the collective bargaining contract or the power of the union, so in that sense, this serious problem remains.

Some districts have, however, handled this issue well, in ways that are replicable elsewhere. District E, for example, has the "marginal teacher" program we described earlier, and it has upgraded the classroom skills of many teachers. A continuous relationship is set up between a district office staffperson and a marginal teacher. They decide jointly on a course of action to improve the teacher's performance, with one option being the transfer of that teacher out of the shcool or even the district if the teacher cannot be helped.

Another strategy that districts have developed has been to train principals in documentation, so that when they do bring up a teacher on charges, the union will be unlikely to overturn their decision. Thus far, districts have not received as much back-up help from headquarters as they would like, and this matter should be further explored.

PARENT PARTICIPATION

One of the disappointments of decentralization has been the limited participation of parents in school affairs. In some formerly middle-class districts, where there was an infrastructure before, there is active parent involvement—in school and district curriculum committees; in reviews of appointments, promotion, and tenure decisions on staff; and in other matters (e.g., school construction, integration, enrichment programs).

Poverty-area districts, however, still have limited parent involvement. Many parents have become discouraged about being able to influence school and district decisions. In a period of budget cuts and declining services, many don't see much role remaining for their districts. And with inflation and declining real income in such areas, where people were already at the bottom end of the scale, more parents are working and holding a second job. They have neither the time nor the energy to become involved in school affairs.

One significant trend has been a widespread pattern of cooptation of parents by schools and the district office. Principals set up parent advisory councils (PACs), for example, to absorb parent leaders and then use them as informants on actions and intentions of those still outside. And sometimes activist parents are given jobs in the district office or as paraprofessionals or school neighborhood workers to blunt their protest activities. This practice often helps a school or district, by incorporating skills that enhance education, but it dilutes parent protest and monitoring activity that may also help improve education.

Headquarters-District Relations

TECHNICAL ASSISTANCE AND MONITORING

In order for decentralization to work, headquarters must play new technical assistance and monitoring roles. It did so poorly on these matters in the early years of decentralization that districts overspent their budgets and were permitted to engage in questionable financial practices without censure. In fact, in one year (1972), the districts overhired so much relative to their allocations that the entire Board of Education budget was expended more than two months before the end of the fiscal year.[7] There were, in addition, some blatant cases of districts engaged in questionable spending practices (no-show jobs, unaccounted-for expenditures, patronage appointments of unqualified people, board members taking long trips) that were allowed to continue for a long period of time.

Headquarters has improved its monitoring and technical assistance considerably since those early days. There is a district management support team, and there are staff from several headquarters departments (e.g., budget, personnel, funded programs, community school district affairs) who have been helpful to districts. Although many of its departments have moved in that direction, more could be done to turn headquarters into a service agency.

Part of the problem between headquarters and the districts is that many district staff and lay persons (e.g., parents, CSB members) distrust headquarters. Such a field-headquarters conflict is characteristic of most big organizations, but it is probably greater when the headquarters is as cumbersome and difficult to deal with as that in the New York City public school system had been. Under a new reform chancellor, who had himself been a local CSB member, headquarters has become more streamlined, better managed, and more responsive; and that seems to bode well for decentralization, depending on how long he stays and on whether his policies and style continue when he leaves.[8]

THE FUTURE OF CENTRALIZED PROGRAMS

A number of governance and policy issues have emerged recently under decentralization. One set of issues relates to those parts of the New York

City school system that are still centralized. Some districts would like to take over control of those functions. A number of high schools around the city, for example, have requested to the districts where they are located and to the chancellor that they be administratively separated from the centralized high school office and be made part of their district. As one community superintendent reported: "Even as recently as a few years ago, you wouldn't have found much support from high schools to become affiliated with districts, but that is all changing now, and there are high schools in almost every borough that are making that request. This is a new development."

Some of the same sentiments exist with regard to special education, that is, to programs for handicapped students. Districts have resented having to deal with a central office that they felt had been poorly managed. These districts have extensive, court-mandated programs that some of them would like to control themselves, subject, of course, to general policy guidelines. District staff and CSB members feel that they know their local needs and capabilities much better than do headquarters administrators.

Some consideration may have to be given, then, to a selective decentralization of these programs. Not all districts want that, nor are all necessarily capable of taking on such added responsibilities. It would be worth experimenting with, however, to see if programs might be provided in more cost-effective ways than under the existing centralized arrangements.

INTEGRATION AND NEIGHBORHOOD STABILIZATION

When decentralization first became a contested issue in New York City, those groups opposing it argued that it would lead to increasing separatism and that whatever integration efforts were already under way would be stifled by local groups trying to build a ethnic power base.[9] This study suggests that desegregation can be accomplished quite effectively by an individual district. We concluded from District G's experience, for example, that when conditions are favorable, a district desegregates its students better than the central board because its staff are much closer to the local situation. They have more firsthand knowledge of local needs. They know the leaders and groups whose support must be mobilized.

They understand how the input of local groups can be secured for the development and implementation of a desegregation program.

Beyond that, District G illustrates how to pursue effectively a neighborhood stabilization strategy to keep an area from tipping, by developing programs that retain and attract black and white middle class. That has rarely, if ever, happened under central board leadership in New York City.[10]

On the other hand, several districts have not taken much initiative on this issue. In those cases, central should play an active role, as it now does, in pressing districts to desegregate, where conditions seem to warrant that and where local groups may be vetoing it. Such conditions would encompass situations where minority-area schools within a district are overcrowded and where schools in white middle-class areas are underutilized. They might also include those situations where schools within an entire minority district are overcrowded, while those in an adjacent white middle-class district are underutilized. Interdistrict plans would then have to be addressed from central, though it should try to get the participating districts—their superintendents, board, and community groups—to take as much of the leadership and initiative as possible. While this may undercut district autonomy and community control, the improved school utilization that might result from it and the potential for improved education would warrant headquarters playing an active role in encouraging such integration efforts.

What is needed most of all after twelve years of decentralization is a careful reexamination of the roles of headquarters and the districts. With the exception of this study and a briefer one by Gittell, the real workings of decentralization have not been analyzed very extensively.[11] Although it is obviously a very delicate balance to maintain, headquarters should play an active leadership and policy role, without at the same time controlling the districts too closely.

The details remain to be worked out, but I would suggest the following general directions: Headquarters should appropriately set standards and policies on such matters as promotions; target populations to be served in bilingual, special education, and other such programs; school utilization; and integration. Moreover, it should be the main evaluation agency for the public schools. It should gather information on a wide range of product and process indicators and publicize it very widely. Some districts would object vehemently, and some would not want certain kinds of information publicized, but that is essential for an enlightened populus and for school administrators, CSBs, and other public officials. As a general rule, then, headquarters should set broad policy and engage in some administrative functions like evaluation, while the districts should be free to develop programs and specify how they should be implemented.

Another headquarters role should be to locate effective programs and to develop a mechanism for publicizing and disseminating them. The chancellor's School Improvement program and a few others like that are examples.

In brief, a central headquarters administrative mechanism should be set up to deal with the problems listed in this epilogue, and there are of course others as well. Headquarters could probably do a lot more, for example, in promoting the kinds of CSB-superintendent relations that contain less of the unproductive conflict that now exists. It could probably do much more to provide a stimulus for involving parents in districts and schools. And it might well help improve the quality of CSBs, by participating in efforts to get parents to vote in greater numbers and in working to revise election procedures so that they are simpler to administer, do not turn away many potential voters, and allow for more knowledgeable local people to get elected.

This is not the place to develop a detailed agenda of needed reforms. It is important to indicate, however, that the time has come to develop a better organizational framework for the New York City schools to deal more effectively with their many problems. This study and its findings are hopefully an important first step.

Source Notes

In keeping with a common tradition in social science where informants who provide confidential interviews are not identified by name, we have no footnote references to such interviews from this study. Instead, in almost every case, the source is otherwise indicated in the text (e.g., as a parent, district office staffperson, principal, or other category of informant).

Statistical data on the districts were provided by staff from appropriate headquarters departments. In most instances, they read off the information to us from computer printouts or documents. Our footnote references relating to those data will not refer to published materials, largely because that would enable the interested reader to identify the particular districts, thereby violating our agreement with the superintendents. We have simply identified the bureau or department that was the source of the information.

CHAPTER 1: INTRODUCTION

1. Indeed, desegregation was barely tried, so strong was the opposition both inside the system and in white areas of the city, as documented in David Rogers, *110 Livingston Street. Politics and Bureaucracy in the New York City Schools* (New York: Random House, 1968).
2. See, for example, Marilyn Gittell, *Participants and Participation* (New York: Praeger, 1967); Rogers, *110 Livingston Street*; and Miriam Wasserman, *The School Fix, NYC, USA* (New York: Outerbridge and Dienstfrey, 1970).
3. The most publicized of these events was the Board of Education's reneging on its stated commitment to establish a desegregated intermediate school (PS 201) in East Harlem. Community leaders saw the initial commitment as a "hoax," given the school's location, and they regarded the central board's handling of it as typical of how it had treated them over the years. The demand for community control of the New York City schools began to some large extent at this school.

4. In addition, the publication of Marilyn Gittell's *Participants and Participation* (New York: Praeger, 1967) and the senior author's *110 Livingston Street* further helped legitimate the demands of community activists that the bureaucracy be made more responsive. Rogers's characterization of the Board of Education headquarters as a "sick, pathological bureaucracy" resonated throughout the many disaffected civic groups of the city and crystallized for them the sentiments they had had for a long time.
5. See, for example, the famous Ford Foundation Bundy Report, *Reconnection for Learning*, New York City Mayor's Advisory Panel on Decentralization of the New York City Schools, 1967. For good historical accounts see Mario Fantini and Marilyn Gittell, *Decentralization: Achieving Reform* (New York: Praeger, 1973), and Joseph Cronin, *The Control of Urban Schools* (New York: The Free Press, 1973).
6. Many of these points are covered in Alan Altschuler, *Community Control* (New York: Pegasus, 1970). See also Henry M. Levin, ed., *Community Control of Schools* (New York: Clarion, Simon and Schuster, 1970).
7. See Wasserman, *The School Fix*, Part II, "The Struggle for Power and Status," for a good historical account.
8. See Frances Fox Piven, "Militant Civil Servants in New York City," *Transaction* (November 1969): 24–28.
9. See Rogers, *110 Livingston Street*, pp. 285–297, for a discussion of the ethnic politics surrounding the Board of Examiners.
10. A good historical account of the political-institutional development of big city school systems is contained in Cronin's *The Control of Urban Schools*. See the senior author's foreward to that book, which we draw on in the sections that follow.
11. Cronin, ibid.
12. These points are discussed in Edward Banfield and James Q. Wilson, *City Politics* (Cambridge, Mass.: Harvard University Press and MIT Press, 1963).
13. Further historical accounts of these developments appear in Mario Fantini et al., *Community Control and the Urban School* (New York: Praeger, 1970), and Fantini and Gittell, *Decentralization*.
14. See Gittell, *Participants and Participation*.
15. A good recent statement of this view appears in Robert L. Bish and Hugh O. Nourse, *Urban Economics and Policy Analysis* (New York: McGraw-Hill, 1975). For their discussion of diseconomies of scale in big-city school systems see pp. 289–294.
16. David Seeley, *Education Through Partnership* (Cambridge, Mass.: Ballinger, 1981).
17. Ibid., p. 116.
18. Henry Mintzberg, *The Structuring of Organizations* (Englewood Cliffs, N.J.: Prentice-Hall, 1979).
19. Low-achieving minority or lower-middle-class white students, for example, may learn better in a highly structured classroom situation, and their parents

may prefer that. Some upper-middle-class students, by contrast, may do well in open classrooms.
20. Mintzberg, *The Structuring of Organizations*, chap. 20.
21. An interesting early discussion on this appears in Michael A. Rebell's "New York's Decentralization Law: Two and a Half Years Later," *Journal of Law and Education* 2, no. 1 (January 1973): 1–41. See also *School Decentralization in New York City*, prepared for the State Charter Revision Commission for New York City, June 1974.
22. These observations are based on a pilot study we did prior to the one on which this book is based.
23. See James P. Gifford and Frank J. Macchiarola, "Legal, Technical, Financial, and Political Implications of School Finance Reform in New York State," *Tulane Law Review* 55, no. 3 (April 1981): 716–734.
24. A good discussion on this point appears in Rensis Likert, *New Patterns of Management* (New York: McGraw-Hill, 1961).
25. This holistic approach was formulated during the study, rather than built into our interview guides in any explicit way.
26. Sociologist Charles Perrow notes in this *Organizational Analysis* (Belmont, Calif.: Wadsworth, 1970), pp. 5–14, that the structure of the organization and its environment are key factors affecting management style, not just the leadership traits and training of the manager.
27. Charles Bidwell discusses this point in an insightful way in his "The School as a Formal Organization," in James G. March, ed., *Handbook of Organizations* (Chicago: Rand McNally, 1965), pp. 972–1022.

CHAPTER 2: DISTRICT A

1. These data were obtained from the Office of Zoning and Integration, school headquarters. All subsequent references to this and other offices and/or bureaus are to those at headquarters.
2. This observation is from fieldwork Rogers did in the 1960s, in the preparation of *110 Livingston Street: Politics and Bureaucracy in the New York City Schools* (New York: Random House, 1968).
3. Daniel Bell and Virginia Held make this point in "The Community Revolution," *The Public Interest* 16 (Summer 1969).
4. Office of Educational Statistics, annual pupil census.
5. For a discussion of the professionalism ideology of teachers see Dan Lortie, "The Partial Professionalization of Elementary Teaching," in Sam Sieber and David Wilder, eds., *The School in Society* (New York: The Free Press, 1973), pp. 315–325.
6. Bureau of Educational Statistics.
7. Data from the Office of Funded Programs, Bureau of ESEA, Title I, indicate very little change in the percent of students from welfare families since 1975.

230 SOURCE NOTES

The same holds for ethnic backgrounds, from data provided by the Office of Zoning and Integration.
8. Bureau of Educational Statistics.
9. Bureau of Attendance.
10. The district office provided these data.
11. Office of Educational Statistics, annual school census, reports on staff ethnic composition.
12. Ibid.
13. Office of School Buidlings.

CHAPTER 3: DISTRICT B

1. From reading score data provided by the Office of Educational Statistics in which districts are ranked.
2. Office of Zoning and Integration.
3. Office of Educational Statistics, annual pupil census.
4. Office of Zoning and Integration.
5. See Gerald Zaltman, Robert Duncan, and Jonny Holbek, *Innovations and Organizations* (New York: Wiley, 1973), for a further disucssion.
6. See, for example, Warren Bennis, "Changing Organizations," *Journal of Applied Behavioral Science* 2, no. 3 (1966): 247–263.
7. From an unpublsihed study provided by district office staff.
8. Ibid.
9. Ibid.
10. Ibid.
11. Summary Report of Staff Ethnic Composition, Office of Educational Statistics.
12. For a general discussion of this characteristic of school systems see Karl Weick, "Educational Organizations as Loosely Coupled Systems," *Administrative Science Quarterly* 21 (1976): 1–19.
13. Office of Educational Statistics.
14. Office of Funded Programs.
15. Office of Educational Statistics.
16. Office of School Buildings.
17. District office staff provided these data.
18. Office of School Buidlings.

CHAPTER 4: DISTRICT C

1. Office of Educational Statistics.
2. Office of Zoning and Integration.
3. Office of Educational Statistics.

4. Office of School Buildings.
5. Office of School Buildings.
6. Office of Educational Statistics, reports on staff ethnic composition.

CHAPTER 5: DISTRICT D

1. From compilations of district staffpersons, using 1970 census data.
2. Office of Educational Statistics.
3. Office of School Buildings.
4. Data compiled by the district office.
5. Office of Educational Statistics.
6. Office of Educational Statistics.
7. Bureau of Attendance.
8. Office of School Buildings.
9. Office of Educational Statistics.

CHAPTER 6: DISTRICT E

1. From district office data.
2. Office of Educational Statistics.
3. Office of Educational Statistics.
4. Office of School Buildings.
5. Data provided by Office of Community School District Affairs.
6. The district office provided this information.
7. Office of Community School District Affairs.
8. See Douglas McGregor, *The Human Side of Enterprise* (New York: McGraw-Hill, 1960), for the original development of these concepts. They refer, respectively, to more authoritarian versus democratic styles of management.
9. Numerous accounts of classrooms in poverty-area schools in New York and other inner cities document this common orientation among teachers, including Miriam Wasserman, *The School Fix: NYC, USA* (New York: Outerbridge and Dienstfrey, 1970).
10. Office of Educational Statistics.
11. Office of Educational Statistics.
12. Bureau of Attendance.
13. Data provided by the district office.
14. Office of School Buildings.
15. Office of Educational Statistics, staff ethnic census.

CHAPTER 7: DISTRICT F

1. Office of School Buildings.
2. Office of School Buildings.
3. Office of Zoning and Integration.
4. Office of Funded Programs.
5. Office of Community School District Affairs.
6. Office of Zoning and Integration.
7. Office of Educational Statistics.
8. Office of Educational Statistics.
9. Bureau of Attendance.
10. Office of School Buildings.
11. Office of Educational Statistics, reports on staff integration.

CHAPTER 8: DISTRICT G

1. Office of Educational Statistics.
2. Office of School Buildings.
3. Office of Zoning and Integration.
4. Office of Funded Programs.
5. Office of Educational Statistics.
6. Office of Funded Programs.
7. District office staff provided these data.
8. Bureau of Attendance.
9. Office of School Buildings.
10. Office of Educational Statistics.

CHAPTER 9: DISTRICT H

1. Office of Educational Statistics.
2. Demographic data and observations of district office staff formed the basis for the discussion here on the district's size and religious and ethnic composition.
3. Office of Zoning and Integration.
4. Office of Zoning and Integration.
5. Office of Educational Statistics.
6. Office of Educational Statistics.
7. Bureau of Attendance.
8. Office of School Buildings.
9. Office of Educational Statistics.

CHAPTER 10: CONCLUSIONS

1. These reading score data were obtained from The Mayor's Management Report, January 20, 1982.
2. Educational researchers and citizen groups have raised many serious questions about the validity of reading tests in the New York City schools. See, for example, Eugene Radwin et al., *A Case Study of New York City's Citywide Reading Testing Program* (Cambridge, Mass.: The Huron Institute, May 1981), and Phyllis Eckhaus, "The Citywide and Beyond: Tests Score Poorly," *The Advocate* (Fall 1981).
3. This is an ideal-type model that characterizes what a highly effective district would be like. See Max Weber, *The Theory of Social and Economic Organization*, trans. A. M. Henderson and Talcott Parsons (New York: Oxford University Press, 1947), pp. 13 ff., for a good discussion of ideal types.
4. A discussion of organizational effectiveness as a concept appears in Robert H. Miles, *Macro Organizational Behavior* (Santa Monica, Calif.: Goodyear, 1980), chap. 12.
5. A large body of literature in the organizational behavior field, emphasizing contingency approaches to management, points to this view. See, for example, Henry Mintzberg, *The Structuring of Organizations* (Englewood Cliffs, N.J.: Prentice-Hall, 1979), and Miles, *Macro Organizational Behavior*.
6. One such factionalized minority district, for example, has had more than ten community superintendents since decentralization began. Its CSBs have undercut each one, and at least one of the boards has been suspended, pending a headquarters investigation of questionable uses of funds and hiring practices.
7. In two poor minority distircts we studied, for example, one black and the other Hispanic, local leaders who later moved on to elected office effectively coalesced community factions. They were instrumental in selecting able superintendents and then helped buffer them from the CSB and militant community groups, while still holding them accountable for their performance. Before this happened, both districts were in so much political turmoil that little education took place.
8. The superintendents in four of the most effective districts we studied have served there since 1973.
9. Local parent and community groups in such districts participated actively in helping develop educational programs. At the same time, they often exercised an effective independent voice in staffing decisions—for example, the selection of the superintendent and the principals.
10. The conflict was usually over the distribution of program funds and power—in other words, over which groups and leaders get what under decentralization.
11. Bell and Held highlight this problem in inner cities in "The Community Revolution," *The Public Interest* 16 (Summer 1969).

12. Districts that had reached some degree of social peace were consistently more effective than those still in the throes of community conflict over who would run the schools and district and how they would be run.
13. One such problem was the conflicts that existed between its regular schools and its alternative ones, as some principals in the former felt threatened by the competition. That conflict had positive effects, however, as it pushed the regular schools to develop new programs in order to retain their students and attract new ones.
14. David Rogers, *110 Livingston Street: Politics and Bureaucracy in The New York City Schools* (New York: Random House, 1968).

CHAPTER 11: EPILOGUE

1. This judgment is based on extensive fieldwork in the districts.
2. From interviews with several CSB members who declined to run in 1977 and 1980.
3. Charles Bidwell, "The School as a Formal Organization," in James G. March, ed., *Handbook of Organizations* (Chicago: Rand McNally, 1965), pp. 972–1022.
4. See *Revising the New York City Charter*, Introductory Report, State Charter Revision Commission for New York City, n.d.
5. Such districts are common in New York City's outer boroughs where there still remain some white middle-class residents who send their children to the public schools.
6. Yet, one can point to District B in the poor Hispanic area, where extraordinary results have been attained under decentralization. It would probably hurt that district, its students, and its community to be consolidated. Its smallness and homogeneity have clearly helped to create a sense of community and to provide a training ground for local leaders, including the superintendent, who have been very effective.
7. This information comes from interviews with headquarters officials who were serving at that time and from management consultants who were working with them.
8. See Joseph P. Viteritti, "Managing 110 Livingston Street," *Urban Education* 15, no. 1 (April 1980): 103–114.
9. See Alan Altschuler, *Community Control* (New York: Pegasus, 1970), for a review of this.
10. David Rogers, in *110 Livingston Street: Politics and Bureaucracy in the New York City Schools* (New York: Random House, 1968), further documents this point.
11. See Marilyn Gittell's chapter, "School Governance," in Charles Brecher and Raymond D. Horton, eds., *Setting Municipal Priorities, 1982* (Montclair, N.J.: Allenheld Osman, 1981), pp. 181–212.

Bibliography

1. GENERAL WORKS (BOOKS AND ARTICLES)

Altschuler, Alan. *Community Control*. New York: Pegasus, 1970.
Bell, Daniel, and Virginia Held. "The Community Revolution." *The Public Interest* (Summer 1969).
Bidwell, Charles. "The School as a Formal Organization." In James G. March, ed., *Handbook of Organizations*. Chicago: Rand McNally, 1965. Pp. 972–1022.
Bish, Robert L., and Hugh O. Nourse. *Urban Economics and Policy Analysis*. New York: McGraw-Hill, 1975.
Cistone, Peter J., ed. *Understanding School Boards*. Lexington, Mass.: Lexington Books, 1975.
Crain, Robert. *The Politics of School Desegregation*. Chicago: Aldine, 1968.
Cronin, Joseph. *The Control of Urban Schools*. New York: The Free Press, 1973.
Fantini, Mario, et. al. *Community Control and the Urban School*. New York: Praeger, 1970.
Fantini, Mario, and Marilyn Gittell. *Decentralization: Achieving Reform*. New York: Praeger, 1973.
Gittell, Marilyn, et. al. *School Boards and School Policy: An Evaluation of Decentralization in New York City*. New York: Praeger, 1973.
Gittell, Marilyn, and T. Edward Hollander. *Six Urban School Districts*. New York: Praeger, 1968.
Kirby, David J., T. Robert Harris, Robert L. Crain, and Christine H. Rossell. *Political Strategies in Northern School Desegregation*. Lexington, Mass.: Lexington Books, 1973.
LaNoue, George R., and Bruce L. R. Smith. *The Politics of School Decentralization*. Lexington, Mass.: D. C. Heath, 1973.
Levin, Henry, ed. *Community Control of Schools*. New York: Clarion, Simon and Schuster, 1970.

Lorsch, Jay, and Stephen Allen. *Managing Diversity and Interdependence.* Harvard Business School, Boston, 1973.
Mayor's Advisory Panel on Decentralization of the New York City Schools. *Reconnection for Learning: A Community School System for New York City.* New York: Praeger, 1969.
Miles, Robert H. *Macro Organizational Behavior.* Santa Monica, Calif.: Goodyear, 1980.
Mintzberg, Henry. *The Structuring of Organizations.* Englewood Cliffs, N.J.: Prentice-Hall, 1979.
Perrow, Charles. *Organizational Analysis: A Sociological View.* Belmont, Calif.: Brooks/Cole, 1970.
Ravitch, Diane. *The Great School Wars.* New York: Basic Books, 1974.
Rogers, David. *Can Business Management Save the Cities: The Case of New York.* New York: The Free Press, 1978.
———. *An Inventory of Educational Improvement Efforts in the New York City Schools.* New York: Teachers College Press, 1977.
———. *110 Livingston Street: Politics and Bureaucracy in the New York City Schools.* New York: Random House, 1968.
Steinberg, Lois Saxebly. *Social Science Theory and Research on Participation and Voluntary Associations: A Bibliographic Essay.* Prepared as part of *Citizen Organizations: A Study of Citizen Participation in Educational Decision Making.* Institute for Responsive Education and Optimum Computer Systems, Inc., July 1977.
Yin, Robert K., and Douglas Yates. *Street-Level Governments: Assessing Decentralization and Urban Services* (An Evaluation of Policy Related Research), prepared for the National Science Foundation, Rand, Santa Monica, California, October 1974.
Zimet, Melvin. *Decentralization and School Effectiveness.* New York: Teachers College Press, 1973.
Zaltman, Gerald, Robert Duncan, and Jonny Holbek. *Innovations and Organizations.* New York: Wiley, 1973.

2. UNPUBLISHED STUDIES AND PAPERS

Byrne, Eileen Elizabeth. "Community Participation After Decentralization in One New York City School District, 1970–1977." Doctoral diss., Fordham University, School of Education, 1979.
Edmonds, Ronald R., and Alan S. Blummer. "The School Improvement Project of the New York City Public Schools." Unpublished paper, November 1978.
Gittell, Marilyn. "New York City School Decentralization: A Retrospective." Draft of an article, April 1980.
Kriftcher, Noel N. "The Educational Power Structure in a Decentralized Community School District." Doctoral diss., Hofstra University.

Levine, Jonathan, and Norman M. Adler. "The Effects of Race, Ethnicity, and Class in the 1975 New York City Community School Board Elections," paper prepared for American Educational Research Association, annual meeting, 1976.

3. AGENCY AND COMMISSION REPORTS

Citizens Budget Commission, Inc. *The Role of Local Community School Districts in New York City's Expense Budget Processes*, vol. 42, no. 1, June 1975.

Cresap, McCormick and Paget, management consultants. *The Community School Boards: How Their Presidents Perceive Them After Six Months in Office*. Done for the Board of Education of the City of New York, February 1971.

Department of City Planning, City of New York. *Public School Enrollment Trends, New York City, 1970–1980*, 1977.

New York City Planning Commission, City of New York. *Community School District Profiles*. July 1974.

State Charter Revision Commission for New York City. *School Decentralization in New York City*. June 1974.

4. BOARD OF EDUCATION REPORTS AND STATISTICAL DOCUMENTS

Office of Community School District Affairs. Data on ethnic composition of community school boards, 1970, 1973, 1975, 1977.

Office of Educational Statistics. Data on promotions and attendance, 1970 to present.

Office of Educational Statistics. Staff ethnic reports from annual school census, 1970–71 through 1977–78.

Office of Funded Programs. Data on reimbursable funds received by districts.

Office of Funded Programs, Bureau of ESEA, Title I. Data on student socioeconomic status, by district, 1971–72 to present.

Office of Planning, Programming, and Budget. Data on district office budget schedules.

Office of Zoning and Integration. Data on ethnic characteristics of students by school and district, 1970 to present.

Office of Zoning and Integration. Data on school utilization, 1970 to present.

Division of Curriculum and Instruction. Data on citywide reading test results, 1970 to present.

School Profiles, 1973–74, 1974–75, 1975–76. Contains a comprehensive statistical description of schools and districts for those years.

Board of elections of New York City. Statistical data on CSB elections, 1970, 1973, 1975, 1977, 1980.

5. INTERVIEWS

Roughly 550 during the period from September 1978 through July 1981. CSB members, superintendents, district office staff, principals, teachers, parents, headquarters staff, business, labor, university officials, civic group leaders, state education department staff.

Index

Alternative schools, 48-53, 61, 73, 208
Antipoverty agencies, 19, 21, 42, 70, 136-137
Arson, 39, 66, 85, 106, 129, 148, 173
Audits, 118, 210
Authority (lay vs. professional), 15

Bakke decision, 145
Bidwell, Charles, 218
Big city school systems, 4-6
Bilingual programs, 21-23, 26, 33, 53-57, 70, 88, 108, 141
Board of Education: *see* District office, relations with headquarters
Board of Examiners, 3
Bureaucracy: types, 9-11

Chancellor, 30, 157
City Commission on Human Rights (NYC), 3
Collective bargaining, 220
Community control, 1-8, 11-12
Community development corporations, 169-170
Community school boards:
  backgrounds, coalitions, 21-25, 43, 70, 82, 90-91, 110-113, 133-140, 150, 156-161
  presidents, 43-44, 54-55, 138-140, 157, 160
  relations with superintendents, 21-25, 42-45, 71-76, 90-92, 113-114, 134-140, 159-161, 178-181, 218-219
  selection of superintendents, 21-24, 43, 71-72, 74, 112-113, 134, 137, 138, 151, 157-159, 178, 180-181
  weaknesses, ineffectiveness, 75, 81-82, 126, 138, 216-218
Congruence (extent of fit) between schools and community, 13, 211
Consultants, 47-48
Council of Supervisory Associations (CSA), 100, 153, 183
Curriculum, 26-28, 48-57, 76-78, 92-98, 115-122, 141-142, 162-165, 186-188

Decentralization:
  a political model, 8-9
  a management view, 9-12
Decentralization Act of 1969, xvi
Desegregation, 49, 110, 155, 164-165, 172, 183-185, 223-224
District characteristics:
  demography, 12, 18-20, 41-42, 69, 87-89, 109-110, 132-133, 150-153, 174-177
  diversity, 68, 83-84
  enrollment, 19, 42, 63, 84, 89, 132-133, 152, 175-176, 184-185, 192
  size, 12, 19, 68-70, 84, 175, 181-183
District lines, 19, 42, 109-110, 182-183, 219
District office:
  bureaucracy, 33-34, 47-48, 82-83, 170, 188-190, 191-192
  relations with community, 29-31, 60-62,

240 INDEX

District office (*Continued*)
  80-82, 100-102, 124-126, 145-146, 169-170, 190-191
  relations with professional staff, 31-32, 57-59, 60-62, 79-80, 99-100, 122-124, 144-145, 167-169
  relations with headquarters, 33, 59-60, 222-223
  relations with schools, 28-29, 50-57, 79, 98-99, 111-112, 142-144, 166-167, 188-190

Effectiveness (indicators for districts and schools), xiv, 13, 15-16, 206-207
  attendance, 38, 66, 85, 105-106, 128, 148, 173, 193
  placement of students in specialized (elite) high schools, 38, 50-51, 66-67, 129
  reading and math scores, 36-37, 51, 64-66, 84-85, 94-95, 104-105, 127-128, 147-148, 171, 192-193
  vandalism, 39, 67, 85, 106, 129, 148-149, 173, 193-194
Elections (community school boards), 216-217
Emergency School Aid Act (ESAA), 66, 163, 165, 211
Ethnic succession politics, xiv-xv, 3, 5, 8-9, 18-19, 21-25, 40-45, 68-71, 87-92, 102-104, 131-140, 150-159, 183-185, 203-204, 219

Ford Foundation, 31, 188
Fiscal crisis (NYC), 12-13, 73, 78

Gittell, Marilyn, xii, 224

Hazen Foundation, 188
Headquarters (Board of Education): *see* District office, relations with headquarters
High schools, 61, 223: *see also* Effectiveness, placement of students in specialized (elite) high schools

Junior high schools, 51, 93-94, 109, 120, 141

Kaufman, Herbert, xii

Lindsay, John V., 31
Linkages (program) of schools with outside agencies, 4, 10, 22, 31, 73, 94, 119, 169-170, 188

Management style: *see* Superintendents
Media:
  Daily News, 77-78
  New York Magazine, 49
  New York Post, 49
  New York Times, 49
Methodology of the study, xii-xiv, 12-15
Mintzberg, Henry, 9
Model districts, 207-214

Neighborhoods, 19, 20, 41-42, 69-71, 88-91, 109-110, 132-133, 151-153, 175-177
New York Urban Coalition, 119

Ocean Hill-Brownsville, 74, 110
Outside (federal and state) fundings, 46, 61, 65, 165

Parent participation and organizations, 29-31, 44, 61-62, 72, 80-82, 101-102, 124-126, 145-146, 169-170, 221
Parochial schools, 19, 91, 154, 184-185
Political clubs, 35, 44, 70-71, 80, 180, 198
Politics: *see* Ethnic succession politics
Pre-requisites for district effectiveness, 197-200
Principals:
  appointment, 92-94, 98, 208, 214
  ethnic composition, 58, 86, 89, 106, 130, 149, 173, 193
  labor relations, 57, 59, 79, 100, 123
  layoffs, 95
  monitoring and evaluation, 58-59, 79, 98-99, 118-119, 143, 168, 190, 220
  political activities in district, 22, 87, 153, 156, 178
  training, 96, 124, 167, 221
Private schools, 19
Problem districts, xiii
Professionalism:
  ideology, 5-6
  professional dominance and power, 2, 74, 179

Scale (economies and diseconomies in districts), 6
Seeley, David, 7-8
Social peace, 9, 19, 83, 131, 150, 205, 207-208; *see also* Ethnic succession politics
Special education, 223
Staff development, 219
STAR reading program, 57
Staffing, 21-25, 26, 35, 38, 40, 43, 57-59, 71, 75, 80, 83
   ethnic integration, 38, 58, 85-86, 92, 102-103, 106, 149, 153-156, 194
Superintendents:
   management style, 13-15, 25-35, 45-64, 76-83, 91-102, 108, 114-127, 140-146, 161-171, 185-192, 200-206

Teachers:
   ethnic composition, 3, 58, 106, 173, 194
   initiatives in classrooms, 50, 52-53, 93, 100, 121-122
   labor relations, 21, 32, 57, 79-80, 122-123, 167-168
   monitoring and evaluation of, 118, 144, 168, 210, 220
   participation in district politics, 22, 70, 87, 112-113, 139, 153, 167, 177
   recruitment, 21, 35, 208
   residing in the district, 88-89, 130, 153, 194
   see also, United Federation of Teachers

United Federation of Teachers (UFT), 21, 32, 53, 73, 80, 90, 100, 112-113, 118, 122, 139, 153, 180, 183
U.S. Commission on Civil Rights, xii
U.S. Office of Civil Rights, 95, 173

Zoning, 164